WEh

AA

THE AA GUIDE TO

Norfolk & Suffolk

WITH CAMBRIDGE

D0101676

L914.26

About the author

A BBC-trained journalist, author and member of the British Guild of Travel Writers, Carole French travels the world in search of inspirational lifestyles, but always loves to come home to her beloved East Anglia. Carole was born in the region and remembers an idyllic childhood spent horseriding in the countryside and taking trips to towns likes Lavenham in Suffolk and the castle in Norwich at weekends.

Carole was first bitten by the travel bug as a child; one of her favourite activities was packing for family beach holidays in Caister-on-Sea and Great Yarmouth, weeks in advance. During her career, Carole has worked with some of the largest media names in East Anglia: Archant Life for which she was editor of its prestigious *Cambridgeshire Life* magazine, the *East Anglian Daily Times* in Suffolk and the *Eastern Daily Press* in Norfolk. Her work has taken her to all corners of the region.

Published by AA Publishing (a trading name of AA Media Limited, whose registered office is Fanum House, Basing View, Basingstoke, Hampshire RG21 4EA; registered number 06112600)
© AA Media Limited 2014

Maps contain data from openstreetmap.org
© OpenStreetMap contributors
Ordnance Survey data © Crown copyright and database right 2014.

A CIP catalogue record for this book is available from the British Library.

ISBN: 978-0-7495-7594-6
ISBN (SS): 978-0-7495-7630-1

All rights reserved. This publication or any part of it may not be copied or reproduced by any means without the prior permission of the publisher. All inquiries should be directed to the publisher.

Cartography provided by the Mapping Services Department of AA Publishing

Printed and bound in the UK by Butler, Tanner and Dennis.

A05140

The contents of this book are believed correct at the time of printing. Nevertheless, the publishers cannot be held responsible for any errors or omissions or for changes in the details given in this book or for the consequences of any reliance on the information it provides. This does not affect your statutory rights. We have tried to ensure accuracy in this book, but things do change and we would be grateful if readers would advise us of any inaccuracies they may encounter by emailing travelguides@theaa.com.

Every effort has been made to trace the copyright holders, and we apologise in advance for any accidental errors. We would be happy to apply the corrections in the following edition of this publication.

Visit AA Publishing at theAA.com/shop

AA

THE AA GUIDE TO

Norfolk & Suffolk

WITH CAMBRIDGE

WE KNOW BRITAIN

CONTENTS

- FINDING YOUR WAY 6
- INTRODUCTION 8
- TOP ATTRACTIONS 12
- HISTORY OF NORFOLK & SUFFOLK 16
- BACK TO NATURE 22
- LORE OF THE LAND 26
- EAST ANGLIAN WATERWAYS 30
- HORSERACING AT NEWMARKET 33

- SUTTON HOO, LAND OF ANGLO-SAXON KINGS 36
- LOCAL SPECIALITIES 38
- BEFORE YOU GO 40
- FESTIVALS & EVENTS 47
- CAMPSITES 48
- A–Z OF NORFOLK & SUFFOLK 50
- ATLAS 288
- INDEX 296

Finding your way

Use the maps below together with the atlas section and the town plans throughout the guide to explore Norfolk, Suffolk and Cambridge. The A–Z section lists the best of the region, followed by recommended attractions, activities and places to eat or drink. The Places Nearby section then lists other points of interest within a short travelling distance to help you explore a little further.

Many of the restaurants that we've included carry an AA Rosette rating, which recognises cooking at different levels nationwide, from the very best in the local area to the very best in the UK. Pubs have been selected for their great atmosphere and good food. You can find more Rosette-rated places to eat at theAA.com.

We're guessing you probably have your accommodation sorted already, but for those who like to play it by ear, we've recommended a few campsites to help you out (see page 48). Caravan and campsites carry the AA's Pennant rating, with the very best receiving the coveted gold Pennant award. If your tastes run more to luxury then theAA.com also lists AA-rated hotels and B&Bs.

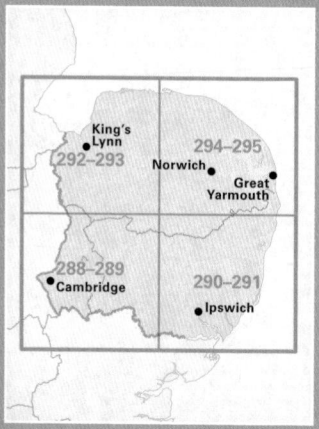

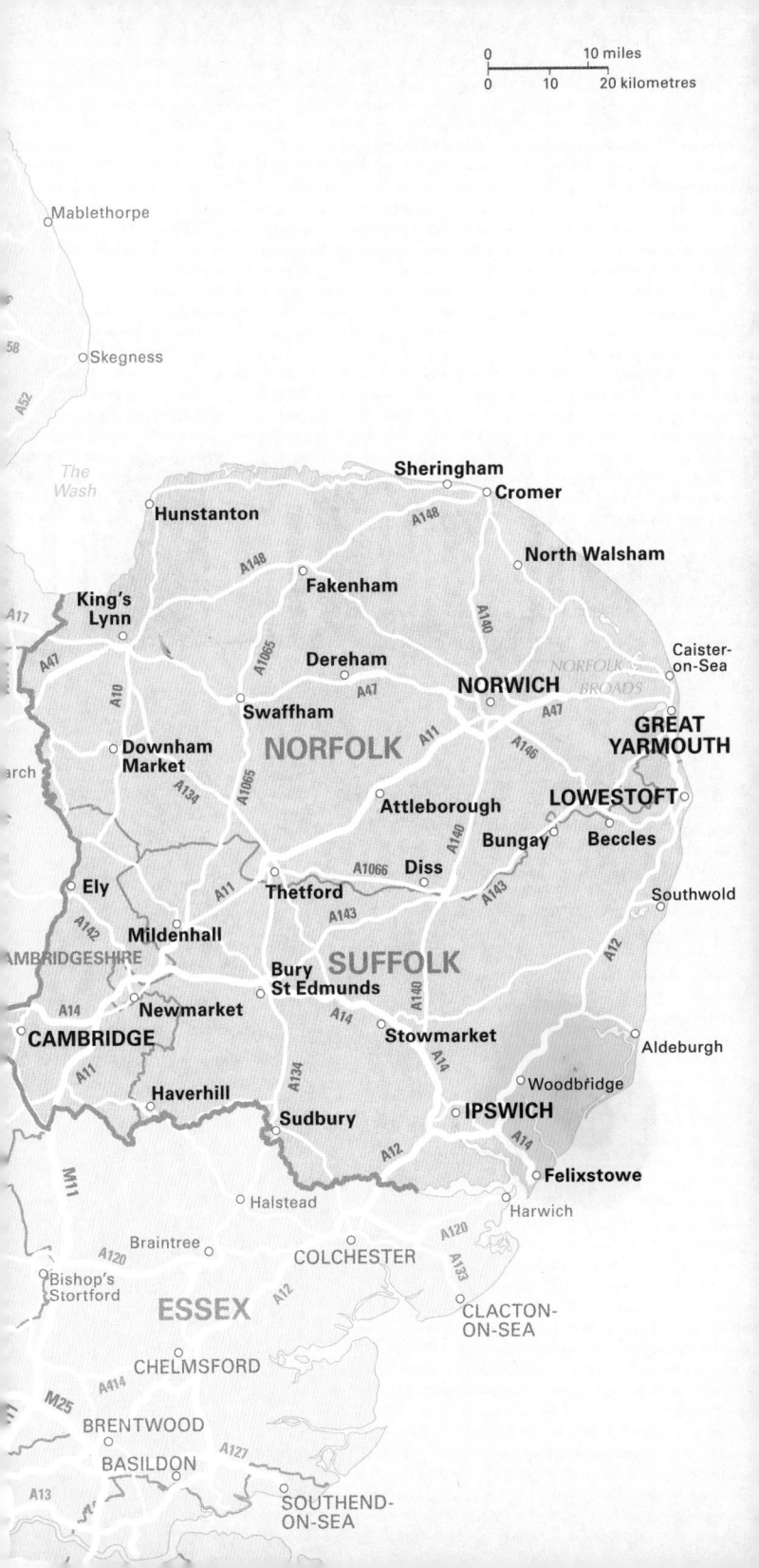
0 10 miles
0 10 20 kilometres
Mablethorpe
Skegness
The Wash
Sheringham
Cromer
Hunstanton
North Walsham
Fakenham
King's Lynn
Dereham
NORWICH
NORFOLK BROADS
Caister-on-Sea
Swaffham
GREAT YARMOUTH
Downham Market
NORFOLK
Attleborough
LOWESTOFT
Bungay
Beccles
Diss
Ely
Thetford
Southwold
Mildenhall
CAMBRIDGESHIRE
Bury St Edmunds
SUFFOLK
Newmarket
CAMBRIDGE
Stowmarket
Aldeburgh
Haverhill
Woodbridge
Sudbury
IPSWICH
Felixstowe
Halstead
Harwich
Braintree
COLCHESTER
Bishop's Stortford
ESSEX
CLACTON-ON-SEA
CHELMSFORD
BRENTWOOD
BASILDON
SOUTHEND-ON-SEA
A52
A17
A47
A10
A1065
A148
A140
A11
A146
A134
A1066
A143
A142
A14
A12
A133
A120
A414
A127
A13
M11
M25

INTRODUCTION

With their landscapes that stretch as far as the eye can see, the counties of Norfolk and Suffolk, and the countryside around Cambridge, are some of the most enchanting places to visit anywhere in England. They have fabulous sweeping skies and sunsets, and countryside dotted with impossibly pretty villages, full to bursting with centuries-old timber-framed cottages and medieval churches; there are vast country estates, ancient archaeological sites, cathedrals, castles and fortresses; and a coastline both tranquil and treacherous.

Add to all this, vibrant cities that will bowl you over, such as Cambridge where for centuries academics have pioneered world-changing advances in medicine, astrology and science, and the county towns of Norwich and Ipswich, and you have a region just waiting to be explored. It's an area full of possibilities for great days out, but you could spend weeks here without running out of things to see and do.

Each of the counties has its own character. Norfolk is characterised by marshland with reedbeds, dykes and creeks, dense wetland woodlands and a landscape dotted with flint-

and-brick villages and pumps, not unlike windmills, that keep water levels safe. Its coast, once a bustling place of tiny quayside streets lined with merchants' houses and fishermen cottages, and harbours full of fishing boats unloading their catches to the cries of seagulls and the hammering of boat-builders, is famous for its biodiversity and wildlife.

Norfolk is now a magnet for holidaymakers too, from exuberant Great Yarmouth, with its legendary end-of-pier seaside fun, to the more genteel Cromer and Lowestoft. Norwich is its administrative, financial and cultural hub.

Suffolk, meanwhile, is full to bursting with pretty villages, such as Kersey and Somerleyton, and quiet fishing and seaside towns, such as Aldeburgh and Southwold. It has rolling rural countryside, lots of market towns and magnificent medieval wool towns, such as Lavenham. Strolling around the streets of Lavenham, England's most complete medieval town, is like stepping into an extremely pleasant time warp.

In contrast, you have Felixstowe, a seriously busy place where container ships load their cargo for trips to Europe, Asia and beyond, and the elegant Bury St Edmunds and Ipswich, both of which have a plethora of shops, restaurants, sports centres and art galleries.

Cambridge, the capital of Cambridgeshire, is a dazzling place of jaw-droppingly gorgeous Gothic colleges, elegant homes, vast open spaces and the Backs, a delicious area dominated by the meandering River Cam where students and visitors punt on the river or party on the greens near King's College and the world-famous King's College Chapel. This is fen country; and one of Britain's most magical sights is nearby Ely Cathedral rising like a massive cruise liner from the flat misty landscape.

Norfolk, Suffolk and the countryside around Cambridge may inspire you to enjoy all manner of outdoor activities too. Here, you can while away some time boating on the inland waterways, cycling, painting, walking or even riding on horseback. Stables offering hacks to experienced riders can be found in most of the larger towns, or if your passion leans more to watching horses being ridden, then there are racecourses at Fakenham, Great Yarmouth and, of course, Newmarket, where racing has been a constant since the time of James I. Over the centuries, trainers and jockeys have come to East Anglia to perfect their skills, including Sir Henry Cecil, Sir Michael Stoute and Saeed bin Suroor, and jockey Frankie Dettori, and the region has even provided inspiration for novels written by former steeplechase jockey turned crime writer, the late Dick Francis.

East Anglia has been an inspiration for centuries. You only have to sit awhile on the grassy riverbank looking across the rippling water to the Flatford Mill to understand what so moved John Constable to immortalise the Dedham Vale on canvas, or stand on windswept Aldeburgh's shingle beach to know exactly how poet George Crabbe and composer Benjamin Britten felt when they penned their great works. East Anglia will be an inspiration to you too.

▸ King's College, Cambridge

TOP ATTRACTIONS

▲ Southwold Pier

For a proper British seaside experience, head to Southwold Pier (see page 246) and its quirky range of attractions – best being the Under the Pier Show, where you can 'Whack a Banker' in a modern take on the penny arcade, before or after taking to the beach.

◀ Fitzwilliam Museum

See works by Rembrandt, Constable, Rubens and Picasso alongside antiquities from the ancient world and a collection of medieval and renaissance illustrated manuscripts at Cambridge's Fitzwilliam Museum (see page 93).

◂ Norwich Castle and Cathedral

Go back in time in Norwich; the magnificent Norman Norwich Castle (see page 215) was built for William the Conqueror, while Norwich Cathedral (see page 216) has the second highest spire and the largest monastic cloister in England.

▸ Imperial War Museum Duxford

If planes are your passion, visit the country's largest aviation and war museum, the Imperial War Museum Duxford. You can see 200 or more planes, naval and military vehicles in original listed wartime hangars (see page 124). Look out for air shows on event days.

◂ BeWILDerwood

One for the kids – and big kids – BeWILDerwood (see page 161) is an adventure park based on a children's story book. Spend a day climbing in treehouses, taking boat trips and meeting the imaginative resident creatures. Fun for the kids too...

Pleasurewood Hills

'Pleasurewood Hills' (see page 191) might sound more like a location from an American sitcom, but this theme park on the Suffolk coast is actually vaguely pirate themed. There's a good mix of adult and kiddie rides.

Africa Alive!

If staycationing gets tiring and you'd prefer to pretend you're on safari, this African-themed zoo (see page 63) will be a big help – though you might still have to imagine the good weather.

Sutton Hoo

No one should come to Norfolk and Suffolk without visiting Sutton Hoo (see page 36 and page 263), site of the discovery of an Anglo-Saxon burial ship that lay hidden here for over 1,300 years. It's considered to be one of the most important archaeological finds in British history.

▲ King's College

Take an early morning walk along the Cambridge Backs and see King's College and King's College Chapel through the thin mist that often blankets the area (see page 89).

▶ Holkham Hall

A palatial stately home surrounded by parklands. The nature reserve is part of the estate as well, as is Holkham beach, Bygones Museum and the Church of St Withburga (see page 154).

◀ Sandringham

One of Britain's several royal residences, there's plenty to see at Sandringham (see page 237): the state rooms, a museum including a collection of royal cars, and lots of parkland and gardens.

HISTORY OF NORFOLK & SUFFOLK

East Anglia has been inhabited for a very long time; certainly, there's plenty of evidence pointing to neolithic man living and thriving here, followed by the Iceni tribes who developed the region from around the 1st century BC and the Romans who established settlements such as *Gippeswic* – present-day Ipswich in Suffolk.

This gloriously flat region, with its shores lashed by the North Sea, is also famously the land of the Anglo-Saxons who arrived here after the Romans had upped sticks and moved on. You can still sense the Anglo-Saxon legacy as you stand on the cliffs at Dunwich – once a prosperous and important Saxon port city now swallowed by the sea – or at Sutton Hoo – where it is widely believed that the first King of the East Angles, King Raedwald, was buried with his ship.

Originally, the Anglo-Saxon Kingdom of the East Angles, or East Anglia as we know it today, comprised just Norfolk and Suffolk. It was formed around the year AD 520 and quickly became one of the most powerful kingdoms in England. King Raedwald (*c.*580–*c.*624), who ruled the kingdom from around 599 until his death, was one of its legendary rulers. Although few documents detailing his reign

▲ Dunwich on the Suffolk Coast

survive today – most having been destroyed when the Vikings invaded East Anglia in the 9th century and targeted the monasteries where important document were kept – what is known of King Raedwald is that he was regarded as a great leader. In fact, at one time he was the most powerful English king in the south of England.

The kingdom grew in size when Ethelthryth, the daughter of the then King of East Anglia, King Anna, married in AD 652 and was presented with the Isle of Ely as a gift. Ethelthryth – who was later canonised as St Etheldreda or Audrey – adored the Isle of Ely, today part of Cambridgeshire, and founded a monastery here.

Over the next few decades, East Anglia was targeted by the Mercians, an Anglo-Saxon tribe from the region that is today known as the Midlands. Mercian kings ruled the kingdom until they were defeated in *c*.825 and East Angles once again became independent. In 869, the Vikings invaded and, having killed King Edmund, who ruled the kingdom from 855 to 869, assumed control. They destroyed the kingdom's monasteries, including the one so lovingly founded by Ethelthryth in Ely.

East Angles, which now covered an area from the coast of Norfolk and Suffolk inland to the fenlands around Ely, was renamed East Anglia by the Vikings. In the early 900s, the

Anglo-Saxons sought to regain the kingdom and defeated the Vikings in battle, only to lose it temporarily again to the Danes. Harold II (*c.*1022–66) was the last Anglo-Saxon king of England. He died at the Battle of Hasting fighting the Norman invasion led by William the Conqueror.

In 1066, William the Conqueror arrived in East Anglia. He too adored the region and decided that Norwich, which by then had grown through Roman and Anglo-Saxon habitation to become the largest city in England after London, was the ideal place in which to build a new royal palace.

William had some fanciful ideas. He had plans drawn up for the grandest palace the country had yet seen; in fact, architecturally it was so ambitious that it must have been the most talked about building of the period. The result was Norwich Castle, a fabulous structure that became the king's favourite palace. You can visit the castle today – its museum is one of the best in the region.

From the Middle Ages to around the time King Charles I ascended the throne in 1625, East Anglia became enormously wealthy as a result of its wool and cloth trade. Wool was exported to far-flung destinations such as Africa and Asia, and to many European countries. In fact, Norwich and towns such as Lavenham and Hadleigh in Suffolk, and Diss in Norfolk were being transformed as more and more churches and large country houses were built by merchants and clothiers who had vast sums of money to spend.

The region's ports were thriving, too. The quaysides at places such as Cley-next-the-Sea and Dunwich were bustling with boats,

▼ Norwich Castle

laden to the gunwales with wool and cloth, preparing for their often perilous voyages. Larger ports, such as those at Great Yarmouth and Lowestoft in Norfolk, and Southwold and Aldeburgh in Suffolk, were also becoming increasingly prosperous through their fishing and shipbuilding industries.

Over time, the region's wool, fishing and shipbuilding industries all but disappeared. The Industrial Revolution in the late 1700s and early 1800s saw manufacturing move to the Midlands and north of England, signalling the decline of the East Anglian wool industry, while the region's fishing and shipbuilding industries gradually diminished due to silting that made it impossible for large sea-going fishing boats to navigate the region's waters and reach its ports. It wasn't until Victorian times and the coming of the railways that the coastal towns were able to reinvent themselves as seaside resorts, while the wool towns sought wealth through independent enterprise.

Meanwhile, in Ely, an abbey built to replace the monastery founded by the Anglo-Saxon Ethelthryth, and destroyed by the Vikings, had become an important place of worship. The isle county became a bishopric, governed by the Bishop of Ely. In 1837, an Act was passed, known as the Liberty of Ely, which saw the county become part of Cambridgeshire. Its county town was Cambridge.

By this time, Cambridge was a thriving place, famous for its colleges and scholars' achievements. The first students arrived as far back as 1209 – they had been studying at Oxford University, but fled when the townspeople turned hostile – they were enraged by stories of two students who were found guilty of murder. Oxford

▼ Ely Cathedral

▲ Front Court, Emmanuel College

University closed. It reopened some time later, of course, but by this time many of its students had settled in Cambridge and had been joined by others. Numbers grew and so a second major place of learning evolved. The two universities have been rivals ever since.

Peterhouse was Cambridge's first college. Founded in 1284 by Hugo de Balsham, the then Bishop of Ely, during the reign of the Plantagenet Edward 1 of England, it is one of the city's smallest colleges. Nevertheless, it has produced a number of famous Petreans. Charles Babbage, who brought us the forerunner of modern-day computers, was a Petrean in the 19th century. Others include newsreader Richard Baker, poet Richard Crashaw, the Duke of Grafton who was Prime Minister from 1768 to 1770, film star James Mason and film director Sam Mendes.

The following century saw the colleges Pembroke, Clare, Trinity Hall, Gonville and Caius, and Corpus Christi opening, as well as 'lost' colleges King's Hall and Michaelhouse. Henry VI drew up plans for the magnificent King's College and King's College Chapel himself, and laid the first stone on 25 July 1446. The project took 70 years to complete.

King's College was joined by many other colleges in the 15th century, most notably Queens' in 1448, St Catherine's in 1473 and

Jesus College in 1496. John Flamsteed, the first Astronomer Royal, studied at Jesus in 1670, as did astronaut Dr Michael Foale, Archbishops of Canterbury Thomas Herring and Matthew Hutton, broadcaster Alistair Cooke, playwright David Hare and HRH Prince Edward who read history from 1983 to 1986.

In 1546 Trinity College was founded through the amalgamation of several smaller colleges and became a centre for science, largely due to the extraordinary work of one of its students, Sir Isaac Newton. Cambridge's colleges have long been pioneering institutions. Girton became the first women's college in Cambridge in 1869, although female students were not awarded degrees until 1947. Today, almost half of all students admitted to the university are women.

In the 20th century, East Anglia was at the forefront of wartime activity. Here, numerous Royal Air Force bases became central to England's war effort during World War II, including RAF Duxford near Cambridge, which is now one of the homes of the Imperial War Museum. On the coast at Orford, the isolated Orford Ness spit was a secret Ministry of Defence testing centre, where radar pioneer Sir Robert Watson-Watt (1892–1973) and a small team of scientists took the first steps in the development of the air-defence system.

BACK TO NATURE

East Anglia is a gloriously flat region, made up almost entirely of marshland with swaying reedbeds, wetland woodlands and a coastline deeply indented by rivers, creeks and dykes. Only a ridge of gently undulating hills in north Norfolk punctuates this idyllic landscape. The varied habitats created over millennia in Norfolk's Broadland and Breckland regions, along Suffolk's Heritage Coast and in Cambridgeshire's fenlands provide a home to a spectacular variety of plants and wildlife.

The Norfolk landscape is incised by the rivers Bure, Waveney and Yare, and dotted with flint and brick villages and windpumps that keep water levels safe. The flat, wet region is resplendent with fish and amphibians, birds, animals and plants, especially in the Norfolk Broads National Park, which covers nearly 120 sq miles of countryside, taking in parts of Cambridgeshire, north Suffolk and almost all of Norfolk. The habitats found here can be divided into four main types: the open broads and rivers, the Fens, the grazing marshes and wet, or carr, woodland.

The waters support a wide variety of plants, providing abundant shelter and food for fish, amphibians, birds and animals. You can

▲ Cley Marshes ▲ Blue heron

see water plants such as water lily, hornwort and bladderwort, and birds, including the great crested grebe, heron, shoveler, tufted and mallard ducks, and the kingfisher.

The grazing marshes, such as those at Halvergate, form the heartland of the Broads. This flat area between the rivers Bure and Yare once formed part of the estuary emptying into the sea, but now lies largely below sea level and the rivers have high embankments to avoid the risk of flooding.

The area is threaded by drainage ditches, known locally as dykes, which were first cut in the 14th century, and these are important for plants, such as water violet, frogbit, arrowhead and the carnivorous bladderwort. If you are lucky you may see damselflies and dragonflies flitting delicately over the channels in summer, and lapwings, redshanks, snipe and wagtails nesting between the grassy tussocks in the wetter, boggier meadows. Herons are often seen standing motionless by the water's edge.

Another important wildlife habitat on the Broads is the carr woodland, which has been described as the closest thing Britain has to a tropical rainforest. It is characterised by wetland-loving trees such as alder, sallow and, in drier areas, silver birch. Inside, these woodlands are dense and swampy, and it is practically impossible to walk through them in any degree of comfort. Birdlife here includes woodpeckers, redpolls, siskins and blackcaps. To the west of the park is Cambridgeshire's supremely flat fenland region, which supports an astonishing number of different plant and wildlife species. In the Wicken Fen National Nature Reserve alone, which is Britain's oldest wetlands park, more than 8,500 species of plants and wildlife have been recorded.

The reserve, which lies on the edge of the Norfolk Broads, is dominated by tall stands of reeds and sedge. It is probably the most important area of the park for wildlife. In fact, the Fens are of international importance for the wide range of plants, insects and birds they support. The rare Norfolk hawker dragonfly and the spectacular swallowtail butterfly frequent these areas.

Overhead, you may be lucky enough to see the ghostly shape of the rare marsh harrier. Another extremely rare bird found deep in the reedbeds is the highly secretive bittern. Its low, booming, foghorn-like call is one of the great sounds of the Fens.

To the south of the national park is Suffolk. Here, the landscape has deep indentations created by the estuaries of the rivers Deben, Orwell and Stour, the Blyth and Alde, and their creeks. When the

▼ Hunstanton cliffs

water of these yacht-strewn rivers flows out to sea, mudflats are created and quickly teem with wading birds.

The coastal region of Suffolk, known as the Suffolk Heritage Coast, is designated as an Area of Outstanding Natural Beauty, a protection that is vital since it suffers badly from silting, crumbling low sea cliffs and tidal shingle spits. Here, you may catch sight of the spoonbill, a long-legged wading bird, the exotic purple heron, or the rare black-and-white avocet – returned some years ago, it is one of the RSPB's greatest success stories. These birds now form one of the country's biggest breeding colonies at the Minsmere RSPB Reserve in Suffolk, which can be found a few miles south of Southwold.

Inland, ancient heathlands of heather and bracken are home to birds and wildlife too, including the rare nightjar, Dartford warbler and woodlark, and Britain's only venomous snake, the adder. Thousands of roosting starlings can be seen flying over the countryside here in the autumn evenings – it's a dramatic and unforgettable sight.

▾ Wicken Fen windmill

LORE OF THE LAND

Across East Anglia, a creature as black as the peaty fenland soil stalks the land. Black Shuck, the devil-dog, leaves his lair at nightfall, finding his way with eyes the size of saucers lit with flames of green or red fire. In Norfolk it's said that anyone setting eyes on Black Shuck is doomed to die, while in Suffolk – where he makes his presence known by the brush of his shaggy coat as he passes by – he's regarded as harmless as long as he isn't approached, but if attacked he will strike a deathly blow. On the plus side, however, he's reputed to care for lonely travellers. At Clopton Hall (where he helpfully guards a hoard of golden treasure) he takes on a particularly odd form, having the head of a monk. Around the coast, for example at Sheringham, he's even said to emerge from the sea.

More bizarre yet is the Dragon of Wissington, in the south of Suffolk, whose image remains painted above the north doorway of the village church. He appeared in nearby Bures in 1405 and was said by a monk to be 'vast in body with a crested head,

◀ Roos Hall, Beccles

▲ Wild man carving, Orford

saw-like teeth and a tail of enormous length' and clothed in arrow-proof armour. Having turned on and devoured the villagers, the beast dived into the River Stour and swam to Wormingford Mere, where it still churns the waters.

Coastal mysteries

Around the coast tales of mystery abound. On the bleak shore at Happisburgh in Norfolk, a hideous legless smuggler, head hanging backwards between his shoulderblades, sweeps silently in from the sea, a sack slung over his shoulder. He glides inland until he comes to a well, into which he drops the sack. This story has a basis in reality: the torso of a smuggler, murdered in a quarrel by his accomplices, was indeed found in a local well.

Just as weird is the Wild Man of Orford. One day, fishermen caught what they thought at first to be a massive fish but was in fact a naked man covered in hair with a long straggly beard; he could talk only in grunts. The astonished fishermen tied him up and took him to the castle where he was kept in the dungeon. His favourite food was raw fish which he would squeeze until the water ran out of it into his hands and then he would drink it. When one day his gaolers took him to the river estuary for a swim, the wild man dived deep, swam under the nets erected to enclose him, and escaped into the open sea, leaping elatedly up and down the water.

As midnight strikes, the Long Coastguardsman makes his way along the coast of Norfolk between Bacton and Mundesley. The nights this phantom likes best – when he's most likely to be seen – are those when it's cloudy and windy. If you listen carefully as a gale abates, you can hear him laughing; at other times you can hear him calling for help.

Norfolk fisherman have always been especially aware of voices from the sea. A voice rising from the deep was a signal to head for home quickly before a deadly storm struck. Equally ominous is the yell of the Shrieking Woman, the spirit of an underwater hag who is heard only when bad times are imminent.

In pursuit of witches

East Anglia is witch country and famous as the centre of 17th-century witch hunts. The self-styled Witchfinder General, Matthew Hopkins, a puritan, arrested hundreds of 'suspects' between 1645 and 1647. It's estimated that around 100 were executed, most of them single women, but among them was an 80-year-old clergyman, John Lowes, accused of using magic to sink a ship. In Bury St Edmunds in 1645, a single trial resulted in 18 executions.

Even before Hopkins' time, women thought to be witches were persecuted. The region's best-known witch, Margaret Read, was burned alive in Kings Lynn's Tuesday Marketplace in 1590. Legend relates that as the fire swept through her body her heart burst out and hit the wall of the house opposite, where a permanent scar on the brickwork remains. Stranger still, her heart then bounced into the River Ouse, where it created a sulphurous, cauldron-like bubbling.

After Hopkins' death the witch hunts continued – in fact, the laws against witchcraft were not repealed until 1736. Two Lowestoft widows, Rose Cullender and Amy Duny, accused of bewitching seven children by infesting them with lice and bringing on fits, as well as overturning farm carts and making chimneys collapse, were brought to trial at Bury St Edmunds in 1662. Furthermore, the children were said to be paralysed, to spit nails and to have had their skin tainted with 'witches' marks'. Despite their protests of innocence the pair were hanged.

Haunted houses

Explore East Anglia and you'll soon find yourself a ghost or three. Roos Hall at Beccles in Suffolk is reputed to be among England's most haunted, with ghosts in the guest room and garden. A phantom coachman drives up to the door each Christmas Eve and the footprint of the devil can be seen on one of the walls. At Oulton High House in the same county, a white-robed woman and a ghostly huntsman, complete with pack of hounds, inhabited the site. The woman may have been a poisoned wife or one who stood by as her husband thrust a sword into the heart of her lover.

Fairies

And there are fairy stories aplenty too. This one is a version of Rumpelstiltskin. At Stowmarket, a girl was once promised that she would be saved from execution by a king who commanded her to spin five skeins of flax a day. As she sat weeping at the impossibility of the task, a Brownie with a ghastly visage appeared and promised to help her if she could guess his name within a month. Every day she guessed wrongly, until the last possible day when she heard him singing, 'Nimmie-nimmie-not, my name is Tom Tit Tot.' Once properly named, the spirit vanished. Not only was she saved from execution, she married the king.

Griston in Norfolk's claim to fame is as the place where the tale of the Babes in the Wood originates. One day in the 1700s, Arthur Truelove, who was dying, passed his small son and daughter into the safekeeping and care of an uncle. In an attempt to make off with their inheritance, the uncle hired two men to kill them. Having a heart, one villain could not complete the task and instead killed his compatriot and left the children to starve. A robin who found their bodies covered them with dead leaves and their ghosts, so the story goes, still wander around the woodland as a reminder of those dreadful deeds.

College legends, city tales

Cambridge, home of the 'light blue' university, boasts many a spooky college tale. At Corpus Christi College, the ghost of Dr Butts, Master from 1626 to 1632, and praised for his bravery as the university's Chancellor in the dreaded plague year of 1630, is still believed to haunt the upper rooms of Old Court. Brought to a desperate low in spirits by the devastating losses that the plague induced, he hanged himself by his garters on Easter Sunday of 1632. In the early 1900s, some students tried to exorcise his ghost but only succeeded in 'ordering up' a mist which slowly coalesced into a human figure. Also stalking the college is the ghost of a student who, in the 17th century, fell in love with the Master's daughter. They were interrupted during a tryst so she hid him in a kitchen cupboard where he suffocated. Heartbroken, she threw herself from the roof of Old Court.

Over at St John's, Dr Wood, Master until 1839, still climbs Staircase O, transmogrified into the impoverished student of his youth. A stranger being stalks Merton Hall (part of the same college) – a large, furry creature shaped like a penguin. Rumour has it that the beast wandered in from Abbey House in Newmarket Road, which itself is haunted by the Grey Lady, the ghost of a nun who reputedly still makes frequent appearances.

To the north, at Ely, a healing tradition goes back to St Etheldreda, who attributed her death from a tumour of the neck to her youthful vanity and love of necklaces. Today, the saint is still invoked for healing throat complaints, and at the church of St Elethdreda, in London's Ely Place, a Blessing the Throats service takes place each year on 3 February.

On misty evenings on Ely's River Ouse, a phantom barge bearing the body of St Withburga drifts along the water, a reminder that her body was stolen from East Dereham and brought to Ely in 974 by an abbot hoping to attract wealthy pilgrims.

EAST ANGLIAN WATERWAYS

Before the proliferation of the canal system in the late 18th and 19th centuries, the movement of freight across large distances had been a practical impossibility, effectively limited to something like 12 miles by both the cost and the poor state of the roads. The only exceptions were those areas lucky enough to be on one of the larger rivers such as the Great Ouse, which flows from central England through parts of Cambridgeshire and Norfolk to the North Sea.

Attempts to find a way of improving river navigation date back to the days of the Romans, perhaps even earlier, with the construction of artificial waterways near Lincoln and Cambridge. From the 12th century onwards the idea was resurrected and small-scale navigation allowed the passage of narrow barges.

The first pound locks in Britain were introduced in 1566, having already been in existence in Holland for 200 years. The domestication of rivers became much easier and their continued development and use increased throughout the 17th century.

The Great Ouse was first made navigable from the sea upstream to Bedford in the 17th century, when the surrounding land was

▲ Horsey Mill

drained by the Dutchman Cornelius Vermuyden (1595–1677) who worked extensively on Cambridgeshire's Fens, creating new waterways in and out of East Anglia. But the river's commercial usefulness had vanished by the late 19th century, and by the turn of the 20th century much of it lay derelict. Mills along its length had long been established, including Houghton Mill, which is still a working mill today.

These projects were not generally government financed but were instead investments made by wealthy merchants, who were driven by the expectation of being able to make even greater profits. Large-scale construction was nevertheless surprisingly slow to get off the ground considering that most of the technical problems had already been overcome in projects undertaken in the 17th century.

It was really only with the construction of the Bridgewater Canal in northwest England in the 18th century that canals began to be built. Their success encouraged the formation of joint stock companies to build others throughout the country. However, this flurry of activity created its own problems. The companies built their canals as they saw fit and according to local conditions. This lack of coordination meant that some canals were open to just about any size of craft, while others were restricted to narrowboats only. Nevertheless, it became clear that canals were useful and construction continued until the 1830s, at which point nearly every town of any importance was within distance of a stretch of navigable water.

East Anglia and central England were the two areas where waterways were particularly important. The Midlands were at the heart of the Industrial Revolution and there are still 130 miles of navigable canal in Birmingham and the Black Country alone. In its heyday, canal transport carried eight million tonnes a year, and even as late as the 1950s a million tonnes a year were still being transported on the waterways.

Ironically, the canal system, with its network linking large industrial sites, was to become instrumental in its own downfall. Waterways were used to transport the coal that powered the steam locomotives on the railways, which were new, much faster and more efficient. Canals were gradually abandoned, and in some cases drained in order to become rail beds.

With one or two major exceptions, commercial traffic has all but died out and the canals have assumed a new role as leisure amenities. And not only on the water – the old towpaths are ideal for walking and cycling, and many tourist offices produce routes and trails to follow. In Norfolk and Cambridgeshire today, the enthusiastic Great Ouse Restoration Society, after many vicissitudes, has been responsible for the reopening of navigation on the greatest river in the area.

▼ The River Ouse at Ely

HORSERACING AT NEWMARKET

Surrounding Cambridge and Ely is a vast landscape that captivated the monarchy. James I, as well as Charles I and Charles II, adored the region. They were all passionate about horses, and James created a summer court at Newmarket. Even the Celtic Queen Boudicca is said to have raced her horses across Newmarket Heath. Today, horseracing and this part of East Anglia go hand-in-hand.

The Suffolk market town of Newmarket, with its elegant red-brick Georgian houses surrounded by flat greens and countryside, is utterly devoted to the sport. The day starts early with the horses being exercised and trained on the various turf gallops on Newmarket Heath and often ends with a discussion of the day's results over dinner in one of the many upmarket restaurants or pubs – this is a town that lives and breathes all things equestrian.

Newmarket's page in racing history really began in 1604, when James I went hunting in the area, and saw its potential for sporting activities. Choosing Newmarket as his base, he leased a local inn, creating what must have surely been the least glamorous of all of Britain's Royal Palaces. The Griffin suffered from subsidence, and eventually collapsed in around 1614 with James I and several members of his court inside it at the time. Fortunately, they were all unharmed and were pulled free.

The King was not deterred, and both the Griffin and the nearby Swan Inn were demolished to make way for a much larger royal residence. With this, Newmarket's status as a sort of royal holiday resort was assured. The first recorded race here took place in 1622 – many more were to follow.

Charles I – who, in fact, was imprisoned in the royal palace at Newmarket before his execution – and his son Charles II were both keen horsemen. Charles II is said to have been interested in the breeding of racehorses and in improving the cavalry stock, which had been severely depleted during the Civil War. He is thought to have made at least two visits a year to the town to ride, during which time he set up both the July Course and the Rowley Mile. A pattern of spring and autumn race meetings was established, which continues to this day.

Newmarket was right at the centre of national horseracing again in 1750 when The Jockey Club set up shop there. This group of horseracing's elite members met to draw up the rules for horseracing, jockeys, trainers, owners and racecourses. Essentially a very exclusive gentleman's club at its inception – its members would largely have come from within the aristocracy – it conjures up delightful images of wealthy peers exchanging racing stories over a cigar in the billiards room; whether accurate or not, who can say? Its intriguing set up of privilege and power is one made use of by the late Dick Francis in his popular racing thriller – well worth a read for anyone interested in horseracing.

▼ Training at Newmarket

The Jockey Club moved to London in the 1960s and still owns 15 of Britain's racecourses, though racing itself is now governed by the British Horseracing Authority.

Back to Newmarket though. At any one time there are over 3,000 thoroughbred horses based here in training in the 50 or so stables, and almost as many owners, trainers, jockeys and stable hands, along with many breeding studs and veterinary practices – Newmarket is a world leader in horse health.

It is also the largest horse breeding and training centre in the country, and has two of the world's finest flat racing racecourses, the one mile two furlong-long Rowley Mile and the mile-long July Racecourse. The latter is next to the National Stud, and is known for its summer party atmosphere. You can see the racecourses on your visit, along with huge swathes of flat greens neatly divided by fencing where horses are trained.

To experience Newmarket at its best, try to plan your visit to coincide with a race day. Both the Rowley Mile and the July Racecourse have a lengthy programme of meetings. Champions' Day, held at the Rowley Mile, is well worth seeing. It is the last major event in the European flat racing season and, arguably, the best single day's racing in its calendar. There are six races of the highest class, making it Newmarket's premier race day.

Champions' Day is the culmination of the October meeting season and provides the last chance for riders to make their mark, and claim almost £1 million in prize money. To splash out, buy a ticket that allows entry to the Members' Enclosure, which provides the best facilities the racecourse has to offer, and the best views of the Finishing Post, Parade Ring and Winners' Circle.

SUTTON HOO, LAND OF ANGLO-SAXON KINGS

One of the most important archaeological sites in Britain, Sutton Hoo near Woodbridge in Suffolk, has revealed such astonishing treasures befitting only a king that its discovery in 1939 opened up a whole new chapter of English history.

The significance of the Anglo-Saxon finds, including a ship and priceless regalia, which had lain undisturbed since the early seventh century, is incalculable. It is an extraordinary site and well worth adding to your itinerary.

Sutton Hoo, a picturesque place surrounded by lovely walks with estuary views, is an Anglo-Saxon ship burial site. Excavation revealed an 89-foot-long heavy oak ship which, although its timbers had rotted, had moulded itself in the soil, together with

▲ The Sutton Hoo mask

its magnificent contents of jewellery, vessels and weapons, all beautifully preserved. Historians think that the ancient burial is probably that of King Raedwald who reigned from around AD 599 to 624.

Among the treasures found in the burial chamber of the ship were a ceremonial warrior's helmet, shield, Byzantine silverware, a set of spears, a purse containing gold coins and a collection of gem-encrusted gold body ornaments, such as buckles, that were so fine as to suggest they could only have been the property of a great person. Particularly significant, and unusual, was a sceptre, traditionally carried only by a ruling monarch. No body was found, but soil analyses suggest that all traces of it would have long since disappeared in the acidic soil.

The Anglo-Saxons were a people from Denmark and Germany who settled in Britain after the Romans had left in the fifth century; 200 years later, Raedwald was one of the first rulers of the Kingdom of East Angles. Anglo-Saxon custom decreed that important people were buried beneath mounds, with precious goods as a sign of their wealth and importance. The burial of an entire ship is unique to East Anglia and Scandinavia, and signifies that the body was that of a prominent person. The ship would have been hauled up the hill from the river, and lowered into a trench with only its stem and stern posts visible above ground. The body and personal processions would have been placed in the ship, and then a mound of earth build around it.

Although few details of Raedwald's reign remain after the destruction of monasteries, which held vital documents, by the Vikings in the nineth century, he was said to have been one of the most powerful kings of the period and Sutton Hoo would have been a fitting memorial to him.

You might be wondering how this extraordinary site was discovered. Well, at one time the land close to the River Deben was owned by amateur archaeologist Edith Pretty (1883–1942) who lived in a modern house on the site. She reported seeing ghostly warriors hovering over mounds on her land and sought the help of local archaeologist Basil Brown to start a dig here. Three of the mounds were empty, thought to have been robbed in the 16th or 17th century, but in the fourth he made the amazing discovery.

A treasure trove inquest declared Edith to be the owner of the finds, which she promptly donated to the British Museum in 1939, still the largest gift to the museum ever made by a living donor.

The National Trust now cares for Sutton Hoo and an exhibition houses some of the finds. There are replicas of the site's most fascinating treasures (which remain in the British Museum) and a full-sized reconstruction of the burial chamber, telling the story of how its treasures lay undisturbed for over 1,300 years.

LOCAL SPECIALITIES

When it comes to food and drink, you'd be hard pushed to find a region with quite so many specialities. Many of the recipes have been handed down through the generations and are supremely tasty with an exciting fusion of flavours. Most are healthy, too – that's if you discount some of the puddings, such as Norfolk's own treacle tart made with lashings of black treacle, flavoured with lemon and topped with a gigantic blob of double cream, which may have a few more calories than, say, fresh fish. But then you're on holiday so a few treats are allowed.

The tart, as well as Norfolk's version of bread pudding made with rum and dried fruit, locally known as Nelson slices, and Norfolk ginger biscuits, are eaten by households up and down the county and can usually be found in souvenir shops neatly packaged in portions for you to take home. The county is also as renowned for its Norfolk turkey, infamously reared at the Bernard Matthews Farms in Great Witchingham near Norwich for more than 60 years, and its world-famous mustard produced at the Colman's of Norwich factory in since 1814 (see page 219).

The coastline yields an abundance of delicacies. Be sure to try samphire, also known as sea asparagus, which grows in the tidal salt marshes off Norfolk; it can be pickled or steamed and served with a knob of butter. Don't miss Cromer crabs, whose habitat is the chalk reef just off the county's coastline, juicy Brancaster mussels from the creeks, or 'stewkey blue' cockles from Stiffkey.

Think of Suffolk pubs and the smooth golden ale that has been brewed by Adnams of Southwold for the past 150 years springs to mind. This family business has been a constant in the town, and is its biggest employer. The range has grown from the original cask ales to include bottled beers and lager, some of which are flavoured with banana and citrus, plus wines made from Merlot and Grenache grapes, and spirits such as barley vodka.

◀ Colman's Mustard Shop, Norwich ▲ Cromer crabs

Suffolk is also famous for its acres of apple orchards and the excellent ciders they produce. The Chevallier family at Aspall Hall Farm has been making cider since 1728. It started as a local brew, but is now an international brand and includes apple juice and vinegars available as far afield as the US and Australia.

In Bury St Edmunds, Greene King is an institution. The family business was founded in 1799 by Benjamin Greene and brews strong vintage ales. It's one of the largest British-owned breweries in the UK with an extensive range of restaurants and pubs.

To accompany all these fine ales and ciders, the county has plenty of food specialities too. Suffolk is known for its top-quality pork produced from herds throughout the county, and oysters from beds that dot the coastal creeks around Orford (see page 228). At Butley Creek, the beds yield oysters so fine that they have long been a delicacy on the menus of Suffolk restaurants. There's a smokehouse here too, founded by Richard Pinney, of Pinney's of Orford, where fishermen smoke trout and mackerel, kippers, eels and salmon over whole oak logs.

To follow, there are cheeses, from the delicately flavoured Suffolk Gold to the more robust Suffolk Blue. Then there are the pies and cakes, including Medley Pie made from kidneys and apples, and Suffolk Harvest Cake with its spicy mix of fruit.

Cambridge has long been associated with puddings and cakes. Trinity College has served a baked cream custard with a burnt sugar topping since the 19th century; its college coat of arms was traditionally burnt into the top of the dessert with a branding iron. But Cambridge is probably best known for afternoon tea. At the Orchard Tea Garden in Grantchester, made famous in a poem by Rupert Brooke (1887–1915), afternoon tea with scones and cakes was served to students who had punted upstream from Cambridge. The tradition of serving afternoon tea, and other delicacies, in the Orchard continues to this day (see page 137).

Farmers' markets found throughout Norfolk, Suffolk and Cambridge provide the perfect opportunity to sample some of the finest specialities of the region and to chat with the producers.

BEFORE YOU GO

THINGS TO READ

Ask someone to name a classic novel set in Norfolk or Suffolk, and they might struggle; there's no dramatic heights to wuther, and no Jane Austen character ever went to Norwich – although David Copperfield was born near Great Yarmouth. But, and Dickens aside, that's not to say the area doesn't have its own share of great literature. George Orwell lived for a time in Southwold in Sussex, while fantasy writers Philip Pullman and China Mieville were both born in Norwich – perhaps there's something in the water. One of the first graduates of the University of East Anglia's famous creative writing course was Booker Prize-winning novelist Ian McEwan – and he was taught there by Malcolm Bradbury (as was Kazuo Ishiguro). Diana Athill and *Black Beauty* author Anna Sewell were also Norfolk-born.

But one of the region's most famous literary connections isn't even a person: it's a line. 'The past is a foreign country: they do things differently there.' is the opening line of *The Go-Between* by L P Hartley. First published in 1953, and granted immortality by its induction to the hallowed halls of Penguin Modern Classics, *The Go-Between* is the story of a young boy's loss of innocence over a long, hot summer spent at the fictional Brandham Hall in Norfolk. Even if you've never read the novel, you'll almost certainly recognise the quote. The film adaptation was also made on location in Norfolk.

A Norfolk summer is also a feature of *The Accidental* by Ali Smith, when a family holiday is upended by the arrival of a mysterious stranger, while in Rose Tremain's *Restoration*, Norfolk is both exile and sanctuary for Charles II's foolish physician and sometime-favourite Robert Merivel.

Meanwhile, in Suffolk, childhood trauma with a Martello tower in the starring role features in *The Twins* by

Saskia Sarginson, a recent Richard and Judy book club pick and the type of holiday read to make you neglect all that actual sightseeing in favour of finding out just what happened...

It's probably against the rules to provide any sort of recommended reading for Cambridge without featuring that university, but *Porterhouse Blue* by Tom Sharpe and *The Liar* by Stephen Fry each take care of proceedings in suitably comedic fashion. If creepy multi-layered literature about science, religion and genius undergraduate musicians is more your thing – and why wouldn't it be? – *The Bellwether Revivals* by Benjamin Wood will have you sleeping a little less soundly in your bed at night.

Crime aficionados meanwhile should try Kate Atkinson's *Case Histories*, the first of – so far – four novels starring typically troubled private-investigator-with-a-past Jackson Brodie, as he attempts to solve three separate – but entwined – old cases in modern-day Cambridgeshire.

THINGS TO WATCH

Did you know that Harry Potter was from Suffolk? That's if you're watching *Harry Potter and the Deathly Hallows: Part I* (2010), at least – Harry's infant home 'Godric's Hollow', which Harry and Hermione visit in their search for the Deathly Hallows, is actually the Suffolk village of Lavenham. A lot of it was either re-created at Pinewood Studios or given a helping hand with CGI, but you'll recognise De Vere House, Harry Potter's birthplace – said to be the second most photographed doorway in Britain, behind 10 Downing Street.

Lavenham's medieval streets also featured in the British horror movie *Witchfinder General* (1968), starring Vincent Price. Less friendly to witches and wizards in this incarnation than in Harry Potter, the town square hosts a witch burning. The film, based on the true story of Matthew Hopkins in the 17th century, also used several other locations in the area, including Dunwich, Kentwell Hall and Orford Castle.

Plenty of properties in the area are well accomplished in the art of pretending to be something else. Holkham Hall's Marble Hall stands in for the entrance hall of Devonshire House in *The Duchess* (2008) – and that wasn't Keira Knightley's only visit to Holkham. She can also be found hanging out on the estate's beach in *Never Let Me Go* (2010), while Gwyneth Paltrow washed up there at the end of *Shakespeare in Love* (1998). Fellow film star Elveden Hall's exotic interiors, meanwhile, host an orgy in *Eyes Wide Shut* (1999), a banquet in Bond movie *The Living Daylights*

(1987), a king's bedchamber in *Stardust* (2007) and an evil villain's lair in *Lara Croft: Tomb Raider* (2001).

It's Ely Cathedral that's the real star, though – it has served as the backdrop for royalty three times in the last decade alone, as Henry VIII's palace, Whitehall and Westminster Abbey, respectively, in *The Other Boleyn Girl* (2008), *Elizabeth: the Golden Age* (2007), and *The King's Speech* (2010).

Incidentally, although largely set at Cambridge University, *Chariots of Fire* (1981) was refused permission to film on location at Caius College as the plot contained accusations of anti-Semitism against them. Eton College in Berkshire stood in, although there's a few establishing exterior shots of Cambridge itself. The film is largely based on true events, so still worth a watch even if you have to squint a bit to see a glimpse of the town.

If you prefer your scenery on the small screen, fans of *Dad's Army* (1968–77) will recognise much of the Norfolk town of Thetford as the fictional Walmington-on-Sea. Thetford, of course, being inland. Look out for the Guildhall, the flint cottages in Nether Row, the church and the Palace Cinema. Walmington-on-Sea's pier can be found at Great Yarmouth.

Norfolkian – if that's a word – Stephen Fry's TV series *Kingdom* (2007–9) was also filmed in Norfolk – and unlike most of the aforementioned, was actually set there as well, even if the town of Market Shipborough was fictional. It's actually Swaffham, though Wells-next-the-Sea, Hunstanton, Dereham, Thetford and – yes – Holkham's beach again all make appearances. The Norfolk accents have been criticised, but for pure East Anglian authenticity, it's still probably your best bet.

▾ Church Bell Gate, East Bergholt

That's with one major exception, of course. Who could forget Norwich's most famous fictional son, Alan Partridge? Seen most recently onscreen in *Alan Partridge: Alpha Papa* (2013), look out for Cromer Pier and Norwich. You could also seek out *Alan Partridge: Welcome to the Places of My Life* (2012) and be taken by Alan on a tour of his beloved Norfolk.

THINGS TO KNOW

Norfolk, Suffolk and Cambridge have a few quirky tales: Legend has it that the church tower of St Michael in Beccles (see page 61), Suffolk, has clock faces on only three sides; the side facing Norfolk is blank because townsfolk didn't want to give their time for free to their neighbours.

It was the presence of ghostly warriors hovering over Sutton Hoo (see page 262) that led to the discovery of the remains of a ship burial containing priceless treasures belonging to the Anglo-Saxon King Raedwald.

If you thought the rolling fields surrounding the burial mounds at Sutton Hoo look like pristine fairways of the finest 18-hole golf course, you'd be right. Sutton Hoo turf is grown especially for golf courses, cricket grounds and sports pitches in dry countries such as Saudi Arabia.

Look out for the 500-year-old timber cage housing the bells of the Church of St Mary the Virgin in East Bergholt (see page 125). They are believed to be the heaviest still rung in England, and are rare in that they are rung by hand by ringers who stand alongside.

Cambridge has one of the world's largest concentrations of sundials. The Old Court of Queens' College (see page 90) has a 17th-century moon-dial. It is one of the finest examples in Britain and

▾ Burial mounds at Sutton Hoo

▲ Trinity College, Cambridge

one of only a few moon-dials in the world.

You are not allowed to walk on the colleges' grass in Cambridge – unless you are a senior member of the college, that is, and only then on your own grass. For instance, Fellows of King's College can't walk on Trinity College's grass (see page 90).

Charles Dickens visited the Norfolk seaside town of Great Yarmouth (see page 139) in 1848, and the town appears in scenes in *David Copperfield*, among them the dramatic shipwreck in which David's boyhood friend Steerforth loses his life.

The Broads Reed and Sedge Cutters Association was formed to protect the age-old trade of reed and sedge cutting. The tall Norfolk reeds, which can grow up to 10 foot, are often used for thatching.

Wherry was the name given to the sailing boats that plied the Broads for centuries, carrying everything from timber to fish. Wherries were shallow-draughted, clinker-built, wooden boats powered by a large gaff sail, traditionally black in colour (see page 208).

Look out for Southwold Jack. Dressed in armour with a sword in one hand and an axe in the other, and standing next to a bell, the figure can be found in Southwold's Church of St Edmund, King and Martyr (see page 247). He is incredibly rare. Today, as in medieval times, he is made to raise his axe, which rings the bell to tell the congregation the service is about to start.

▲ Sundial at Front Court, Queens' College

THINGS TO PACK

The one thing you'll need to pack for a break in Norfolk, Suffolk and Cambridge is a good pair of walking boots. There's so much to see and do that your feet may take a bit of a pounding. But don't let all this talk of walking put you off visiting if you are a wheelchair user; East Anglia has been extremely conscientious in making all areas, including museums and churches, accessible for everyone. You'll find ramps, wide doors and so on to help you get about easily, with the exception of some of the old castle ruins and archaeological sites, although even these have been adapted reasonably well in recent years. Clothing should be light and comfortable, especially if walking or travelling by car, bus or train during the summer months. Take swimwear if you're planning to spend time on the beach or in a hotel swimming pool. Summer evenings can get a bit cooler so a jacket or jumper is advisable.

In winter, as in the rest of the UK, it's advisable to be mindful of weather conditions, and take note of forecasts that suggest heavy rain, frost or snow. Pack accordingly. Coastal areas can be extremely windy at any time of the year, so again you may need an extra layer of clothing. Evening dress should be smart casual, especially if you plan to dine in a restaurant or go to the theatre.

If you're planning to venture out into the countryside, you'll need waterproof clothes and suitable boots. Don't forget to carry your mobile phone, a torch and plenty of water. East Anglia has some wonderful walks, but always be mindful of a handful of risks, such as slippery cliff paths, tidal conditions if walking on the seashore, and farmyard machinery or livestock. Some areas, like heaths and marshland, can be tricky, especially in winter months when fog can descend quickly. In summer, you should always wear a hat to protect yourself from the sun, and drink plenty of water.

BASIC INFORMATION

It's easy to get about East Anglia, whether you are driving your own car or a hired vehicle, or you plan to use public transport.

Driving from London and the south, you'll probably find yourself taking the M25 for a short while, before turning off on either the A12, which takes you into Essex and onwards to Suffolk and Norfolk as far as Great Yarmouth, or the M11/A11 where you can easily reach Cambridge and the network of roads, including the A47, A10, A1065 and A14, which will take you into the heart of the region.

From the north of England and the Midlands, you'll need to navigate to the A14, which runs from Rugby in Warwickshire, right through to Felixstowe, passing through Cambridge and Ipswich.

The M25, M11, A12 and A14 are busy roads, especially at junctions and during peak weekday times when people are travelling to work. They all have service areas, so if you get stuck in traffic it may make sense to stop for a break before continuing your journey. All these roads pass through rolling countryside, which will at least make your journey more pleasant.

The region is well served by the railway network. Greater Anglia, for instance, connects the most northern regions of Norfolk – with stations at King's Lynn, Sheringham and Cromer – with Ely, Cambridge and Newmarket to the west and with the coastal towns of Great Yarmouth, Lowestoft and Felixstowe, via Bury St Edmunds, Ipswich and Norwich, and many smaller stations along the routes.

Similarly, long-distance bus/coaches, such as National Express, operate out of major hubs, like Birmingham, Manchester and Victoria in London, straight into the region's main towns and cities. In turn, buses provide an easy way to travel to the villages, or you could take a taxi.

As far as accommodation goes, East Anglia has plenty to offer. There are city centre hotels and many on the coast, such as at Southwold, Aldeburgh, Lowestoft and Great Yarmouth, have fantastic views over the sea. You will find cosy guest houses and inns with rooms too. The region also has a good selection of campsites (see pages 48–9).

FESTIVALS & EVENTS

The people of Norfolk, Suffolk and Cambridge will hold a festival at the drop of a hat, so there's always something going on if you fancy mingling with locals and having a fun day out. Here's a round-up of the best:

- **Norfolk and Norwich Food and Drink Festival**
  norfolkfoodanddrinkfestival.co.uk
  One of the biggest festivals of its kind in the country. Every summer there are hundreds of stalls selling everything from delicious Cromer crab, Brancaster mussels and 'stewkey blue' cockles to Norfolk's black treacle tarts.

- **Beer festivals**
  Elsewhere in Norfolk, beer festivals are a regular event in the diary, as are the seafood festivals at Cromer and Sheringham, and traditional folkloric events at Ludham, Cley, Holt, Wells and Worstead.

- **Aldeburgh Festival**
  aldeburgh.co.uk
  The most famous music festival in the region, if not the country, is held every summer at the Snape Maltings, a gorgeous 19th-century former granary on the Suffolk coast. Founded in 1948 by Benjamin Britten and Peter Pears, it now attracts world-class musicians.

- **Literature and Arts festivals**
  Southwold, Stowmarket and Ipswich all host regular literature and arts festivals. Ip-Art (ip-art.com) in Ipswich stages acts ranging from top comedy performers to music, literature, film and theatre.

- **Cambridge festivals**
  Cambridge hosts a Folk Festival (cambridgefolkfestival.co.uk), a Jazz Festival (cambridgejazz.org), a Comedy Festival (cambridgecomedyfestival.com) and a Film Festival (cambridgefilmfestival.org.uk).

- **Summer in the City**
  is a Cambridge favourite, and features a series of musical events held in the city's parks, while the Strawberry Fair transforms Midsummer Common into a fairground.

- **Ely Folk Festival**
  In Ely, the Ely Folk Festival (elyfolk.co.uk) attracts people from far afield, which is not surprising as the line-up includes jamming sessions, workshops and craft demonstrations.

- **Saints and harvest festivals**
  East Anglia's many churches host a number of festivals. Norwich Cathedral and Ely Cathedral, in particular, are famous for their rich festival pageantry.

CAMPSITES

For more information on these and other campsites, visit theaa.com/self-catering-and-campsites

The Old Brick Kilns ►►►►►

old-brick-kilns.co.uk
Little Barney Lane, Barney, NR21 0NL | 01328 878305
Open 15 Mar–15 Dec (restricted service Easter-Sep)

A secluded and peaceful park approached by a quiet, leafy country lane. The site is on two levels with its own boating and fishing pool and plenty of mature trees. There's outdoor chess and draughts and you can also book a massage. Due to a narrow access road, no arrivals are accepted until after 1pm.

Rose Farm Touring & Camping Park ►►►►►

rosefarmtouringpark.com
Stepshort, Belton, NR31 9JS
01493 780896 | Open all year

A former railway line is the setting for this very peaceful, beautifully presented site, which has some nice rural views and many bright flower beds. Customer care is truly exceptional and the quality cafe (open in peak season only) is popular.

Clippesby Hall ►►►►►

clippesby.com
Hall Lane, Clippesby, NR29 3BL
01493 367800 | Open all year

This lovely country house estate and its attached campsite has secluded pitches hidden among the trees or in sheltered sunny glades. There's a coffee shop with Wifi, a bar and restaurant and family golf. You can also try your hand at volley ball and table tennis, or hire a bike and take to the cycle trails. There are pine lodges and cottages available for holiday lets.

Seashore Holiday Park

haven.com/seashore
North Denes, Great Yarmouth, NR30 4HG | 01493 851131
Open Mar–Oct

Bordered by sand dunes and with direct access to a sandy beach, Seashore Holiday Park is located in Great Yarmouth and close enough to the Norfolk Broads for day trips. Facilities include excellent water activities and bike hire for children and lively evening entertainment for adults.

Two Mills Touring Park ►►►►►

twomills.co.uk
Yarmouth Road, North Walsham, NR28 9NA | 01692 405829
Open Mar–3 Jan
This intimate, beautifully presented park is set in superb countryside. The 'Top Acre' section is maturing and offers panoramic views over the site. The very friendly and helpful owners keep the park in immaculate condition. Please note this park is for adults only.

Westwood Caravan Park ►►►►

westwoodcaravanpark.co.uk
Old Felixstowe Road, Bucklesham, IP10 0BN | 01473 659637 & 07436 813545 | Open Mar–15 Jan
This constantly improving park is in the heart of rural Suffolk. All buildings are of traditional Suffolk style, and the toilet facilities are outstanding. The landscaping is also exceptional. There's a spacious room for visitors with disabilities and plenty of space for children.

Moon & Sixpence ►►►►►

moonandsixpence.eu
Newbourn Road, Waldringfield, Woodbridge, IP12 4PP
01473 736650 | Open Apr–Oct (restricted service low season – club, shop, reception open limited hours)
This well-planned site is located in a sheltered valley position around an attractive boating lake. Toilet facilities are housed in a smart Norwegian style cabin, and there is a laundry and dishwashing area. Leisure facilities include two tennis courts, a bowling green, fishing, boating and a games room. It has an adult-only area, and a strict 'no groups and no noise after 9pm' policy.

Cakes & Ale ►►►

cakesandale.co.uk
Abbey Lane, Theberton, Leiston, IP16 4TE | 01728 831655
Open Apr–Oct (restricted service low season club, shop & reception limited hours)
A large, well spread out and beautifully maintained site on a former World War II airfield. The spacious touring area has plenty of super pitches, and there's a good bar, football nets and a volleyball court.

Heathland Beach Caravan Park ►►►►

heathlandbeach.co.uk
London Road, Kessingland, NR33 7PJ | 01502 740337 | Open Apr–Oct
A well-run and maintained park set in meadowland, with level grass pitches. There's direct access to the sea and beach, good provisions for families, a heated swimming pool and three play areas, and a well-stocked fishing lake.

Run Cottage Touring Park ►►►►

run-cottage.co.uk
Alderton Road, Hollesley, IP12 3RQ
01394 411309 | Open all year
Located in the peaceful village of Hollesley, this landscaped park is set behind the owners' house; for the 2014 season the site will be improved and extended.

SANDERLIN
MATRIX

A–Z of Norfolk & Suffolk

VISIT THE MUSEUMS | GET OUTDOORS | EXPLORE BY BIKE | GO BACK IN TIME | TAKE A TRAIN RIDE | MEET THE WILDLIFE
TAKE IN SOME HISTORY | HIT THE BEACH | EAT AND DRINK | GET INDUSTRIAL | VISIT THE GALLERIES | GO CANOEING
TRY HORSE-RIDING | PLACES NEARBY | CATCH A PERFORMANCE | GO ROUND THE GARDENS | TAKE A BOAT TRIP

Aldeburgh

With its timber-framed cottages dating back to Tudor times, many in shades of pink and yellow, Georgian houses and a shingle beach that stretches as far as the eye can see, Aldeburgh, in Suffolk, is every inch the quintessential sleepy English holiday resort. You'll start to relax the moment you arrive. Away from the coast, the town is surrounded by countryside, with neighbouring hamlets barely specks on the horizon. But don't mistake its importance – Aldeburgh is well and truly on the map, thanks to just one man.

Celebrated composer and conductor Benjamin Britten (1913–76), one of the most famous figures of 20th-century British classical music, adored Aldeburgh and made his home here. Born in Lowestoft, the son of a local dentist, he grew up a stone's throw from the sea. He began composing at the age of five. After studying at the Royal College of Music, he moved to the United States and, as coincidence would have it, began reading the works of Aldeburgh poet George Crabbe (1754–1832). Crabbe, who had lost two brothers to the sea, and whose father was a salt-master, wrote with passion about the lives of Suffolk fishermen. Inspired by Crabbe's work, Britten returned to Suffolk and purchased the Old Mill in Snape, which was to become his home. Here he wrote *Peter Grimes*, an opera based on Crabbe's 'The Borough'. The opera is magical and gritty; you can almost hear the waves breaking on Aldeburgh's shingle beach as the bitterly cold wind comes in on the tide, echoing the anguish of the fisherman Peter Grimes. Britten's lifelong partner, the operatic tenor Peter Pears, took the lead when it was first performed in 1945.

Britten and Pears founded the Aldeburgh Festival in 1948, which is considered one of the finest music festivals in the world. It is housed in former maltings at Snape. The couple lived in Aldeburgh for the rest of their lives, first on the seafront at 4 Crabbe Street – look out for the plaque which tells you that this was Britten's home from 1947 to 1957 – and then in the larger Red House, a farmhouse on the outskirts of town. They are buried side by side in St Peter and St Paul church.

This part of the Suffolk coast also held attractions for writers, including Daniel Defoe, Wilkie Collins and Edward FitzGerald, translator of the fatalistic *Rubaiyat of Omar Khayyam*. Thomas Carlyle wrote approvingly of Aldeburgh's shingly beach and clear water, and novelist EM Forster enjoyed the bleakness as well as the beauty of the place.

While you're in Aldeburgh, be sure to take a look at the Moot Hall, which is a glorious red-brick Tudor building on the seafront, containing a small museum telling the story of

▲ Aldeburgh beach

Aldeburgh. If you walk along the shingle beach from here you'll come to the Martello tower, which was one of a string of defensive towers built along the coast in the 19th century.

On the beach itself is a sculpture, entitled *The Scallop*, dedicated to Benjamin Britten. It's 12ft high so you can't miss it, but don't mention it to the locals as it's not popular. Although you're encouraged to sit on it and look out to sea, many people consider it looks incongruous in the natural surroundings.

Aldeburgh, which means old fort, has a fascinating history. It was a bustling and prosperous medieval port with a flourishing fishing industry and shipbuilding workshops that were among the best in the country. It was here that Sir Francis Drake's ships, the *Greyhound* and the famous *Golden Hind*, were built. Like so many towns along the east coast, Aldeburgh fell into decline when the harbour silted up. Its fishing and shipbuilding days diminished to a point when only local fishermen, and smugglers, could navigate its waters in their tiny boats. In Victorian times its fortunes took a brief upwards turn when it became a fashionable, yet select, holiday resort.

Today, Aldeburgh lies on the banks of the River Alde, at a point where it diverts away from the sea and runs parallel with the coast, separated by the shingle ridge of Orford Ness. It is in an Area of Outstanding Natural Beauty. The shingle is home to many species of rare invertebrates, particularly spiders and beetles.

TAKE IN SOME HISTORY

Martello Towers

visit-aldeburgh.co.uk
Slaughden Road, IP15 5NA

The area's Martello Towers date from around 1810, built to defend against a Napoleonic invasion. The largest, now converted into a holiday home, stands on Orford Ness shingle split, a short walk along Aldeburgh's seafront. There's another at Bawdsey cliffs.

VISIT THE MUSEUMS

The Red House

brittenpears.org
Red House, Golf Lane, IP15 5P2
01728 451700 | Open Jun–Sep, Tue–Sat 2–5; Jan–May & Oct–Dec Tue–Fri 2–5

You can join a tour at the Red House, once the home of Benjamin Britten and Peter Pears and now the headquarters of the Britten-Pears Foundation. See their house, the gallery which has an exhibition that gives you a wonderful introduction to their music, and their studio cleverly created with excellent acoustics within a former hayloft. Exhibits include Britten's piano.

The Aldeburgh Museum

aldeburghmuseumonline.co.uk
Moot Hall, Seafront, IP15 5DS
01728 454666 0 | Open Apr–May & Sep–Oct 2.30–5 daily; Jun–Aug 12–5. Closed Nov–Mar

The little museum inside the Moot Hall on Aldeburgh's seafront tells the fascinating story of the town's history. You can take tours from here too. This Grade I listed timber-framed, flint-and-brick hall was built in Tudor times and would have been the focal point of Aldeburgh's market square. It now stands in isolation, almost on the shingle beach where fishermen draw up their boats, but would almost certainly have once been surrounded by similar Tudor buildings that have vanished into the sea. On its gabled wall is a sundial with the date 1650; it was added around 130 years after the hall was built. The building was restored in 1854 and Jacobean-style chimneys added. As well as the museum, it houses the council chamber, as it has done for the past 400 years.

ENTERTAIN THE FAMILY

Kid's Treasure Trail

Moot Hall, Seafront, IP15 1BH
07976 252334

Youngsters (and mums and dads too) can join the Kid's Treasure Trail, which tests skills of observation with clues on plaques, signposts and buildings. The story of Aldeburgh is told along the way.

PLAY GOLF

Aldeburgh Golf Club

aldeburghgolfclub. co.uk
Saxmundham Road, IP15 5PE
01728 452890 | Open daily including Bank Holidays

Good natural drainage provides year-round golf in links-type conditions on this heathland course. There are fine views over the Suffolk Coast and Heaths to be had.

EAT AND DRINK

Regatta Restaurant ❁

regattaaldeburgh.com
171 High Street, IP15 5AN
01728 452011

Regatta has been going for two decades, drawing in local foodies with its bright and breezy ambience, stylish seaside-themed decor with murals of yachts on choppy waters on the walls and, of course, its excellent dishes and use of locally sourced raw materials. The sea is just a pebble's skim away, so it is only right that super-fresh fish landed on the beach in Aldeburgh is showcased in Robert and Johanna Mabey's cheery bistro. A blackboard of fresh fish specials bolstering the à la carte selection is sure to tempt you. There's an extensive wine list and the liqueur selection adds the finishing touch.

Wentworth Hotel ❁❁

wentworth-aldeburgh.com
Wentworth Road, IP15 5BD
01728 452312

A grand country house in a peaceful location overlooking Aldeburgh's pebble beach, the Wentworth is one of the town's premier hotels and restaurants. Oozing tradition, its restaurant has claret-coloured walls hung with portraits, a thickly carpeted floor, crisp napery and sea views. The cooking has its roots in the traditional English repertory, with local produce the mainstay – think meat from Suffolk farms and fish landed on the beach that morning.

The White Lion Hotel ❁

whitelion.co.uk
Market Cross Place, IP15 5BJ
01728 452720

Unpretentious brasserie dining is the deal at the White Lion, Aldeburgh's oldest hotel

▾ The Moot Hall, Aldeburgh

located next to the shingle beach, and it's all built on fine Suffolk ingredients. In fact, sourcing doesn't get more local than the fish landed just a few steps away, which turns up on the plate as exemplary haddock in Adnams beer batter with crisp golden chips and chunky tartare sauce. Bathed in a dramatic cobalt-blue light by night, the sparkling-white building revels in a fresh contemporary look inside, while its beautifully carved inglenook in the bar and oak panels in the restaurant still hold pride of place.

Top 10 experiences

- Take a punt on the **River Cam** and see the **Mathematical Bridge**, page 88
- Stroll along **Britannia Pier** in **Great Yarmouth** and experience the wind in your hair, page 145
- Enjoy the tranquillity and wildlife of the **Norfolk Broads**, page 203
- Let your imagination take you back to Anglo-Saxon times at **Sutton Hoo**, page 262
- See seals bobbing in the waters off **Blakeney Point**, page 62
- Wonder at **Ely Cathedral**, rising like a massive ship from the flat landscape of the Fens, page 126
- Pass under the magnificent gatehouse and stroll around **Abbey Gardens** in Bury St Edmunds, page 77
- See a Norfolk windmill – one of the prettiest is **Bircham Windmill** with its massive white sails, page 138
- The sunset from **Hunstanton beach**, page 162
- Follow in the footsteps of royalty at **Sandringham House**, page 236

PLACES NEARBY

Thorpeness is a five-minute drive along the coast and is a peaceful and lovely place in which to unwind, while Orford lies to the south of Aldeburgh and is an important wildlife area (see page 228). The Minsmere RSPB Nature Reserve is close by (see page 238), and the small village of Leiston – where you can visit the Long Shop Museum and abbey ruins – is a short drive inland. No visit to Aldeburgh would be complete without a visit to the Snape Maltings. For refreshments, try the Parrot and Punchbowl Inn in Aldringham or the Crown Inn in Snape.

Leiston Abbey

leistonabbey.co.uk
Leiston, IP16 4TD | 01728 831354
Open at any reasonable time

For hundreds of years this mostly 14th-century abbey – originally founded in 1182 – was used as a farm and its church became a barn. A Georgian house, now used as a school for young musicians, was built into its fabric and remains of the choir, the church transepts and parts of the cloisters still stand.

Long Shop Museum
www.longshopmuseum.co.uk
Main Street, Leiston, IP16 4ES
01728 832189 | Open Apr–Oct Thu–Tue 10–5, Sun 11–5
Discover the magic of steam with a visit to the world-famous traction engine manufacturers, Richard Garrett engineering. See the traction engines and road rollers in the very place that they were built. Soak up the atmosphere of the Long Shop, built in 1852 as one of the world's first production line engineering halls. This is an award-winning museum with five exhibition halls full of items from the glorious age of steam, covering 200 years of local, social and industrial history.

Snape Maltings
snapemaltings.co.uk
Snape, Aldeburgh, IP17 1SP
01728 688303 | Open 10–5
The former 19th-century maltings complex at nearby Snape has been turned into one of the country's leading music venues and a smart shopping outlet. Here you can buy upmarket goodies, and take a break in the tea room or the pub. The hall itself is housed in a converted red-brick warehouse and hosts a regular programme of classical, jazz and folk concerts, featuring the world's finest musicians. Here, too, the famous Aldeburgh Music Festival, founded by Britten and Pears in 1948, takes place every June. The complex stands amid reeds and marshes on the outskirts of Aldeburgh.

The Parrot and Punchbowl Inn and Restaurant
parrotandpunchbowl.co.uk
Aldringham Lane, Aldringham, IP16 4PY | 01728 830221
If you thought bizarre pub names were a late 20th-century fad, think again. Originally called the Case is Altered, this 16th-century pink-washed smugglers' inn became the Parrot and Punchbowl in 1604 when Aldringham was a centre for smuggled contraband. East Anglian-brewed ales from Adnams and Woodforde's, and Suffolk's Aspall Cyder all feature in the bar line-up. The good-value menu includes daily specials and vegetarian meals. There are roasts on Sundays and quiz nights.

The Crown Inn
www.snape-crown.co.uk
Bridge Road, Snape, IP17 1SL
01728 688324
It must be the abundant old beams, brick floors, fine double settle and large inglenook fireplace that help make this 15th-century, former smugglers' inn so atmospheric. The absence of gaming machines and background music also contributes and then, of course, there's the food. Teresa and Garry Cook know exactly where their produce comes from: they rear

their own quail, poultry, Suffolk lamb, rare-breed pigs and Anglo-Nubian goats; they source Limousin beef from a nearby farm and game from local shoots. Orford fishermen do their bit too. From the Cooks' allotment come vegetables and herbs, and they forage enthusiastically. Pre- or post-concert meals are available for those going to Snape Maltings. There's also a spacious garden.

Baconsthorpe

Baconsthorpe is a sleepy village that lies just a few miles from Holt and the coastal town of Sheringham in one of Norfolk's wildest and most remote spots. Here, huge skies and an ever-changing landscape provide interest for its 250 or so inhabitants. The village is perhaps best known for the remains of its once magnificent 15th-century castle, now owned by English Heritage. It once formed part of fortified quadrangle-style manor house built by Sir John Heydon, a wealthy landowner and political ally of William de la Pole, the first Duke of Suffolk, during the Wars of the Roses (1455–85). In the village, the medieval Church of St Mary contains a magnificent 16th-century glass window and artefacts dating back six centuries.

TAKE IN SOME HISTORY

Baconsthorpe Castle

www.english-heritage.org.uk
NR25 6LN | 01799 322399
Open at any reasonable time

Baconsthorpe Castle was the home of wealthy Sir John Heydon, who had it built around the 1460s to protect himself and his family during the Wars of the Roses. He was a supporter of the first Duke of Suffolk, but is said to have changed his allegiance a few times for his own gain, thus upsetting a number of influential people. The exact date when work started on the castle is not known, since Sir John did not apply for the statutory royal licence necessary to construct a fortified house. He built the house anyway, to a quadrangle design with towers and a collection of buildings around an inner courtyard, with the fortification added later. A three-storey gatehouse was built as a focal point in the middle of the south wall, and an outer gatehouse had a drawbridge over which visitors could cross the moat. It was a lavish home. In the 1560s, Sir John's grandson added the outer gatehouse, which was inhabited until the 1920s, when one of the turrets fell down.

Visiting the site today, you can see many of the walls and the gatehouses, which remain in fairly good condition and give an insight into how grand this house once was. The red-brick and knapped-flint remains are reflected in the lake, which still partly embraces the castle as a moat, offering a dramatic view and a great photo op.

PLACES NEARBY

Be sure to visit Holt (see page 155) and Sheringham (see page 239), two of the prettiest places in the Norfolk coastal region, and the Blakeney National Nature Reserve for great views (see page 62).

Banham

Banham lies in the southernmost regions of Norfolk, not far from Diss (see page 117), in an area rich in forest and agricultural countryside. This historic, yet modern, town with plenty of amenities such as shops and schools, revolves round its parish church of St Mary the Virgin. An impressive Grade I listed building made of Norfolk flint, its construction began in the early part of the 14th century, but it took many decades for it to be completed because a huge number of local masons died in the Black Death of 1349 and a shortage of the craftsmanship and skills needed ensued. Banham is also the home of Banham Zoo, which you'll find has everything for a great day out from tigers and leopards, zebras and horses to an adventure playground and restaurants.

ENTERTAIN THE FAMILY

Banham Zoo

banhamzoo.co.uk

The Grove, NR16 2HE

01953 887771 | Open Jan–mid-Mar and mid-Oct–Dec daily 9.30–4; mid-Mar–mid-Jul and mid-Sep–mid-Oct 9.30–5; mid-Jul–mid-Sep 9.30–7

Set in 50 acres of magnificent parkland and gardens complete with winding pathways, rest areas and lakes, Banham Zoo is one of the best in the region. You can see hundreds of animals ranging from big cats, such as cheetahs, ocelots and the gorgeous Snow Leopard, to birds of prey; and from giraffes, zebras and red kangaroos to shire horses, snakes and monkeys. Tiger Territory is a purpose-built enclosure for Siberian tigers, including a rock pool and woodland setting; you can also visit Lemur Island and Tamarin and Marmoset Islands, or take the woodland walk to see the flamingoes. The Farm Barn, with its domestic animals, is popular with children, as is the adventure play area, though the skytrek – aerial trekking on zip wires – is not for the faint-hearted. The zoo has restaurants, baby-changing facilities, locker hire and a souvenir shop to complete your day out.

Bawburgh

Bawburgh, a few miles outside Norwich in Norfolk, is associated with St Walstan who, legend has it, was responsible for many miracles. A special day of celebration is held every year at the village's Church of St Mary and St Walstan, on the nearest Sunday to 30 May, the day he died.

As the story goes, St Walstan was a charitable man who is said to have given his belongings to those less fortunate than himself. He dedicated his life to farming and livestock, and his knowledge became legendary. When he died in 1016 he was brought to Bawburgh from the village of Taverham, where he worked, on a cart pulled by two white oxen. Along the route, springs bubbled up to provide water for the animals. Walstan's shrine at Bawburgh's church became a place of pilgrimage for farmers. Throughout medieval times the cult grew and extended to counties beyond Norfolk, and eventually he was declared a patron saint of farmers and husbandry.

The Church of St Mary and St Walstan, a Grade I listed building, is unusual in having a round tower.

Bawburgh's other claim to fame is a mill in the centre of the village that was the original home of Colman's mustard (see page 219).

PLAY GOLF

Bawburgh Golf Club

www.bawburgh.com
Glen Lodge, Marlingford Road, NR9 3LU | 01603 740404
Open daily including Bank Holidays

A challenging 18-hole course with its mixture of parkland and heathland, Bawburgh Golf Club's main feature is a large hollow that meanders down to the River Yare, creating many interesting tee and green locations.

EAT AND DRINK

The Kings Head

kingshead-bawburgh.co.uk
Harts Lane, NR9 3LS
01603 744977

The Kings Head stands opposite Bawburgh's pretty village green, just yards from the River Yare. This 17th-century free house has bags of traditional charm. There are solid oak beams, bulging walls, wooden floors and comfy leather seating. Owners Anton and Pam Wimmer have been welcoming locals and visitors alike for nearly 30 years. The pub is named after Edward VII who, says Anton, invested the Edwardian era with a reputation for delicious if somewhat upholstered pleasures. 'We aim to continue this philosophy,' he says. Behind the bar are East Anglian ales and ciders, including Woodforde's Wherry. The monthly menus and daily changing specials are firmly rooted in local markets. Many of the dishes can be made gluten- or dairy free on request.

Beccles

As you stand in the centre of Beccles it's hard to believe that this historic – it was given its charter by Elizabeth I in 1584 – yet modern community-minded market town was once a thriving Saxon port. That's because it now stands some six miles from the sea. Beccles was at one time on the coast and all that could be seen looking east was water. In time, land was reclaimed and wherries plied up and down the waterways.

Beccles lies in the Waverley Valley at the southernmost extremity of the Norfolk Broads, although the town itself is rooted across the county border in Suffolk. The name Beccles is a combination of 'beck', a Scandinavian word meaning stream, and 'leas', meaning meadow. In fact, that's what medieval Beccles must have been for many years – largely a beautiful meadow by a stream.

The attractive parish church, St Michael's, has a 97-foot bell tower, which dates from the 16th century and is Perpendicular Gothic in style. Interestingly, it is not actually attached to the church building, but stands independently. Locals have dubbed it Beccles Bell Tower, and whenever you're arranging to see someone in town, you will almost always set the meeting place as the tower. According to legend, the church tower has clock faces on only three sides; the side facing Norfolk is blank because the inhabitants of Beccles did not want to give the time to their neighbours for free.

Horatio Nelson's mother, Catherine Suckling (1725–67), married his father, the Reverend Edmund Nelson, curate of Beccles, at St Michael's church in May 1749. Horatio was born in Burnham Thorpe, Norfolk, the sixth of eleven children, in 1758 and is best known for his naval career that ended with his death at the Battle of Trafalgar in 1805. Suffolk poet George Crabbe (1754–1832) was also married in St Michael's, in the 18th century.

PLAY GOLF

Beccles Golf Club

club-noticeboard.com/becclesgc
The Common, NR34 9BX
01502 712244 | Open Mon–Fri some Sun and Bank Holidays & Sat pm

Beccles' heathland course was founded in 1899 and welcomes visitors. A 9-hole course with fast greens, it has gorse bushes, but no water hazards or bunkers to hinder you.

PLACES NEARBY

Henstead Exotic Garden

hensteadexoticgarden.co.uk
Church Road, Henstead, NR34 7LD
07715 876606 | Open May–Oct, Wed 2–5 plus some Sun in Aug, Sep & Oct

The Henstead Exotic Garden really lives up to its name. For years, Andrew Brogan's 400-year-old cottage had been sheltered by a 10-foot yew hedge on one side and dense ancient woodland on the other, so when he moved here in 2000 a micro-climate was already established. Andrew wanted to create an exotic garden in which all the plants – with the sole exception of a red ensete banana – would be left outside to survive the fierce East Anglian winters. As much as 50 tons of rocks, stones and hardcore were needed to create the foundation of the garden and the volume of plants he has established since then is impressive: 10 large tree ferns, *Dicksonia antarctica*, which grow 12 inches every 10 years, 15 large bananas, 50 large palms, including six different types, all growing in the ground unprotected, over 100 bamboos and countless yuccas, puyas and ferns that cover tiers of rocks, low stone walls and curved paths.

The garden now extends into part of the adjoining ancient woodland, which is full of huge oak, yew and holly trees. Three large ponds, one stocked with koi carp and golden orfe, attract dragonflies. Pheasants strut around the garden as if it were their own, their red, green and blue plumage a camouflage against the colourful foliage. A visit to this garden is well worth the detour.

Africa Alive!
See highlight panel opposite

Blakeney

Blakeney is one of the many brick-and-flint villages that line the north Norfolk coast in an Area of Outstanding Natural Beauty. It is an important area for birds and wildlife, especially around the harbour, known as Blakeney Haven, and Blakeney Point, a strip of shingle where grey and common seals can often be seen bobbing in the waters.

The town was mentioned in the Domesday Book of 1086. At that time it was a small harbour, but from early medieval times through to relatively recently it has been a prosperous port, trading in grain and fish, and later in gold and silver. Sadly, like so many ports in the region, it went into decline when its sea channels began to silt up. Only small boats can now navigate the waters from the quayside out past Blakeney Point. While merchants decried the slow accumulation of salt marsh and sand bars over the decades, birds began to flock here in their thousands. So much so that by Victorian times Blakeney had become known as the place to go shooting.

Today, Blakeney's harbour and the surrounding marshes from Cley Beach to the tip of the sand and shingle peninsula of Blakeney Point are owned by the National Trust; it was one of the first nature reserves to be safeguarded in Britain.

Africa Alive!

africa-alive.co.uk
Whites Lane, Kessingland, NR33 7TF | 01502 740291
Open daily from 9.30. Check website for seasonal opening hours
Set in 100 acres of dramatic parkland in Kessingland, a few miles from Beccles towards the coast, Africa Alive! is one of Suffolk's most exotic animal wildlife parks. Here you can explore the sights and sounds of Africa, see giraffes, rhinos, cheetah and hyenas, and get a bird's-eye view of the lion enclosure. Attractions include daily feeding, talks and animal encounter sessions, a magnificent bird of prey display and a free journey round the park in a jeep.

▲ Blakeney harbour

Among the species of bird found here, including some that are vulnerable and rare, are Pallas's warbler, yellow-breasted bunting, subalpine warbler and red-spotted bluethroat. The Blakeney National Nature Reserve is open for you to visit. If you enjoy walking, the 45-mile North Norfolk Coastal Path, which opened in 1986, runs right along Blakeney's quayside. It's a lovely place to walk. A bright summer day will show you glittering streams, grasses waving gently in the breeze and yachts bobbing in the distance. By contrast, a wet and windy day in winter will reveal the stark beauty of this place, with the distant roar of white-capped waves pounding the beach.

In the centre of the village, look out for the large Gothic-style Church of St Nicholas. With its hilltop location and two huge towers, the most westerly of which has mighty flint buttresses, you shouldn't miss it. The towers are landmarks; the smaller of the two is lit at night and has long been used as a beacon to guide boats in past the Point to the harbour.

GET OUTDOORS

Blakeney National Nature Reserve

nationaltrust.org.uk/blakeney
Morston Quay, Quay Road, NR25 7BH | 01263 740241
Open daily dawn to dusk

Join the many walkers who flock to the Blakeney National Nature Reserve to enjoy the exercise, the peacefulness and the uninterrupted views of the unspoilt coastline with their changing tides and abundance of wildlife. If you're lucky you may see Arctic terns, skylarks, redshanks, oyster catchers and the thriving colonies of seals.

SEE A LOCAL CHURCH

St Nicholas' Church

A landmark Grade I listed church and one that has especially interesting architectural features, St Nicholas can trace its origins back to the 13th century when it was built at around the same time as Blakeney friary. The earliest part of this church is its deep, two-bay chancel, which dates from the period, while its 100-foot-long nave and its west and east towers are 15th century.

Take a look inside; it has the most beautiful hammerbeam rib-vaulted roof. There are only a handful of other churches with a roof built to this style, and few that look quite so dramatic. There's a seven-light window too, which is rare, and on the walls you can make out pre-Reformation graffiti that would have been done by the hand of merchants. The east tower is lit up at night and has an almost ghostly presence. It's very dramatic.

EAT AND DRINK

The Blakeney Hotel

blakeneyhotel.co.uk
The Quay, NR25 7NE
01263 740797

The Blakeney's quayside terrace is one of north Norfolk's gems on a sunny day, with a big-sky panorama sweeping across the estuary and salt marshes to Blakeney Point, and the cries of wading birds providing a soulful soundtrack. When the weather forces you inside the lovely flint-faced hotel, the restaurant still has that view, and is a shipshape venue with an easygoing, friendly ambience. The kitchen is clearly on good terms with local suppliers, showing off their wares to great effect in uncomplicated modern ideas – local crab, perhaps, on Bloody Mary jelly with avocado, cucumber salad and basil oil, or Brancaster oysters with raspberry shallot vinegar and lemon. Given the setting, fish is a good bet; meat is handled deftly, too. Finally, the pudding trolley trundles in, bearing comfort in the shape of warm spiced bread pudding with maple syrup.

The Blakeney White Horse
blakeneywhitehorse.co.uk
4 High Street, NR25 7AL
01263 740574
Dating from the 17th century, the Blakeney White Horse is a former coaching inn that today oozes 21st-century chic following a stylish refurbishment a few years back. It's tucked away among Blakeney's flint-built fishermen's cottages, a short, steepish amble up from the small tidal harbour. All around are glorious views over creeks, the Glaven Valley estuary, acres of marram grass-covered dunes, sea lavender, samphire, mussel beds and, on the horizon, the shingle ridge of Blakeney Point. Owners Francis and Sarah Guildea offer an à la carte and daily specials menus. Locally sourced food is a given, especially the lobster, crab and mussels from village fishermen, meats and game from Norfolk estates, soft fruit, salads, asparagus and free-range eggs from local smallholders, while rod- and line-caught mackerel and sea bass find their way through the kitchen door in summer.

The Kings Arms
blakeneykingsarms.co.uk
Westgate Street, NR25 7NQ
01263 740341
Tucked away in a tiny street, this thriving free house is the perfect refreshment stop following an invigorating walk, time spent birding or a boat trip to the nearby seal colony. An excellent selection of real ales, including Norfolk-brewed Woodforde's Wherry, is backed by menus featuring locally caught fish and seasonal seafood. Musical theatre stalwarts Howard and Marjorie Davies have run The Kings Arms since 1976 and pictures from their showbusiness days adorn the walls, adding a real sense of fun to the welcoming atmosphere of this 17th-century inn.

Blickling

see **Cromer**, page 108

Blythburgh

Blythburgh lies on the Suffolk coast in an Area of Outstanding Natural Beauty. An old Saxon town, it is quiet and peaceful, and surrounded by a tidal river, marshes, heathland, small woodlands, pastures and arable fields. The tidal section of the River Blyth flows just to the north of the village, reaching the sea at Southwold. Over the years, the sea walls have been breached and the land not reclaimed, creating a tidal lagoon, Blythburgh Water, which is immensely popular with coastal

▾ River Blyth, Blythburgh

birdlife as a safe habitat. The town is probably best known for the goings-on at its cathedral-like 15th-century church, which is often used as a venue for the Aldeburgh Festival (see page 52) – and for being the birthplace of actor Ralph Fiennes.

SEE A LOCAL CHURCH

Holy Trinity Church

holytrinityblythburgh.org.uk

Church Lane, IP19 9LL

Holy Trinity Church in Blythburgh has a mixed history. Famously, it was hit by a bolt of lightning in August 1577, bringing its steeple crashing to the ground. The devil was blamed for this deed. On the same day, Black Shuck, the legendary devil-dog of the marshes, is said to have run through the church, killing two parishioners. The damage to the roof meant that for a time congregations had to worship beneath umbrellas.

On a happier note, the church is sometimes referred to by locals as the Cathedral of the Marshes, lending credence to the claim that Blythburgh was once much larger than it is today. But even though Blythburgh has always been small, it attracted sufficient wealthy piety to build a large church. It also had an important Augustinian priory founded here in 1130, which probably accounts for the size and splendour of the church.

In 1412, Henry IV granted permission for the church to be rebuilt, transforming it into one of Suffolk's finest Perpendicular churches. The tower remains from the earlier building. The exterior is an amazing mix of flint and glass, with intricate decorative stonework and carving along the parapets of the porch and south aisle. Set into the east end are enigmatic carved letters.

If you step inside you'll see the aged wooden roof, still with its original faded paintwork, stretching the entire length of the church. On it are the 12 wooden angels celebrated in Blythburgh's town sign. There used to be more, and some of those that remain have had to be repaired or renewed.

One story tells that they were fired at by Puritans trying to dislodge them. Shot has been found in the roof timbers, but this probably dates from the 18th century, when people were paid to shoot at the jackdaws that inhabited the church.

In the chancel are stalls carved with figures of saints and the Apostles, which may have been part of the base of the rood screen. Each carries his own symbol so that he can be recognised. The figures are beautifully made and very sophisticated, with neatly combed beards and hair.

Look out for the clock jack, which rings to signal the start of services; it dates from 1682 and stands on a shelf near the altar.

Brancaster

Brancaster, together with the villages of Brancaster Staithe and Burnham Deepdale, form a community that hugs the north Norfolk coastline, on the edge of the protected Brancaster Manor salt marsh owned by the National Trust.

Each has stunning vistas over glorious tidal marshes to Scolt Head Island, a four-mile long sandbar thst is home to a nature reserve rich in birdlife. The villages are peaceful and picturesque with lots of brick-and-flint cottages that give this area its distinct look.

Many of this region's unspoiled villages have imposing, often circular, church towers, such as St Mary's in Burnham Deepdale – one of six medieval churches found within two miles of each other.

The reason for the distinctive round towers, which are so common in Norfolk, was not, as is often stated, that they were a form of defence against invaders, but simply because the absence of any other workable building stone made local flint the best available material. This knobbly and uneven stone is usually hammered and split open to reveal its black interior, a process known as knapping. Working with this stone meant that it was easier to build circular towers than masonry-faced square ones.

Brancaster is said to have been where Horatio Nelson (1758–1805), the famous admiral noted for his bravery in the Napoleonic wars of the 19th century, learned to sail as a boy. He was born in the nearby village of Burnham Thorpe. Local folklore says his nurse haunts the village's pub, the Ship.

ENTERTAIN THE FAMILY

Brancaster Activity Centre

nationaltrust.org.uk/brancaster
Brancaster Staithe, PE31 8BW
01485 210719 | Open daily 9–5

Make for the Brancaster Activity Centre in Brancaster Staithe, owned by the National Trust, where the family can really let off steam. Activity courses include sailing, kayaking and raft building as well as photography and art courses. The centre is Grade-II listed and was converted from a former pub and various outbuildings in the late 1990s.

PLAY GOLF

Royal West Norfolk Golf Club

rwngc.org
PE31 8AX | 01485 210087
Open Mon–Fri except Bank Holidays

One of the most famous courses in the UK, the fine links are laid out in a grand manner with sleepered greens, cross bunkers and salt marshes. The tranquil surroundings include a harbour, the sea, farmland and marshland, inhabited by many rare birds. For a great part of the year, the club is cut off by tidal flooding that restricts the amount of play.

EAT AND DRINK

The Jolly Sailors

jollysailorsbrancaster.co.uk
Brancaster Staithe, PE31 8BJ
01485 210314

The focal point of the village, the 18th-century 'Jolly' is the brewery tap for the Brancaster microbrewery, both run by father-and-son team, Cliff and James Nye. In the Harbour Snug you can look out over the water, read local books, and play darts and board games. The Nyes' Brancaster ales aren't obligatory – you'll also find Woodforde's and Adnams. Pub food is typified by open-fired pizzas, pie of the day, Cromer crab with salad, and spiced veggie burger. The beach-themed ice cream hut in the garden is an attraction. A beer, real cider and music festival begins in mid-June.

The Ship Hotel

shiphotelnorfolk.co.uk
Main Road, Brancaster, PE31 8AP
01485 210333

Set in a prime coastal location close to Brancaster beach, TV chef and hotelier Chris Coubrough's stylish gastro-pub continues to attract walkers, beach lovers and families with its appealing menus of modern pub food prepared from fresh produce sourced from local farmers and fisherman. Be tempted by smoked haddock, cockles and leek chowder or local venison casserole. Wash it down with a pint of Bitter Old Bustard and relax in the bar and dining rooms, where you can expect rug-strewn wood floors, wood-burning stoves, shelves full of books, scrubbed wooden tables and a distinctly nautical atmosphere.

The White Horse

whitehorsebrancaster.co.uk
Main Road, Brancaster Staithe, PE31 8BY | 01485 210262

While this neat, traditional but much-extended inn comes with a big bolt-on conservatory restaurant and decked terrace, the real show-stopper here is its location on the north Norfolk coast, offering knock-your-socks-off views over the tidal salt marshes. The brasserie-style dining room is a relaxed spot – all natural wood tables

▸ The coast at Brancaster

and seascape tones – and takes in the vista, while the kitchen doesn't disappoint, bringing fashionable modernity to great regional produce. Given the location, marine life has its say; as well as Brancaster oysters or mussels, there's pan-fried sea bass. The menu makes the best of Norfolk's land larder, too: try pan-roast Norfolk pheasant breast teamed with Brancaster braised vegetables, new potato fondant, sautéed kale and jus. There's a separate bar menu too.

PLACES NEARBY

Pop into the Hoste at Burnham Market or the Lord Nelson at Burnham Thorpe for a bite, and further afield take in Wells-next-the-Sea (see page 275) and the magnificent Holkham

10 top nature reserves

- **Blakeney National Nature Reserve,** page 65
- **Dingle Marshes RSPB Nature Reserve,** page 259
- **Holkham National Nature Reserve,** page 152
- **Horsey Mere Nature Reserve,** page 159
- **Minsmere RSPB Nature Reserve,** page 238
- **Orford Ness National Nature Reserve,** page 231
- **Pensthorpe Nature Reserve,** page 129
- **Ranworth Broad,** page 259
- **Titchwell Marsh RSPB Nature Reserve,**page 73
- **Wicken Fen National Nature Reserve,** page 279

Estate (see page 152). In North Creake, you can visit the ruins of Creake Abbey; and only a couple of miles away are the RSPB Titchwell Marsh reserve and the Titchwell Manor Hotel.

Creake Abbey

english-heritage.org.uk
North Creake, NR21 9LF
0870 333 1181 | Open at any reasonable time

The ruins at North Creake once formed part of an Augustinian abbey founded here in 1206. They stand in 40 acres. The abbey was originally founded as a hospital by local landowners Sir Robert and Lady Alice de Nerford; it later became a priory. Henry III elevated the priory to an abbey. Today, the ruins, which are beautifully preserved – albeit smaller than they once were due to a massive fire in 1484 that saw much of the building collapse – provide a backdrop to a monthly farmers' market, and a food hall, cafe, craft workshops and studio complex.

The Hoste ◎◎

hostearms.co.uk
The Green, Burnham Market, PE31 8HD | 01328 738777

A couple of miles back from the heritage north Norfolk shoreline, Burnham Market has acquired the kind of gentrified reputation that has seen it nicknamed Little-Chelsea-on-Sea. The Hoste is a historic whitewashed inn, partially covered in climbing foliage in the shape of a trident. Recent extensive refurbishment has introduced a lodge dining area influenced by New Zealand restaurant style, and an open kitchen. Great emphasis is laid on sourcing as much produce from within a 30-mile radius as possible, transforming it into an essentially simple modern idiom that avoids unnecessary frippery. Look out for the Brancaster oysters (in straightforward options of red wine vinegar, garlic and parsley, tempura or Bloody Mary).

The Lord Nelson

nelsonslocal.co.uk
Walsingham Road, Burnham Thorpe, PE31 8HN | 01328 738241

This pub started life in 1637 as the Plough and was renamed the Lord Nelson in 1798, to honour the village's most famous son. Located facing the delightful cricket ground and bowling green, it has an atmospheric interior that has changed little over the past 370 plus years; you can even sit on Nelson's high-backed settle. Drinks are served from the taproom, with real ales drawn straight from the cask. In the cosy bar you can also partake of unique rum-based tipples such as Nelson's Blood. The kitchen aims to cook dishes with balance between flavours, so that the quality of the ingredients shines. Children will enjoy the huge garden. From May to September, weekend walking tours of Nelson's village are available.

RSPB Nature Reserve Titchwell Marsh
rspb.org.uk
PE31 8BB | 01485 210779
Mar–Oct daily 9.30–5; Nov–Feb daily 9.30–4
Titchwell Marsh is one of the RSPB's most popular reserves. Here, hundreds of thousands of migrating birds pass through in spring and autumn and many stay during winter, providing an opportunity to see various species of ducks, waders, seabirds and geese. If you are really lucky you may catch sight of the RSPB emblem, the avocet. The reserve, which lies on the coast, is a great day out for the entire family.

Titchwell Manor Hotel ❁❁❁
titchwellmanor.com
Titchwell, Brancaster, PE31 8BB
01485 210221
A former Victorian farmhouse overlooking the coastal marshes, Titchwell Manor has been turned into an intimate and stylish boutique hotel. The neat little red-brick building has been owned by Margaret and Ian Snaith for over 15 years and, this being a real family business, son Eric looks after the food side of things. Eric's highly inventive seven-course tasting menus are served in the contemporary Conservatory Restaurant – an atmospheric setting for dinner with its twinkling lights wrapped around the ceiling beams, soft background music and views over the walled garden. If you need any clarification of the menu or have any questions about the 100-bin wine list, the staff will be happy to assist; alternatively, you could just sit back and enjoy. The pick of north Norfolk's larder, including local fish and seafood, plus flowers and herbs grown in the hotel's own garden, is showcased in dishes that are complex, innovative and as pretty as a picture.

Bressingham
see **Diss**, page 118

Bungay
The small market town of Bungay occupies a hilltop location surrounded by marshes and the valley of the River Waveney, which means you'll get fabulous views from here across the Suffolk countryside towards the sea. The Anglo-Saxons and Romans identified it as an excellent spot from which to defend their territories, and the Normans went a step further and built a castle. You can visit Bungay Castle (see page 74), which was built in 1165 and dominates the centre of the town. The Bungay Museum is also worth visiting.

TAKE IN SOME HISTORY

Bungay Castle

www.visit-sunrisecoast.co.uk
6 Cross Street, NR35 1AU
01502 533600 | Open daily 10–4

Built in the third century AD by the Romans, as one of a chain of forts along the Saxon Shore, sections of the massive walls still stand including walls, parts of the keep and the twin towers of the gatehouse, and learn about its history in the Bungay Castle Visitor Centre.

VISIT THE MUSEUM

Bungay Museum

suffolkmuseums.org
Broad Street, NR35 1EE
01986 896788 | Open Mon–Fri 9–1 and 2–4.30

This small museum is worth taking a look at for it has some interesting prehistoric, Anglo-Saxon and Roman pottery and tools found in the area, along with a model and descriptive boards that tell the story of Bungay Castle. Bungay had a vital printing industry at one time, and machinery from that period is also on display.

PLAY GOLF

Bungay and Waveney Valley Golf Club

club-noticeboard.co.uk
Outney Common, NR35 1DS
01986 892337 | Open daily including Bank Holidays

The heathland course of the Bungay and Waveney Valley Golf Club, lined with fir trees and gorse, has excellent greens all-year-round, with easy walking.

PLACES NEARBY

In the nearby village of Flixton, the Norfolk and Suffolk Aviation Museum is well worth a visit to see its remarkable collection of aircraft and war memorabilia. A little further afield, the Halesworth Airfield Museum offers a smaller collection.

Halesworth Airfield Museum

halesworthairfieldmuseum.org.uk
Sparrowhawk Way, Upper Holton
Halesworth IP19 8NH | 01986 875084 | Open 2–5 Sun and Bank Holidays Apr–Oct

This interesting museum has at its heart a collection of memorabilia dedicated to the period it served as an airfield during World War II.

Norfolk and Suffolk Aviation Museum

aviationmuseum.net
The Street, Flixton, NR35 1NZ
01986 896644 | Open Apr–Oct Sun–Thu 10–5; Nov–Mar Tue–Wed and Sun 10–4

Situated in the Waveney Valley, East Anglia's Aviation Heritage Centre contains collections from, among others, the 446th Bombardment Group USAAF, RAF Bomber Command and the Royal Observer Corps. It houses over 60 historic aircraft. A section is dedicated to the RAF Air Sea Rescue and Coastal Command. Among the displays are Decoy Sites and Wartime Deception, and Fallen Eagles – Wartime Luftwaffe Crashes. A former Ipswich Airport hangar made by Norwich company Boulton and Paul is a feature.

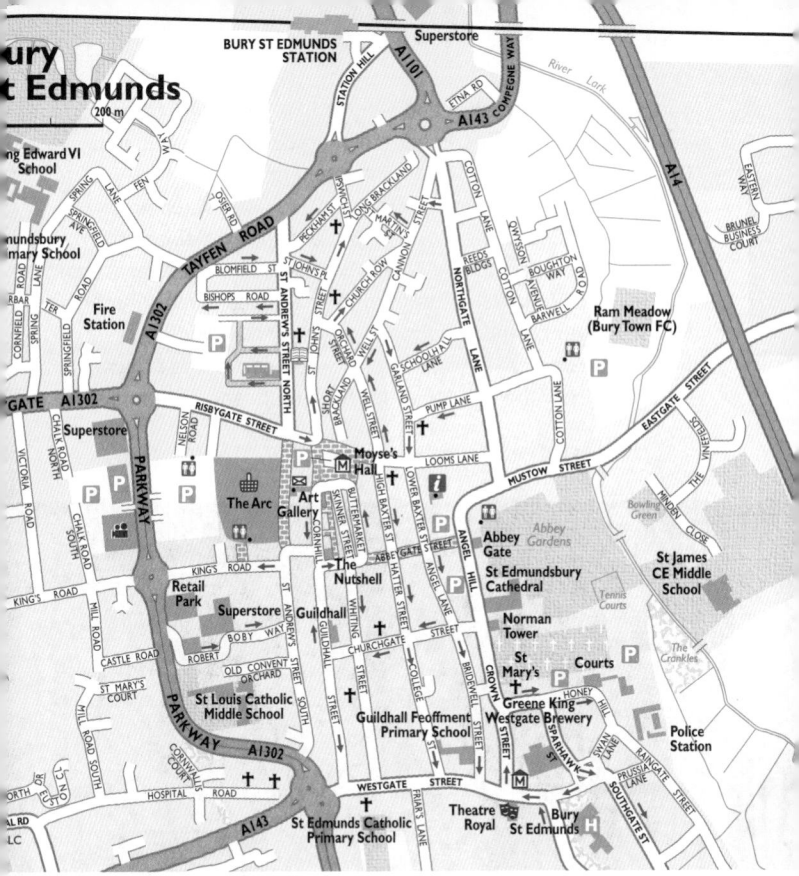

Bury St Edmunds

Bury St Edmunds is one of Suffolk's most prominent, elegant and imposing towns. It has a long and prosperous history dating back way before Saxon times when it was a royal town. Sigebert, the Saxon King of the Angles (East Anglia), and later a saint, lived here for a time, and founded a monastery in 633. The town grew in stature, and remains significant to this day.

The town takes its name from Edmund, also King of East Anglia from around 855 until 869. It is said he loved the town and was a popular king, but few documents relating to his reign remain since the Vikings destroyed much of the region, including the churches where important documents were kept.

When Edmund died, an abbey was built in his honour, housing his tomb, and became a place of pilgrimage. Miracles were attributed to him and he became patron saint of England in the Middle Ages. The abbey, along with the town, grew to become one of the most powerful and wealthiest in Europe.

Take a stroll around Bury, as it's affectionately known. The centre is quite compact, although a little steep in places. You'll be able to see the remains of the abbey and its magnificent gatehouse, its cathedral and leafy streets lined with the most beautiful Norman flint, Elizabethan timber-framed, elegant Georgian brick and Victorian Bath stone houses.

There are several museums for you to visit, including Moyse's Hall Museum, glorious gardens that are ablaze with colour all year round, and walks alongside the River Lark. Look out, too, for St Mary's Church, the burial place of Mary Tudor, Queen of France and the younger sister of Henry VIII. Just beyond the church is the Norman Tower, part of the original abbey and now the bell tower for St Edmundsbury Cathedral.

▾ Cathedral Church of St James

▲ Abbey Gardens

TAKE IN SOME HISTORY

St Edmundsbury Cathedral

stedmundsbury.gov.uk

Abbey House, Angel Hill, IP33 1LS

01284 748720 | Open daily 8–6

St Edmundsbury Cathedral began life as the parish church of St James and was upgraded when the diocese of St Edmundsbury and Ipswich was created in 1914. Tours are available from just inside the entrance. Also inside are an interesting art gallery and an exhibition area displaying some of the cathedral's treasures.

VISIT THE MUSEUM

Moyse's Hall Museum

moyseshall.org

Cornhill, IP33 1DX | 01284 757160

Open Mon–Sat 10–5 (last entry at 4), Sun 12–4; closed Bank Holidays

Moyse's Hall is a 12th-century Norman house built of flint and stone which now serves as a local history museum. Among the fascinating exhibits are memorabilia of the Murder in the Red Barn, an infamous crime of 1827 that took place in nearby Polstead, Suffolk. Other collections include the history of Bury St Edmunds, the Suffolk Regiment, fine art, toys, clocks and timepieces.

GO ROUND THE GARDENS

Abbey Gardens

stedmundsbury.gov.uk

Mustow Street, IP33 1XL | Open Mon–Sat 7.30–dusk. Sun 9–dusk; see website for a full list of opening times throughout the year

Enter the gardens through the magnificent gatehouse of the abbey dedicated to St Edmund. There are herb and sensory gardens, a rose garden and a delightful riverside walk.

Top 10 cathedrals and churches

- **Ely Cathedral**, Ely, page 126
- **Norwich Cathedral**, Norwich, page 216
- **St Edmund, King & Martyr**, Southwold, page 247
- **St Edmundsbury**, Bury St Edmunds, page 77
- **St Margaret's**, King's Lynn, page 178
- **St Mary**, Mildenhall, page 195
- **St Mary Magdalene**, Sandringham, page 237
- **St Mary the Virgin**, East Bergholt, page 125
- **St Michael**, Beccles, page 61
- **St Nicholas' Chapel**, King's Lynn, page 179

GO TO THE THEATRE

Theatre Royal

www.theatreroyal.org
Westgate Street, IP33 1QR
01284 769505 | Open daily

The Theatre Royal, which dates from 1819, is owned by the National Trust and is the only surviving Regency playhouse in Britain. It's still in daily use and you can catch a theatrical experience here most evenings. Tours of the theatre, last just over an hour, are available and are run throughout the year. There are regular 'Self Explore' sessions, which are dependent on the theatre's rehearsal schedule. Check before you visit.

SEE A LOCAL CHURCH

St Mary's Church

stmarystpeter.net
Honey Hill, IP33 1RT
01284 754840 | Open all year
Mon–Fri 10–4 (10 to 3 in winter)

Mary Tudor (1496–1533), the younger sister of Henry VIII and grandmother of Lady Jane Grey, was reburied in St Mary's after being moved from Bury St Edmunds abbey when her brother announced the Dissolution of the Monasteries. You might think the church is named after her, which is a popular misconception. In fact, it refers to the Virgin Mary. The church dates from the 12th to the 16th centuries, and has one of the finest hammerbeam angel roofs in the country.

PLAY GOLF

Bury St Edmunds Golf Club

www.burystedmundsgolfclub.co.uk
Tut Hill, IP28 6LG | 01284 755979
Open daily including Bank Holidays

The nine-hole pay-and-play undulating course of the Bury St Edmunds Golf Club is full of character with some challenging holes.

Suffolk Golf and Spa Hotel

bespokehotels.com
Fornham St Genevieve,
IP28 6JQ | 01284 706801
Open daily including Bank Holidays

Here you can play the classic parkland course with the River Lark running through it. It is criss-crossed by ponds and streams and has been upgraded in recent years.

EAT AND DRINK

The Angel Hotel

theangel.co.uk
Angel Hill, IP33 1LT
01284 714000

This former Georgian coaching inn on the historic town square includes Charles Dickens among its former visitors. Covered in deep-green creepers and purple-pink wistaria, it is a quintessential British inn, albeit at the grander end of the spectrum. As well as the period features, the interior strikes a more contemporary note, nowhere more so than in its stylish, pine-floored Eaterie restaurant, with its stunning artworks and views across the square to the cathedral.

Clarice House

claricehouse.co.uk
Horringer Court, Horringer Road, IP29 5PH | 01284 705550

Sybaritic spa pampering is often the first item on the agenda for many of the guests at Clarice House, followed by an appetite-stimulating stroll through the splendid grounds of the Jacobean-style country house, and then a meal in the smart oak-panelled restaurant, a suitably sumptuous backdrop for uncomplicated modern European cooking.

The Nutshell

thenutshellpub.co.uk
17 The Traverse, IP33 1BJ
01284 764867

Measuring just 15 foot by 7 foot, this unique pub has been confirmed as Britain's smallest by Guinness World Records; yet somehow more than 100 people and a dog managed to fit inside in the 1980s. It has certainly become a tourist attraction and there's lots to talk about while you enjoy a drink – such as the mummified cat and the bar ceiling, which is covered with paper money. There have been regular sightings of ghosts around the building, including a nun and a monk who apparently weren't praying! No food is available, though the pub jokes about its dining area for parties of two or fewer.

Pea Porridge

peaporridge.co.uk
28–29 Cannon Street, IP33 1JR | 01284 700200

Originally two cottages, then a bakery (the oven still in situ), Pea Porridge is now a homely and unpretentious three-roomed restaurant with wooden floors, pine tables, exposed bricks and an open fire. A strong streak of invention and innovation runs through the menu.

PLACES NEARBY

Bury St Edmunds is in the heart of Suffolk and as such is within easy reach of some fabulous places of interest. You will be spoilt for choice. You could visit Ickworth House in the village of Horringer, once the home of nobility, and Wyken Hall, a wonderful medieval house standing in an estate that was occupied by the Romans. In nearby West Stow, you'll find an Anglo-Saxon Village. If you fancy a game of golf, why not head for nearby Flempton Golf Club, or for a bite to eat try Theobalds in Ixworth, the White Horse in Whepstead, the Cadogan Arms in Ingham, the Leaping Hare in Stanton or the Plough in the pretty village of Rede.

Ickworth House

nationaltrust.org.uk/ickworth
The Rotunda, Horringer, IP29 5QE | 01284 735270
Open Mar–Nov Mon–Tue, Fri–Sun 11–5 and Thu 12–3

This beautifully elegant neoclassical country house is set in acres of parkland. Its unusual rotunda effortlessly dominates the landscape. Owned by the National Trust, the house gives you the chance to see restored rooms, including the servants' quarters. An exhibition hall above the rotunda contains priceless treasures collected over centuries by the succession of owners, which have included the Marquises of Bristol. The Georgian silver collection is considered the finest in private hands. The 1,800 acres of parkland, some landscaped in the 'Capability' Brown style, features Italianate and kitchen gardens, cycle trails, walking trails and a children's playground. Outdoor and indoor events are planned throughout the year – see website for details.

West Stow Anglo-Saxon Village

weststow.org
West Stow Country Park, Icklingham Road, West Stow, IP28 6HG
01284 728718 | Open daily 10–5

Located in the 125-acre West Stow Country Park with a river, a lake, woodland and heath, plus many trails and paths and children's play areas, this interesting centre on the site of an excavated pagan Anglo-Saxon settlement makes a fine day out. The village is a reconstruction of the settlement, which dates from around AD 420–650. There are seven buildings on the site, including the Anglo-Saxon Centre displaying some of the finds, such as tools and pots, unearthed here. The visitor centre houses a west Suffolk archaeology exhibition. A full programme of special events runs throughout the year.

Wyken Hall

www.wykenvineyards.co.uk
Wyken Road, Stanton, IP31 2DW
01359 250287 | Garden open Easter–Sep Sun–Fri 2–6

Wyken Hall is a half-timbered medieval manor house with multiple gables, banks of octagonal brick chimneys and an almost indefinable roof line. The garden is a plant-lover's dream, its mood changing from restrained to wild in areas that blend seamlessly into the surrounding meadows and woodland of the Suffolk countryside. Wyken Hall is also famous for its wines, and a

▲ West Stow Anglo-Saxon Village

woodland walk takes you to the south-facing vineyard. It was planted in 1988 and now produces award-winning wines.

The house is private, but you are free to wander around the garden. You will see low, clipped diamond-shaped box hedges, sculptural topiary pyramids and cubes, all planted as focal points. There are lawns and a rose garden planted with a collection of old-fashioned blooms. A lake offers a different environment again. Rocking chairs and benches are dotted around, allowing you to relax in this most perfumed and peaceful of gardens.

Flempton Golf Club
flemptongolfclub.co.uk
Flempton, IP28 6EQ
01284 728291 | Open daily including Bank Holidays
The Flempton Golf Club course has gorse and wooded areas to offer some challenges. There's little water but it's surrounded by woodland and Suffolk Wildlife Trust lakes.

Theobalds Restaurant ❁❁
theobaldsrestaurant.co.uk
68 High Street, Ixworth,
IP31 2HJ | 01359 231707
A Tudor inn in a village to the north of Bury St Edmunds, Theobalds has an abundance

of uneven oak timbers, an inglenook fireplace and plain whitewashed walls. Simon Theobald is an assiduous country chef, seeking out the best of seasonal produce, and letting it lead the transformation of his menus through the year.

The White Horse

whitehorsewhepstead.co.uk
Rede Road, Whepstead, IP29 4SS
01284 735760

Stylishly made over in recent years, this mustard-yellow village inn now sits comfortably at the gastro-pub end of the spectrum, but without losing any of the features one hopes for – the interior is a series of smart and cosy rooms with a copper-sheathed bar serving Suffolk ales, and there are exposed beams, a huge inglenook, country-style tables and chairs, artwork on the walls and soothing colour schemes. The kitchen here appreciates the value of top-class local ingredients, follows the seasons keenly and cuts no corners, making everything from scratch.

The Cadogan Arms

thecadogan.co.uk
The Street, Ingham, IP31 1NG
01284 728443

The interior of this former coaching inn has been reworked and spruced up with a stylish decor, subdued lighting, upholstered sofas and chairs and a curved bar dispensing real ales. Flexibility is the name of the game, with grazing boards for snackers and a lunch menu of sandwiches and dishes such as local ham, eggs and chips. The kitchen moves up a couple of gears in the evening, showcasing the skills and nifty presentation of this stylish gastropub.

The Leaping Hare Restaurant and Country Store

wykenvineyards.co.uk
Wyken Vineyards, Stanton, IP31 2DW | 01359 250287

It is hard to think of a more appealing way to acquaint yourself with the foodie delights of Suffolk than to explore the local wine trail and turn up for lunch at Wyken Vineyard's Leaping Hare Restaurant. The 1,200-acre estate keeps food miles to an absolute minimum, supplying game, meat from its herd of Red Poll cattle and flock of Shetland sheep, fruit, herbs and veg from the kitchen garden, and wine from the seven-acre vineyard, while a farmers' market brings more to the doorstep every Saturday. The setting is a striking 400-year-old timbered barn with a soaring raftered ceiling, wood-burning stoves, exposed wall beams, wooden floors, leaping hare-themed paintings and tapestries, and large windows opening on to fields and ancient woodlands. A simple modern approach to cooking lets the flavours shine through.

The Plough
www.redeplough.co.uk
Rede, IP29 4BE | 01284 789208
Tucked away on the village green is this part-thatched, 16th-century pub, easily identified by an old plough and a weeping willow at the front. On long-standing landlord Brian Desborough's ever-changing blackboard menu look for diced Highland beef in cream with wholegrain mustard and whisky sauce; minted local venison in chilli sauce with potato and cheese topping; and sea bass fillets in cream with bacon, butterbean and sweetcorn sauce. The bar serves Fuller's, Adnams, Ringwood and Sharp's ales and 10 wines by the glass. At 420 feet above sea level, Great Wood Hill near Rede is actually Suffolk's highest point (and a good place for walking) – a fact verified by Guinness World Records.

Caister-on-Sea

One of Norfolk's most popular seaside destinations, located just up the road from Great Yarmouth, Caister-on-Sea is lively yet refined. Known simply as Caister by locals, it dates back to Roman origins and was a naval base from around AD 200 through to the end of the fourth century. There are Roman remains, now owned by English Heritage, if you fancy delving into the town's ancient past. Caister is also famous for its

▼ Caister Castle

lifeboat station – there's been one here since the 1790s and its crews have saved thousands of lives. The phrase 'never turn back' has been attributed to Caister's lifeboat crews following a thwarted rescue in dangerous seas in 1901. Caister is also home to Great Yarmouth's racecourse.

VISIT THE MUSEUM

Caister Castle Car Collection

caistercastle.co.uk

Castle Lane, NR30 5SN

01664 567707 | Open mid-May–Sep Sun–Fri 10–4.30

The car enthusiasts in your family will be thrilled by the exhibits on show in this lovely museum housed in the moated 15th-century Caister Castle. The museum's display of rare vintage, classic and sports motor vehicles dates from the late 19th century through to the present day and is the largest private collection in the country. It includes the first real motor car in the world, the 1893 Panhard et Levassor. There is also the first Ford Fiesta off the production line and the Lotus belonging to British Formula One racing driver and world champion Jim Clark (1936–68). The castle itself was built in 1432 by English knight Sir John Fastolf (1378–1459) and is notable for being one of the earliest brick constructions in

▾ Church of St Peter and St Paul, Burgh Castle

the country. You can climb to the top of its 90 foot-high tower. The spectacular castle and countryside view is worth the effort.

GO BACK IN TIME

Caister Roman Fort
english-heritage.org.uk
0870 333 1181 | Open at any reasonable time
The Caister Roman Fort remains give a fascinating insight into the town's defence connections. Here, a Roman naval base stood for some 150 years or so until the Romans withdrew from Britain. Infantry and cavalry personnel would have been stationed here, as well as sailors. It occupied an island that has since been covered with silt, at a point where four rivers, including the Waveney and Yare, met. There would have been barracks, workshops and stables. Now managed by English Heritage, the partially excavated site includes the south gateway, a town wall built of flint with brick courses and part of what may have been a seamen's hostel.

GO TO THE RACES

Great Yarmouth Racecourse
greatyarmouth-racecourse.co.uk
Jellicoe Road, NR30 4AU
01493 842527
Located on the fringes of Caister towards Great Yarmouth, this racecourse hosts 24 flat-racing fixtures a year. The left-handed oblong course is one mile (five furlongs) in length. There is a full range of hospitality features for race days, and the complex is often the venue for craft and antiques fairs, and concerts.

PLACES NEARBY

Visit the remains of Burgh Castle (see page 148), a fort built by the Romans overlooking Breydon Water to the ever-cheerful and lively Great Yarmouth (see page 139). In nearby Filby you can see wildlife at the Thrigby Wildlife Gardens.

Thrigby Wildlife Gardens
thrigbyhall.co.uk
Thrigby Hall, Filby, NR29 3DR
01493 369477 | Open daily from 10 (closing times vary)
Located in the grounds of one of Norfolk's most attractive country houses, the 18th-century Thrigby Hall, this wildlife garden has tigers, primates and reptiles. There are hundreds of birds, from cockatoos and owls to wetland species; there is even a red panda. There are tropical bird houses, a unique blue willow-pattern garden and tree walk, and a summer house as old as the park. The enormous jungle swamp hall has special features such as underwater viewing of large crocodiles. The garden has an animal and tree adoption scheme, with all money going to its Thrigby Conservation Fund which supports leading environmental projects around the world.

A1307
HUNTINGDON ROAD
VICTORIA ROAD
A1134
MADINGLEY ROAD
A1303
QUEEN'S ROAD
NEWNHAM ROAD
BARTON ROAD
A603
ALL SOULS LA
OXFORD RD
RICHMOND ROAD
HALIFAX ROAD
CANTERBURY STREET
ST STEPHEN'S PLACE
WEST ROAD
PRIOR FIELD
CANTERBURY ST
NORTH ROAD
BERGAMO LANE
HISTON ROAD
B1409
BERMUDA ROAD
BERMUDA TERRACE
Histon Road Cemetery
TRENCH'S ROAD
HARVEY GOODWIN AVENUE
TIMETTEN AVENUE
ARTHUR STREET
CLARE STREET
HEALE STREET
ST LUKE'S STREET
HILDA STREET
ALPHA ROAD
HERTFORD STREET
MACRAE AVENUE
CHESTERTON LANE
Ascension Parish Burial Ground
STOREY'S WAY
Botany Field Station
Greenwich House
Archaeological Unit (UoC)
Trinity Hall Ground
Wychfield (Trinity Hall)
Fitzwilliam College
Churchill College
CHURCHILL ROAD
Moller Centre
Music Centre
Churchill College
Murray Edwards College
Blackfriars
St Edmund's College
ANTON PLACE
SHELLY ROW
CASTLE STREET
Cambridgeshire County Council (Shire Hall)
Register Office
Cripps Co (Magdalen
The Colony (Clare)
Kettle's Yard
St Giles
Lucy Cavendish College
LADY MARGARET RD
ALBION ROW
ST PETER'S ST
Westminster College
NORTHAMPTON ST
Magdalene College
MAGDALENE
Cambridge & County Folk
St John's Co
FULLER WAY
PRESCOTT AVENUE
THE CARPTON DR
CLERK MAXWELL ROAD
WEDGELEY CLOSE
BULSTRODE GARDENS
Isaac Newton Institute for Mathematical Science
Girton College (Wolfson Court)
St John's College School
CLARKSON ROAD
WILBERFORCE ROAD
Emmanuel College Sports Ground
Cambridge Lawn Tennis Club
Pavilion
STACEY LANE
St John's College Playing Fields (private)
St John's College
COCKCROFT PL
St John's College School
GRANGE ROAD
Burrell's Field (Trinity)
Trinity Sports Ground
Athletics Track
ADAMS ROAD
Trinity College
Garret Hostel Bridge
GARRET HOSTEL LA
Trinity Hall
Wilberforce Road Sports Ground
West Court (Clare Hall)
SYLVESTER ROAD
University of Cambridge
Robinson College
HERSCHEL ROAD
Memorial Court (Clare)
Clare College
The Backs
River Cam
King's Bridge
King's College
Kings College School
Kings College Gardens Dept
St Chad's (St Catharines)
University Rugby Ground
Cripps Court (Selwyn)
WEST ROAD
Concert Hall & Faculty of Music
Harvey Court (Gonville & Caius)
St Catharin Colle
Queen's The College
Queen's College
Univers of Cambrid
Emma
CRANMER ROAD
DANE DRIVE
WOOTTON WAY
University of Cambridge
Selwyn College
Corpus Christi Sports Centre
Leckhampton Corpus Christi
PINEHURST SOUTH
PINEHURST
PENARTH PLACE
Classical Archaeology
SILVER STREET
Darwin College
SIDGWICK AVENUE
Ridley Hall
Newnham House (Corpus Christi)
GOUGH WAY
SPENS AVE
SELWYN GARDENS
Newnham College
NEWNHAM WALK
MALTING LA
STUKELEY CLOSE
PEARCE COURT
WORDSWORTH GROVE
Gwen Raverat House
CHAMPNEYS WALK
Newnham College Sports Field
Darwin College (Frank Young House)
Gonville & Caius College Sports Ground
Cambridge Cycle Hire
Sheep's Green
Stone Bridge
Wolfson College
King's & Selwyn Colleges Recreation Ground
Kaplan International College
St John Ambulance
Lammas Land
Pavilion
St Marks Newnham
Cambridge Model Engineering Society
SELWYN ROAD
FULBROOKE ROAD
Downing College Sports Ground
Newnham Croft School
MILLINGTON ROAD
Pavilion
South Green Lodge (St Catharines)
Pavilion
Cambridge RUFC
Newnham Croft
Pavilion
Pavilion
Pembroke College Sports Ground
St Catharine's & Christs' Sports Fields
Queen's College Owlstone Croft Residence
Recreation Ground

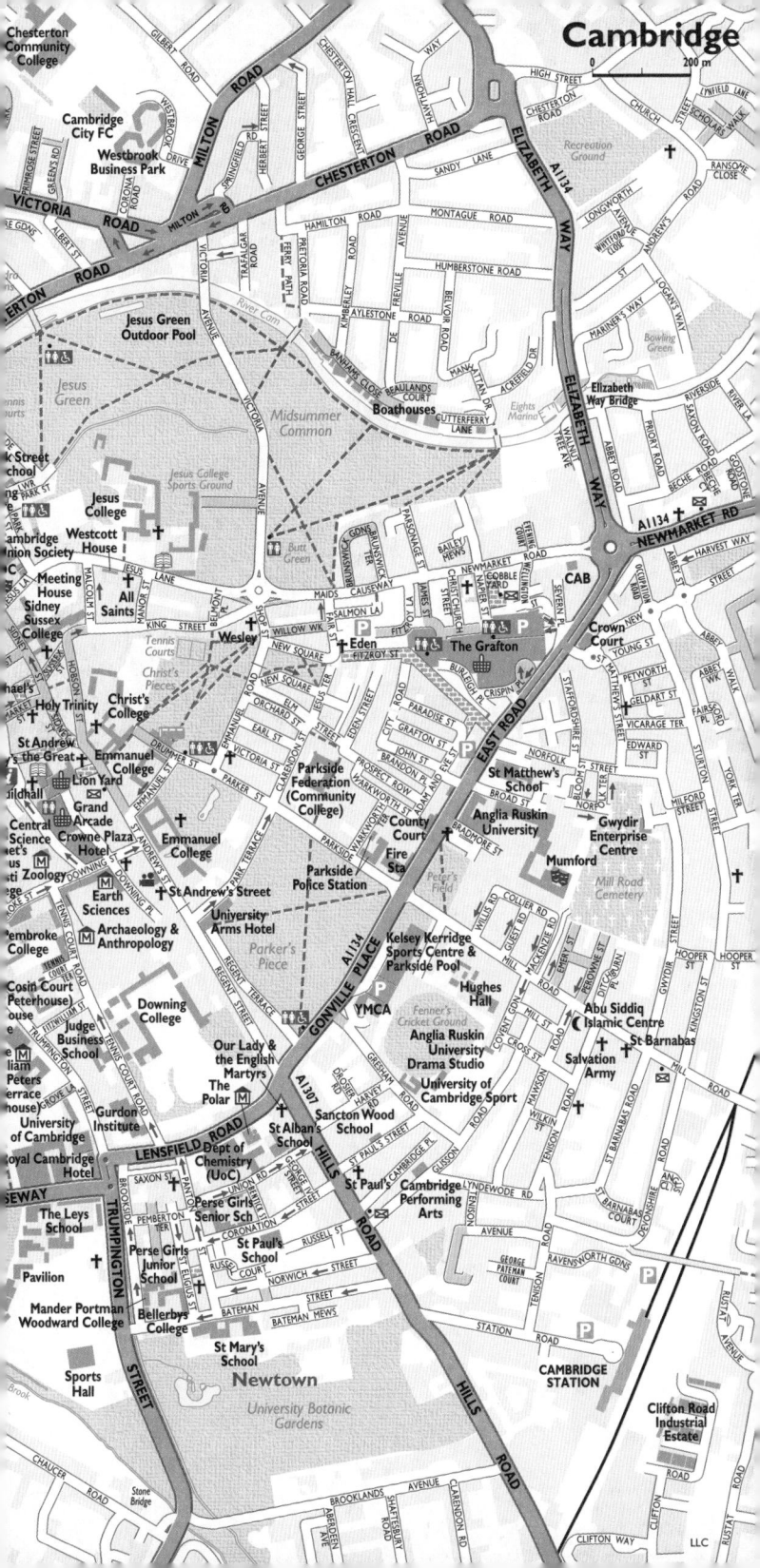
Cambridge
0
200 m
Chesterton Community College
Cambridge City FC
Westbrook Business Park
MILTON ROAD
CHESTERTON ROAD
VICTORIA ROAD
ELIZABETH WAY
A1134
HIGH STREET
CHURCH STREET
Recreation Ground
SANDY LANE
HAMILTON ROAD
MONTAGUE ROAD
HUMBERSTONE ROAD
AYLESTONE ROAD
River Cam
Jesus Green Outdoor Pool
Jesus Green
Midsummer Common
Boathouses
Elizabeth Way Bridge
Bowling Green
Jesus College Sports Ground
Jesus College
Westcott House
Butt Green
Meeting House
Sidney Sussex College
All Saints
Wesley
Eden
The Grafton
CAB
NEWMARKET RD
Crown Court
Tennis Courts
Christ's Pieces
Holy Trinity
Christ's College
St Andrew's the Great
Emmanuel College
Lion Yard
Parkside Federation (Community College)
St Matthew's School
Anglia Ruskin University
Gwydir Enterprise Centre
Grand Arcade
Central Science Laboratories
Crowne Plaza Hotel
Emmanuel College
County Court
Fire Sta
Mumford
Mill Road Cemetery
Parkside Police Station
St Andrew's Street
Earth Sciences
Zoology
University Arms Hotel
Archaeology & Anthropology
Pembroke College
Parker's Piece
Kelsey Kerridge Sports Centre & Parkside Pool
GONVILLE PLACE
Hughes Hall
YMCA
Fenner's Cricket Ground
Abu Siddiq Islamic Centre
Cosin Court (Peterhouse)
Downing College
Judge Business School
Anglia Ruskin University Drama Studio
St Barnabas
Salvation Army
Our Lady & the English Martyrs
The Polar
University of Cambridge Sport
Gurdon Institute
University of Cambridge
Sancton Wood School
St Alban's School
LENSFIELD ROAD
Royal Cambridge Hotel
Dept of Chemistry (UoC)
HILLS ROAD
St Paul's
Cambridge Performing Arts
The Leys School
Perse Girls Senior Sch
Perse Girls Junior School
St Paul's School
Pavilion
Mander Portman Woodward College
Bellerbys College
TRUMPINGTON STREET
St Mary's School
Newtown
Sports Hall
University Botanic Gardens
CAMBRIDGE STATION
Clifton Road Industrial Estate
EAST ROAD
Stone Bridge
LLC

Cambridge

Colleges and capers

You could be forgiven for feeling overwhelmed by Cambridge. With its hauntingly beautiful Gothic architecture displayed in grand style on the facades of most of its colleges and chapels, its vast open areas, fabulous shopping and cafes, its energetic arts scene and busy streets that will leave you breathless, Cambridge is a pulsating fusion of the traditional and the contemporary. It has played a major role in English history and world academia since before the Roman Empire.

A prosperous and influential market town occupying an elevated location – something of a curiosity in the famously flat fenlands of Cambridgeshire – the city was one of the first in England to be granted a town charter, while the University of Cambridge and its illustrious alumni have pioneered advances in the fields of medicine, astrology, architecture, the arts and sciences.

Yet Cambridge, a pretty place with the River Cam snaking its way through the city centre, manages to retain a feeling of peaceful friendliness. You'll be sure to find this comforting if it's your first visit and even just a little bit bizarre, given the city's huge importance.

▲ Left to right: King's College; the River Cam; Cambridge University

It's easy to explore the city centre on foot or bicycle. Hours spent slowly browsing in its cobbled streets and passageways could be one of the most relaxing experiences of your holiday. It's a great way to see the city's amazing architecture up close. Some of the university buildings were the work of the famous 18th-century architect Sir Christopher Wren, whose other great claim to fame is St Paul's Cathedral in London.

Another good way of seeing Cambridge is to join walkers and joggers along the banks of the River Cam, an area affectionately known as the Backs. Early morning is a lovely time of day to be here. A thin mist blankets the area, lending the river and the back of the college buildings an eerie half-light, until the sun rises high enough to illuminate the building in shafts of clear light. From here you can see the much-photographed King's College and King's College Chapel, which together dominate the city and could be consider the iconic view of Cambridge – it's certainly the view that appears in all the brochures.

Cambridge's atmosphere is refined without doubt, but it is lively and entertaining too. Most evenings you'll find small groups of students singing in harmony and dancers or jugglers

▲ The Mathematical Bridge, Queens' College

bringing a smile to the faces of passersby. The joviality around Silver Street, where students help excited visitors into punts on the River Cam, is an experience in itself. You'll catch yourself beaming from ear to ear.

Hopping aboard a punt is one of the 'must have' experiences of a visit to Cambridge. The River Cam has busy stretches of water and quiet, almost hidden, places where you can easily dream away a few wistful hours. You can hire a punt and set out on your own – it's not easy to steer a punt, though – or you can hire one that is 'chauffeured', usually by a student, leaving you free to sit back, enjoy the atmosphere and see the city from a whole new perspective.

From the river, you'll see colleges and bridges, including Queens' College's Mathematical Bridge, which got its name from its geometrical construction. It was widely thought to have been designed by Sir Isaac Newton, who studied at Trinity College in the late 17th century. He was said to have built it without nails, but when students disassembled it for a jest they found they couldn't put it together again and so had to use

bolts. It is, however, one of the more fanciful yarns told in Cambridge, not least because Newton had been dead for over 20 years when the bridge was first built.

Around 3.5 million visitors a year are drawn to the city, but far from frowning upon the invasion, you'll find residents helpful and pleased to point you in the direction of the best cafe, gallery or market stall. The city offers lots to do, from browsing in the second-hand bookshops that seem to occupy a prime spot at every turn, to visiting museums and galleries, enjoying the theatre, taking a sightseeing tour or having a long leisurely break at any one of the many pubs, buzzy cafes and multi-cultural restaurants that befit a university city.

The Fitzwilliam Museum in Trumpington Street holds an exhaustive collection of antiquities found in and around the city, and is a must-see if you want to learn more about Cambridge's ancient history. If studying the flora of Cambridgeshire is your passion, then head for the Cambridge University Botanic Museum. You may prefer to visit an art gallery or exhibition hall – Kettle's Yard in Castle Street is a favourite – or discover handmade jewellery, organic produce or designer goodies in and around the city's centuries-old market square.

▲ Trinity College

Music, theatre and live entertainment are popular in Cambridge. The Cambridge Corn Exchange and the Cambridge Arts Theatre promote the more traditional arts, the emphasis being on ballet, opera and orchestral concerts. More contemporary works are performed at the La Raza, the Cambridge Junction and the West Road Concert Hall, plus the ADC Theatre, famously the home of the Cambridge Footlights comedy troupe that once had actress Emma Thompson, comedians Alexander Armstrong, Peter Cook and John Cleese and television's *Downton Abbey* creator and writer Julian Fellowes treading its boards.

Whatever you do during your stay in Cambridge, you will inevitably succumb to the fascination of the colleges and want to know more about them. There are 31 colleges making up the University of Cambridge, all dotted around the city centre. Dating from the 13th century, Peterhouse is the oldest college building, but it is perhaps the predominantly Tudor colleges along King's Parade and Trinity Street, and King's College, together with King's College Chapel, that dominate the city. The Chapel is famous the world over for its superb choir and the Christmas Eve Festival of Nine Lessons and Carols.

You will find that many of the colleges welcome visitors out of study and exam times and the Tourist Information Office (01223 322640) in Wheeler Street, just off the Market Square, has leaflets with information and routes around the city for you to follow. Joining students and Fellows in the courtyards of the colleges, engaging in stimulating conversation and admiring the architecture and achievements of Cambridge is what time spent in this beautiful city is all about.

Fitzwilliam Museum

fitzmuseum.cam.ac.uk
Trumpington Street, CB2 1RB | 01223 332900 | Open Tue–Sat 10–5, Sun and Bank Holiday Mondays 12–5

Cambridge's foremost museum with over a half a million exhibits, the Fitzwilliam is one of the finest in Europe. It was founded in 1816 by the wealthy musical antiquarian and art collector, Richard Fitzwilliam, the seventh Viscount Fitzwilliam of Merrion (1745–1816), who was an alumnus of Trinity College. He felt the university needed its own art museum and library, and on his death donated a priceless collection of works including Renaissance pieces by Italian painters Palma Vecchio, Titian and Veronese, 144 rare Dutch paintings, engravings by artists such as Rembrandt and sheet music signed by German composer Handel.

The Fitzwilliam became the museum of the University of Cambridge, and remains to this day one of the oldest public museums in Britain. You'll easily find it along the main thoroughfare, Trumpington Street, for it is housed in a monumental neoclassical mansion, a Cambridge landmark. Its magnificent collection has grown over the years and spans centuries and civilisations from as far back as 2500 BC to the present day. Among the exhibits are works by Rubens, Constable, Picasso and Monet, along with antiquities from Ancient Egypt, Greece and Cyprus, rare Oriental works of art and medieval coins.

The museum's own Courtyard Cafe serves morning coffee, light lunches and afternoon tea, and is sure to provide a welcome break.

10 famous colleges in Cambridge

- Clare College
- Corpus Christi College
- Girton College
- Gonville and Caius College
- Jesus College
- King's College
- Pembroke College
- Peterhouse
- Queens' College
- Trinity College

VISIT THE MUSEUMS

Kettle's Yard

wwwkettlesyard.co.uk
Castle Street, CB3 0AQ
01223 748100 | Open Tue–Sun 1–4.30; winter Tue–Sun 2–4 and Bank Holiday Mondays 12–5

The fresh and bright interior of this fine country house-turned-gallery on the outskirts of the city centre provides the perfect backdrop to a varied collection of contemporary art. You'll see paintings by local artists, sculptures, ceramic pieces and furniture. It hosts a programme of practical workshops, many aimed at children.

The Museum of Cambridge

folkmuseum.org.uk
2–3 Castle Street, CB3 0AQ
01223 355159 | Open Tue–Sat 10.30–5, Sun and Bank Holidays 2–5

A pretty 17th-century timber-framed former inn houses the Museum of Cambridge, one of the city's most popular museums. A country and folkloric museum, it aims to present a glimpse of the everyday lives of the county's people from early times through to the present day, with nine room settings, including a kitchen and a playroom. There are more than 20,000 exhibits amassed from private homes. Children, especially, will love the display of toys that would have been an essential part of youngsters' lives centuries ago. This delightful museum was founded in 1936 to help generations understand their local heritage and is particularly family friendly with plenty of hands-on experiences and games for children. There are temporary exhibitions too, talks, events and kids' activities throughout the year, plus a tea room open on Saturdays.

The Polar Museum, Scott Polar Research Institute

www.spri.cam.ac.uk
Lensfield Road, CB2 1ER
01223 336540 | Open Tue–Sat 10–4 except Bank Holiday weekends

Located within this international centre for polar studies, the museum has one of the best collections of journals, photographs, maps and even items of clothing that chronicle the most important Arctic and Antarctic expeditions ever undertaken. Special emphasis is placed on Captain Scott and on the exploration of the Northwest Passage. Other exhibits include Inuit work and the art of the polar regions, as well as displays on current scientific exploration. The museum has a regular programme of exhibitions in addition to its permanent displays. Public lectures run from October to December and February to April.

University Museum of Archaeology and Anthropology
maa.cam.ac.uk
Downing Street, CB2 3DZ
01223 333516 | Open Tue–Sat 10.30–4.30 Sun 12–4.30
The museum is part of the Faculty of Archaeology and Anthropology of the University of Cambridge and houses exhibits spanning two million years of human civilisation. It was established in 1884 and is still housed in its 1916 building in the Downing Street in the city centre. Some of the highlights are Pacific material collected on Captain Cook's voyages of exploration, a 46-foot-high totem pole from Canada and some of the earliest stone tools ever found. Find out about local, national and world archaeology in the archaeology galleries, which include painted pottery from Peru, gilded Anglo-Saxon brooches and Roman altar stones.

GO ROUND THE GARDENS

Cambridge University Botanic Garden
www.botanic.cam.ac.uk
1 Brookside, CB2 1JE
01223 336265 | Open Apr–Sep 10–6; Feb–Mar and Oct 10–5; Nov–Jan 10–4
The university's Botanic Garden comes as something of a surprise. This 40-acre oasis of beautifully landscaped gardens and glasshouses is close to the bustle of the city centre and yet if it's peace you're after then you'll find it here. The garden opened on its present site in 1846, and showcases a collection of some 8,000 plant species, including nine national collections, among them geraniums and fritillarias.

▾ Cambridge University Botanic Garden

This Grade II heritage landscape features rock gardens full of alpine species, gardens of winter and autumn varieties, and even a tropical rainforest. You can relax in the Scented Garden, enjoy beds of herbaceous varieties and, best of all, see the finest collection of trees in the east of England.

GO TO THE THEATRE

Cambridge Corn Exchange

cornex.co.uk
Wheeler Street, CB2 3QB
01223 357851 | Box office open Mon–Sat 10–6, Sun performance days only

Just minutes from the market square the Corn Exchange hosts around 300 performances a year, so whatever your preference you'll be sure to find the perfect evening out, from stand-up comedians and contemporary singers to symphony orchestras and ballet companies.

Cambridge Arts Theatre

cambridgeartstheatre.com
6 St Edwards Passage, CB2 3PJ
01223 503333 | Box office open Mon–Sat 12–8

If you're visiting over the festive season, be sure to take the family to the theatre's pantomime. It's a Cambridge institution. Or catch a touring musical show fresh from the West End. Comedy dramas and plays featuring top international actors, and concerts and dance performances are held here throughout the year.

ADC Theatre

adctheatre.com
Park Street, CB5 8AS
01223 300085 | Open Mon–Sat 1–7. During university term time the main show commences at 7.45 Tue–Sat, followed by a late show at 11

If you fancy finding out how the likes of actors Sir Ian McKellen, Emma Thompson, Stephen Fry and Hugh Laurie, to name but a few, came to get the performing bug, then book a show at the ADC. This pretty, white- and blue-washed period building, a few minutes' walk from the city centre, has hosted the university's Amateur Dramatic Club (ADC) since the late 1800s. The club itself was formed in 1855. Shows are a superb mix of comedy sketches, stand-up and satire

PLAY GOLF

Gog Magog Golf Club

gogmagog.co.uk
Shelford Bottom, CB22 3AB
01223 247626 | Open Mon–Tue, Thu–Fri, Sun and Bank Holidays

Founded in 1901, Gog Magog Golf Club has two-well established courses, each with plenty of hazards to be a challenge. Both are chalk downland courses and because they are at such a high elevation afford panoramic views of the countryside surrounding the city. The view of Ely Cathedral in the distance is mesmerising. The nature of the ground ensures good winter golf too. The area has been designated a Site of Special Scientific Interest.

EAT AND DRINK

The Anchor

Silver Street, CB3 9EL
01223 353554

This attractive pub is situated at the end of the medieval lane that borders Queens' College in the heart of the city. Hard by the bridge over the River Cam, in fine weather the riverside patio is an ideal spot for enjoying one of a range of Greene King ales and guest beers, while watching the activities on the water. The more adventurous can hire a punt for a leisurely trip to Grantchester, and on return sample a choice of hearty meals from a range that includes lasagne, homemade pies and roast beef.

Cambridge Blue

the-cambridgeblue.co.uk
85–87 Gwydir Street, CB1 2LG
01223 471680

This is a friendly 1860s backstreet pub, built to serve a terrace that housed railway workers.It has an unexpectedly large sun-trap garden and an amazing range of beers, from 200 bottled beers from around the world to a mind-boggling choice of 14 real ales from microbreweries on handpump in the taproom – try a pint of Oakham Inferno or Woodforde's Wherry. Inside are two real fires, plenty of memorabilia and a lively, buzzy vibe. Good-value pub grub made on the premises comes in the form of steak-and-kidney pie; fish pie; sausages and mash; a daily curry; and a range of filled ciabatta sandwiches and jacket potatoes (plus there are always vegetarian options). Popular beer festivals take place in February, June and October each year.

10 comedians who studied at Cambridge

- Clive Anderson
- Alexander Armstrong
- David Baddiel
- John Cleese
- Peter Cook
- Jimmy Edwards
- Eric Idle
- Hugh Laurie
- Bill Oddie
- Griff Rhys Jones

Free Press

freepresspub.com
Prospect Row, CB1 1DU
01223 368337

A pub for over 120 years, the Free Press gets its name from the time when part of it was a printing press which produced a free Cambridge newspaper. Now a haunt for students, academics, locals and visitors, this atmospheric and picturesque backstreet pub near the city centre has open fires and a beautiful walled garden – and no music, mobile phones or gaming machines. Visitors are attracted by first-rate real ales and great homemade food.

10 famous Cambridge alumini

- **Charles Babbage**, computer inventor
- **Cecil Beaton**, photographer
- **HRH Prince Charles**
- **Michael Foale**, astronaut
- **David Frost**, television presenter
- **Germaine Greer**, writer
- **Sam Mendes**, film director
- **Isaac Newton**, mathematician
- **Sylvia Plath**, writer
- **Emma Thompson**, actress

Hotel Felix ❁❁

hotelfelix.co.uk
Whitehouse Lane, Huntingdon Road, CB3 0LX | 01223 277977

A bow-fronted Victorian villa is the setting for a rather distinctive boutique hotel, in which the battleship-grey interiors are offset with splashes of abstract-art colour, and outdoor tables on a terrace overlooking the attractive gardens make the most of the punting weather. Contemporary brasserie cooking is the draw in the restaurant, Graffiti.

Midsummer House ❁❁❁❁❁

midsummerhouse.co.uk
Midsummer Common, CB4 1HA
01223 369299

The setting is idyllic: on the edge of Midsummer Common with the River Cam flowing by, the Victorian villa that houses the Midsummer House restaurant sits in a countrifie spot which makes it hard to believe you're still within the city's boundary. It's been a restaurant for many years, r since 1998 by chef Daniel Clifford, who's worked with unwavering enthusiasm in th time to put Midsummer Hous on the gastronomic map. Everything about Midsumme House – not just the creative contemporary cooking – mak it the kind of place where you want to spend a good deal of your time. It's decorated in a sleek, modern style with a conservatory dining room overlooking an immaculately maintained walled garden. Clifford's cooking bears the hallmarks of a chef trained i the French classics. There ar three menus to choose from – the Classic, Market and Ta of Midsummer – each chang with the seasons.

The Old Spring

theoldspring.co.uk
1 Ferry Path, CB4 1HB
01223 357228

You'll find this bustling pub i the leafy suburb of De Frevill just a short stroll from the Ri Cam and its many boatyards which makes its splendid decked patio popular as a post-workout refreshment s for rowers. The bright and ai interior offers rug-covered wooden floors, comfy sofas a large family tables. Sip a pint Abbot Ale, one of several rea ales on tap, or one of 20 wine by the glass while choosing from over a dozen main courses plus specials.

The Punter
thepuntercambridge.co.uk
3 Pound Hill, CB3 0AE
01223 363322
Two minutes' walk from the city centre, this beautifully renovated coaching house is popular with visitors, locals and students alike. Drinkers can enjoy local ales while diners tuck in to well-priced rustic food among the eclectic mix of pine furniture. Serving bar snacks, a three-course set menu and a daily-changing seasonal menu, dishes might include venison and pork terrine with homemade pickle; half roast guinea fowl with truffle mash, spinach and wild mushrooms; and chocolate terrine with rhubarb compôte. Pots of home-grown produce are sold in the delightful courtyard garden.

Restaurant 22
restaurant22.co.uk
22 Chesterton Road, CB4 3AX
01223 351880
As the name implies, look out for that number 22, with its cream frontage and green door and shutters, to track down this converted Victorian town house restaurant on Chesterton Road. Inside, the small dining room is filled with white-linen-decked tables, decorated with flickering candles. The cooking keeps things sensibly simple too, but with an appealing contemporary European sheen.

PLACES NEARBY

Madingley, an unassuming village on the outskirts of Cambridge, has two sites of particular interest, Madingley Hall, an elegant 16th-century country mansion that houses Cambridge University's Institute of Continuing Education, and which is not open to the public, and the Cambridge American Cemetery and Memorial.

Cambridge is ideally located for visiting so many great places. There's heritage at Ely (see page 126) and Houghton Mill, the idyllic country houses at Anglesey Abbey in Lode and Hemingford Grey, and wildlife at Wicken Fen National Nature Reserve (see page 279). Or you can see the planes at Duxford (see page 124), take afternoon tea in Grantchester (see page 137) or enjoy a traditional pub lunch at the Queen's Head in Newton.

Also nearby is Wandlebury, an area of beautiful grasslands, and chalk slopes that is heaven for walkers and nature lovers. You can see the remains of the Wandlebury Ring, an Iron Age fort on the Gog Magog Downs.

Anglesey Abbey, Gardens and Lode Mill
nationaltrust.org.uk/angleseyabbey
Lode, CB25 9EJ | 01223 810080
Open house Wed–Sun 11–5, garden daily 10.30–5.30, mill Wed–Sun 11–4 (times can vary)
This Jacobean-style house, standing in *c.*114 acres of landscaped gardens just a few miles outside Cambridge, dates

from 1600 and is built on the site of a 12th-century Augustinian priory. It contains an idiosyncratic collection of art depicting the tastes of wealthy politician Urban Huttleston Broughton (1896–1966), the first Baron Fairhaven, who purchased the Abbey in 1926.

Among the many paintings you'll see works by Claude Lorraine, set alongside fine examples of furniture, silver and tapestries and one of the largest collections of clocks found in any National Trust property. The domestic quarters of the house have been recently restored to provide the latest collection of exhibits. You can get a glimpse of how the below stairs staff would have lived and where they worked.

The priory is surrounded by a landscaped garden that has been designed over the years to provide year-round floral interest and contains an arboretum with more than 100 pieces of sculpture, most of which take the form of mythical or biblical characters. The watermill in the grounds, Lode Mill, has milling days on the first and third Saturday of each month, provided the water levels are adequate. You can see how wheat has been ground in the same way here for around a 1,000 years, and then buy some to take home to make bread. Anglesey Abbey has its own restaurant, Redwoods, in the grounds, which serves light meals and snacks, including scones made with flour ground at Lode Mill.

Cambridge American Cemetery and Memorial

www.abmc.gov
Madingley Road, Coton
01954 210350

This sprawling, peaceful memorial garden commemorates predominantly American servicemen who died in World War II. You can find it along Madingley Road, a main thoroughfare out of Cambridge, between Coton and Madingley.

▼ Cambridge American Cemetery and Memorial

Castle Acre

see **Swaffham**, page 265

Castle Rising

see **King's Lynn**, page 182

Cley next the Sea

Cley next the Sea is a curiosity in so far as it's nowhere near the sea. To be fair, it was once. Up until about the 17th century its quayside on the River Glaven was a bustling place of boats laden with wool and cloth; then marshland was reclaimed to provide pastures, and its harbour silted up. There's still a little quayside next to the river, but no boats now of any size. You can see the brick-and-flint cottages that once lined the quayside, but now they stand a mile or so from the coast.

▾ Cley Windmill

Cley, as it's commonly abbreviated, or Cly as it's pronounced by the locals, lies in the Norfolk Coast Area of Outstanding Natural Beauty. It's on a strip of land along the sea's edge, no more than two miles long, built up along the north Norfolk coast over the past thousand years by sediment brought down by the rivers. Creeks wind their way muddily to the sea among banks of shingle and sand. Birds haunt the area in multitudes, and almost the entire coastline is protected by nature reserves. Here, you may catch sight of rough-legged buzzards and little terns, avocets and even the odd oystercatcher.

The most prominent feature of the landscape here is the white-sailed windmills, such as the village's own 18th-century red-brick tower mill with its brilliant sails and conical wooden cap. These windmills were often used not to grind corn, as is usually assumed, but to drain the salt marshes to create more land for agriculture. Cley Windmill is now one of East Anglia's more unusual bed-and-breakfast places.

Among the attractive houses in the village is Whalebone House, with panels of flint in the walls framed by whale vertebrae. To the south, where the old harbour stood, the medieval Church of St Margaret is one of Norfolk's finest, built on a grand scale and a witness to Cley's prosperity at that time.

In the centre are shops selling local foods and crafts. Look out for Cley Smokehouse for food and Made in Cley, which has some contemporary souvenirs. Both are in the High Street.

Cley is a great place if walking is your passion. A minor road runs northwards from the village through the marshes and takes you to Cley Eye on the coast. From here there is a walk of three miles or so along a narrow shingle spit to the National Nature Reserve at Blakeney Point, which is best known for its colonies of seals.

SEE A LOCAL CHURCH

St Margaret's Church

Holt Road, NR25 1RT

St Margaret's is a richly decorated Grade I listed church dating from medieval times when Cley was a prosperous and thriving port. It overlooks the village green and is one of the largest in the region.

The tower, which can be seen from almost everywhere in Cley, remains from the 13th century and there are large 15th-century windows in the aisles. Take a minute to look at the 15th-century two-storey south porch's beautiful fan-vaulted roof with carved bosses. Inside, you can see its 500-year-old bench ends depicting mythical creatures, its seven sacraments font, and, from the 17th century, the pulpit and altar table. The royal arms dates from Charles II's reign and was repainted for Queen Anne.

EAT AND DRINK

The George Hotel

www.thegeorgehotelatcley.co.uk
High Street, NR25 7RN
01263 740652

The George's beer garden backs on to the salt marshes of the north Norfolk coast, which prove a paradise for birders. Indeed, this old hotel has been an ornithological focal point for many years. Ask to see its 'bird bible', a record of sightings kept by visiting observers. The welcoming bar is home to several real ales, including Yetman's from just along the coast at Holt. You can snack in the lounge bar or dine in the light, painting-filled restaurant. The daily-changing menu offers only the best of local fresh ingredients, and fish and seafood are a real strength. From here, the village's famous mill and Blakeney Haven are just over a mile away.

PLACES NEARBY

The Salthouse Dun Cow

salthouseduncow.com
Coast Road, Salthouse,
NR25 7XA | 01263 740467

Situated in a quiet coastal village within an Area of Outstanding Natural Beauty, this traditional brick-and-flint pub probably originated as a cattle barn built around 1650. Today it overlooks some of Britain's finest salt marshes, so expect to share it, particularly the front garden, with birders and walkers. The interior decor reflects the surrounding farmland and seascapes. Local suppliers provide high-quality produce for select menus prepared from scratch, especially fresh shellfish and game from local shoots. Samphire, asparagus and soft fruit are all sourced from within five miles while the beef comes from cattle reared on the salt marshes.

Cromer

Cromer, known as the Gem of the Norfolk Coast – a motto you will see everywhere you go – is an ancient town best known for its superb crabs. Cromer crabs are caught on long lines from little clinker-built boats that chug out to sea regardless of the weather. Once the pots are out, the fishermen must collect them the following day, even when a gale is raging. Tractors haul the boats to and from the water's edge. You can spend some time here watching them; it makes for an interesting diversion. The crabs are said to be the best in the country and every traditional Cromer restaurant, bar none, has them on the menu. Be sure to have a taste.

Cromer has long been a fashionable sort of place. It is said that when a bathing machine was advertised at Cromer in 1779, word got round and soon wealthy Norwich families, including the banking families of Gurney and Barclay, bought holiday homes here. The Victorian era bought even more wealth, aided by the railway in 1877. As now, families would think nothing of spending days on the sandy beach, eating the local crab.

Walking around Cromer, especially along its quintessential English seafront, is a delight. The Pavilion Theatre is one of only a few surviving end-of-the-pier theatres in the country. Original fishermen's cottages have been turned into a history and geology museum. Look out, too, for the RNLI's museum near the pier that tells the amazing story of Coxswain Henry Blogg (1876–1954), who served as a lifeboatman for 53 years and was awarded more medals and commendations than any other in Britain.Cromer's fine 14th-century church, St Peter and St Paul, which has Norfolk's tallest tower, is worth a visit.

VISIT THE MUSEUMS

RNLI Henry Blogg Museum

rnli.org/henryblogg

The Rocket House, The Gangway, NR27 9ET | 01263 511294

Open Apr–Sep Tue–Sun 10–5; Oct–Nov and Feb–Mar 10–4

The Royal National Lifeboat Institute's Henry Blogg was an old man when he died, but when you hear about his exploits in plucking imperiled sailors from the treacherous seas you'll wonder how he managed to cheat death for so long. His bravery is legendary; he launched 387 times and was awarded more medals and commendations than any other lifeboatman in Britain. You can learn more about Blogg at the museum dedicated to him. A lifeboat has been stationed at Cromer since 1804, and this museum at the bottom of The Gangway covers local lifeboat history and the RNLI in general too. The main exhibit is the Watson-class lifeboat *HF Bailey*, the boat Henry Blogg coxed.

Cromer Museum
museums.norfolk.gov.uk
East Cottages, Tucker Street, NR27 9HB | 01263 513543
Open Mon–Fri 10–4, Sat 12–4, Sun 1–4 (closed Sun Nov–Mar)
A handful of 19th-century fishermen's cottages, one of which has period furnishings, have been turned into a museum of the area's history and geology. There are pictures and exhibits from Victorian Cromer, with collections illustrating local natural history, archaeology, social history and geology. A highlight is the collection of bones from the West Runton elephant – a 600,000-year-old fossilised mammoth discovered in the crumbling cliffs nearby.

▼ Cromer beach and pier

GO TO THE THEATRE

Pavilion Theatre

cromer-pier.com

Cromer Pier, NR27 9HE

01263 512495

From good old-fashioned seaside specials with belting singers, family-fun comedians and a bevy of colourfully costumed dancers, concerts and events, the Pavilion Theatre at the end of Cromer Pier is the place to go for a lively night out. You'll often find entertainers on the pier itself. Walking along the 496-foot-long pier before and after the show, or simply to take in the bracing air, is an experience in itself.

SEE A LOCAL CHURCH

Church of St Peter and St Paul

Church Street, NR27 9HA

The impressive Church of St Peter and St Paul, whose 160ft tower is Norfolk's tallest by far, was built in the 14th century, at a time when Cromer was hugely prosperous. The town later went through a period of decline, during which time the chancel was demolished and by the 19th century the church was almost derelict. Respected Victorian architect Sir Arthur Blomfield came to the rescue in the 1880s when Cromer had regained its prosperity, and rebuilt the chancel and repaired the nave and tower.

Today, the church is a popular, friendly place, its enormous nave full of light and space. There is excellent glass at the east end made by the English Arts and Crafts movement's designer William Morris's company, and elsewhere there is modern glass celebrating and commemorating local places and people. The outside of the church is magnificent, with superb architectural detailing, and the great tower is an attraction in its own right because of the available views from the top.

PLAY GOLF

Royal Cromer Golf Club

www.royalcromergolfclub.com

145 Overstrand Road, NR27 0JH

01263 512884 | Open daily including Bank Holidays

This challenging course has spectacular views out to sea and overlooks the town. Strong sea breezes affect the clifftop holes, the most famous being the 14th, which has a green in the shadow of a lighthouse.

EAT AND DRINK

The Red Lion

redlion-cromer.co.uk

Brook Street, NR27 9HD

01263 514964

Built in the 19th century, when Cromer was fast becoming a popular seaside resort, this hotel overlooks the pier and Blue Flag beach. Although used by the armed forces during World War II, it mercifully retains much of its Victorian interior. For real ale drinkers, the bar is heaven, with Bees Wobble, Humpty Dumpty Railway Sleeper and Adnams Broadside – and many more at the autumn beer festival.

PLACES NEARBY

The Amazona Zoo with its collection of unusual species, the grand Felbrigg Hall, Wolterton Park at Erpingham and the impressive Blickling Estate owned by the National Trust are all a short drive from Cromer. If you fancy playing golf, the Mundesley Golf Club is a 10-minute drive away, while the Links Country Park Hotel and Golf Club is a little further in West Runton. For refreshments en route, try the Saracen's Head in Wolterton, the Walpole Arms in Itteringham, or Sea Marge Hotel or the White Horse, both in Overstrand.

Amazona Zoo
amazonazoo.co.uk
Hall, Cromer NR27 9JG
01263 510741 | Open Apr–Oct daily 10–5
On the outskirts of Cromer lies one of the area's most endearing animal complexes. The Amazona Zoo presents rainforest creatures in an idyllic wooded setting created on the site of former brick kilns. The zoo's work is devoted to the conservation of rare species and habitats.

Felbrigg Hall
nationaltrust.org.uk
Felbrigg, NR11 8PR | 01263 837444
Open Mar–Nov daily 11–5
Set in the tranquil Norfolk countryside, this great 17th-century house is one of the best in East Anglia. It was begun in the 1620s by a lawyer, Frances Windham, whose grandson William made modifications and filled the rooms with pictures, including many seascapes, he had acquired on a tour of Italy. Intricate plaster ceilings and a fine library are further highlights of the interior. Less grand, perhaps, but equally fascinating is the kitchen, with its array of household implements, utensils and gleaming copper pots and pans.

Outside, the walled garden contains a functioning dovecote and the National Collection of Colchicums. There is free access to the estate, where way-marked trails thread their way past venerable trees. The nearby 15th-century parish church, standing alone, has box pews, memorial brasses and interesting family monuments.

Wolterton Park
manningtongardens.co.uk
Erpingham, NR11 7LY
01263 584175 | Park open daily, summer Fri 2–5 (last admission 4)
Covering some 800ha, this estate contains managed conservation areas, 18th-century landscaped gardens, and Wolterton Hall, built in the 1720s for Horatio Walpole, younger brother of Britain's first prime minister, Sir Robert Walpole. Special events include music, drama, history, costume and textile, art and craft exhibitions and there are themed Sundays throughout summer.

Blickling Estate
nationaltrust.org.uk/blickling ,
Blickling, Aylsham, NR11 6NF
01263 738030 | Open Feb–Nov 9–5 (times can vary), park all year dawn–dusk. Open Bank Holidays
There are 55 acres of grounds for you to wander in on the sprawling Blickling Estate, including woodland and a lakeside walk, a formal parterre, topiary yew hedges, a Secret Garden, an orangery, and a dry moat filled with roses, camellias and other plants. Its focal point in the resplendent Blickling Hall, a red-brick country mansion flanked by dark yew hedges and topped by pinnacles. It is one of the great houses of the region and once home to the Boleyn family in the early 16th century. It is a magical sight.

Inside Blickling Hall, you can visit the Great Hall where stunning reliefs of notable residents, including Anne Boleyn and her daughter, Elizabeth I, adorn the staircase. You visit the Long Gallery where ladies of the court once walked for exercise when the weather was bad in the days before it was transformed, in 1745, into what is today one of the country's finest country house libraries. It contains a remarkable collection of some 12,000 books.

On your visit look out, too, for Blickling Hall's South Drawing Room with its spectacular Jacobean plaster ceiling and fireplace, along with the Dining Room, the kitchens, State Bedroom and the exquisite Chinese Bedroom with its authentic Oriental furniture and decorations amassed by owners since the 18th century. Throughout the hall are some quite stunning paintings and tapestries.

You could easily make a day of it at Blickling Estate. There's the Hobart Restaurant, where light meals are produced almost entirely from produce grown or reared on the estate, and the Muddy Boots Café for light snacks and drinks.

Links Country Park Hotel and Golf Club
links-hotel.co.uk
West Runton, NR27 9QH
01263 838383 | Open daily including Bank Holidays
This parkland course of has superb views of the north Norfolk coast and is ideal for all levels of golfer.

Mundesley Golf Club
mundesleygolfclub.com
Links Road, NR11 8ES
01263 720095 | Open daily including Bank Holidays
This club has an undulating downland course with panoramic views. The small fast greens and tight fairways make for a pleasurable visit.

The Saracen's Head
saracenshead-norfolk.co.uk
Wolterton, NR11 7LZ
01263 768909
The privately owned Saracen's Head lies deep among the

fields down country lanes – and you do find yourself wondering why there's a pub in such a lonely spot. The answer is that it was once a coach house, built in 1806 for neighbouring Wolterton Hall. You can eat in one of the bars, where Suffolk and Norfolk real ales are on hand pump, or in the restaurant, where sample dishes might be roast Norfolk pheasant with Calvados and cream, and baked Cromer crab with apple and sherry. For a really quiet drink or meal, sit out in the sheltered courtyard garden.

The Walpole Arms
thewalpolearms.co.uk
Itteringham, NR11 7AR
01263 587258
Owned by a local farming family, this renowned rural dining venue is tucked away down narrow lanes on the edge of Itteringham, close to Blickling Hall. Its oak-beamed bar offers local Woodforde's and Adnams ales on tap, while menus champion top-notch meats and produce from the family farm and local artisan producers.

Sea Marge Hotel ❀❀
mackenziehotels.com
16 High Street, Overstrand, NR27 0AB | 01263 579579
Terraced lawns lead down to the coast path and beach from this 1908-built mansion. The property has been lovingly restored, with many original features retained, notably a minstrels' gallery. It's a friendly and relaxing hotel, with helpful staff serving in the restaurant. The menu, with a handful of choices for each course, is an appealing package of contemporary ideas.

The White Horse Overstrand ❀❀
whitehorseoverstrand.co.uk
34 High Street, Overstrand, NR27 0AB | 01263 579237
This family-run Victorian inn in the village of Overstrand goes from strength to strength, with food occupying an ever-prominent place at the heart of the operation, whether it is glammed-up old favourites in the bar, themed grill, Spanish or Italian nights, or vibrant modern dishes in the recently converted Barn restaurant. Large wrought-iron chandeliers hang from ceilings with original oak roof trusses above rustic Norfolk flint walls and solid oak tables in a clean-cut contemporary setting that suits the modern food which features top-class local and seasonal produce.

Dedham Vale

Beautiful Dedham Vale

With endless rural landscapes that so inspired 19th-century artist John Constable (1776–1837), the Dedham Vale is a 35-sq-mile designated Area of Outstanding Natural Beauty on the Suffolk–Essex border. At its heart you can see the wide meandering River Stour dotted with sailing boats of all shapes and sizes. Sometimes you will even spot an old Thames barge with its deep red sails straining against the power of the wind. These magnificent vessels were used to transport goods on the River Thames in London during the 19th century, and some have been preserved to provide pleasure tours.

The Stour runs inland from its estuary at Manningtree and at this point marks the counties' boundaries. On the Suffolk side, you can visit the pretty village of East Bergholt (see page 125), where the famed 19th-century painter John Constable was born in June 1776. A plaque marks the spot where his family home, East Bergholt House, once stood.

Once you've found the plaque, walk the few yards to the village's church, the 16th-century Church of St Mary the Virgin where the painter was baptised. Wander around the gardens and you will find the tomb of his parents, Golding and Ann Constable. Don't miss the timber cage just off to the left which houses the bells of this spire-less church. It was built in 1531 as a temporary home for the bells, which are thought to be the heaviest still rung in England at approximately 4.25 tons, and remains their home to this day.

▼ Cloth Hall, Dedham ▶ The River Stour

Almost opposite the church you'll see Flatford Road and, if you head down here and park where indicated, you can visit Flatford Mill. This large, red-brick 18th-century watermill was once owned by Constable's wealthy father and made famous in the painter's work, *The Hay Wain*. You can't go in, sadly, as today it is an environmental studies centre, but you can see how beautifully the Grade I listed building has survived the ravages of time. Then gaze across the mill pond to the whitewashed Willy Lott's cottage.

Willy Lott was a local farmer who lived here for 84 years and is said to have never travelled further than the churchyard of East Bergholt, where he is buried. You can walk to his cottage, and also to Bridge Cottage, which appears in many of Constable's paintings. Both are owned by the National Trust and open for you to visit. Times vary so do check before setting out if you want to go inside. At Bridge Cottage you can join a guided tour.

On the Essex side of the river you can visit Manningtree, one of Constable's favourite places – he painted *The Ascension* for its church; it now hangs in nearby Dedham's church – and the village of Dedham itself, where he went to school.

Dedham is a picture postcard village dominated by its church, St Mary the Virgin. A mighty structure with a 131-foot-high tower and a lavishly carved Galilee porch, the church towers above the village and was the focal point in many of Constable's paintings. It has stood on the site since 1492 and was built through the efforts of two leading wool merchants of the time. Dedham was a prosperous village in the 13th and 14th centuries, and had a thriving weaving industry so the church was built, to some extent, as a consequence of the village's wealth.

▸ Willy Lott's Cottage, East Bergholt

You can visit the church before enjoying an afternoon cream tea – Dedham is famous for its cream teas. Look out for the church's interior features, many are quite extraordinary, including its octagonal font engraved with emblems of the Four Evangelists, the Lion, Man, Bull and Eagle, with angels and little cherub heads around its edge. If you ask the vicar he'll tell you it dates from the 14th century. Behind the font is a rare window depicting Faith, Hope and Charity, and if you look up you will see a wonderful wood ceiling.

The Dedham Vale, which also includes the villages of Stratford St Mary, whose church stands isolated across the busy dual carriageway of the A12, Polstead, Nayland and Stoke-by-Nayland, is an important RSPB breeding ground. If you have a keen eye for spotting birds you'll see blackcaps, nightingales and grey plovers; at low tide waterfowl tread delicately among the precariously lopsided yachts.

Unspoiled areas like the valley of the River Stour are rare in East Anglia, yet here you can see the landscapes that so captured the imagination of one of the country's foremost artists.

VISIT THE MUSEUM AND GALLERY

Flatford Mill, Willy Lott's Cottage and Bridge Cottage
nationaltrust.org.uk/flatford
East Bergholt, CO7 6UL
01206 298260 | Open Mar–Dec, times vary
An 18th-century watermill once owned by the artist John Constable's father, Flatford Mill lies next to the River Stour and is at the heart of the Dedham Vale. Nearby are Willy Lott's Cottage and Bridge Cottage, which you can visit – made famous in the painter's works. Displays tell the story of Constable's life.

Dedham Art and Craft Centre
www.dedhamartandcraftcentre.co.uk
High Street, Dedham, CO7 6AD
01206 322666 | Open daily 10–5 (Sat–Sun in summer 10–5.30)
Housed in a converted church, this centre has three floors of artisans' displays. You can see demonstrations of woodturning and pottery, painting and glass decorating, and buy the perfect souvenir to take home. Its tea room specialises in local vegetarian dishes.

TAKE A WALK

If you head for East Bergholt you can take a leisurely walk along its main street and see where John Constable was born. His childhood home, East Bergholt House, is no longer there but a plaque on railings marks the spot. His first studio is nearby and further along is the church where his parents are buried. On the opposite side of the road you'll see a signpost to Flatford. Head down here for Flatford Mill, Bridge Cottage and Willy Lott's Cottage. The highlight of walking around here is that you get to stand in the places where Constable produced some of his finest paintings, such as *The Cornfield*, *The White Horse* and *Boat-Building Near Flatford Mill*.

EAT AND DRINK

The Haywain
thehaywainrestaurant.com
Burnt Oak Corner, East Bergholt, CO7 6TJ | 01206 299194
Eating at this compact fine dining restaurant – it sits only 20 people – elegantly created within a 17th-century Grade II cottage, is an experience. It's cosy, the staff are friendly and the menu mouthwatering. It has a good wine list too. Enjoy honey-roasted quail to start, corn-fed chicken to follow and a tempting chocolate terrine to finish from the choice available.

Marlborough Head Inn
marlborough-head.co.uk
Mill Lane, Dedham CO7 6DH
01206 323250
Tucked away in glorious Constable Country, this 16th-century building was once a clearing-house for local wool merchants. In 1660, after a slump in trade, it became an inn. Today it is as perfect for a pint, sofa and newspaper as it is for a home-cooked family meal. There is a terrace and walled garden.

▲ St Mary the Virgin's Church, Dedham

Le Talbooth ◎◎
milsomhotels.com
Gun Hill, Dedham, CO7 6HP
01206 323150
Confit duck followed by rump Suffolk lamb or Dedham Vale Chateaubriand, and accompanied by a glass of something seriously special is sure to tempt you if you fancy dining à la carte in one of the finest restaurants in East Anglia. Le Talbooth is housed in a stunning 15th-century timber-framed country house with lawns and gardens right beside the River Stour.

The Red Lion
The Street, East Bergholt, CO7 6TB | 01206 298332
This atmospheric period inn offers delicious pub fare, such as sandwiches and baguettes, main meals and vegetarian options – its vegetarian chestnut casserole is a speciality on the menu, which changes daily according to the seasons.

Denver

The village of Denver, which lies on the banks of the Great Ouse in Norfolk, has some really pleasant walks for you to enjoy, including one that takes you past its beautifully restored 19th-century windmill, a landmark of the village, and the mighty sluice gate on the river.

In fact, Denver's claim to fame is that it was the first village to have a sluice, in 1651. This area of the Fens is extremely flat and sluices are essential for drainage and to stop villages like Denver being flooded. If you're sporty, there are boats to hire on the river or you can play a round of golf at the Ryston Park Golf Club.

Denver's most famous resident was Captain George Manby, who was born in the village in 1765 and is best remembered for his work in establishing the forerunner of the modern fire extinguisher. The village lies on the Fen Causeway, a 24-mile long Roman road that runs between Denver and Peterborough.

PLAY GOLF

Ryston Park Golf Club

club-noticeboard.co.uk/rystonpark
Ely Rd, PE38 0HH | 01366 382133
Open Mon–Fri except Bank Holidays

This mature nine-hole parkland course has two challenging par fours to open. Water features come into play on holes five, six and seven. The course is well wooded with mature trees and an abundance of wildlife. The club house is well equipped for refreshments.

Dereham

Dereham can trace its roots back to Neolithic times. Most of its earliest buildings were lost in fires, but look out for Bishop Bonner's cottage, built in 1502 and said to have been the home of the notorious Edmund Bonner (1500–69) Bishop of London who persecuted heretics relentlessly in Mary I's time and died as a prisoner of Elizabeth I.

PLAY GOLF

Dereham Golf Club

derehamgolfclub.com
Quebec Road, NR19 2DS
01362 695900 | Open daily including Bank Holidays

On the outskirts of Dereham this friendly club has a nine-hole parkland course and 17 different tees. There's a lounge bar and dining area.

EAT AND DRINK

Darby's Freehouse

darbysfreehouse.com
Elsing Road, Swanton Morley, NR20 4NY | 01362 637647

This large country house, divided into cottages in the late 19th century and then, in 1988, converted into a pub which has recently been refurbished. The pub menu, mostly locally supplied, includes sharing boards and vegetarian and children's selections.

PLACES NEARBY

The Gressenhall Farm and Workhouse is just outside Dereham – follow the brown signs from the town centre. If you like country golf courses, then head for the Mattishall Golf Course.

Gressenhall Farm and Workhouse
museums.norfolk.gov.uk
Gressenhall, NR20 4DR
01362 869263 | Open Mar–Nov daily 10–5
This superb museum of Norfolk life provides plenty for families to do: there's a woodland adventure playground, a working farm with rare breed animals, a dairy complete with a milking machine and a workhouse where daily Victorian life is re-created. All this is set in 50 acres of pristine parkland.

Mattishall Golf Course
mattishallgolfclub.co.uk
South Green, Mattishall, NR20 3JZ
01362 850111 | Open daily including Bank Holidays
Mattishall has the distinction of having the longest hole in Norfolk at a very demanding 638 yards par five. This nine-hole course can be played as 18 holes. Facilities include a large practise putting green next to the main course.

Diss

Diss is a delightful Norfolk market town that almost straddles the county's border with Suffolk. Timber-framed cottages and smart Georgian properties line many of its town centre streets. The town can trace its roots back to the time of Edward the Confessor (c.1003–66), one of the last Anglo-Saxon kings of England, when daily life revolved around a wealthy Crown estate. Over the centuries Diss became a centre for the wool industry and enjoyed great prosperity; some of grand wool merchants' houses remain to this day.

Look out for the 14th-century Church of St Mary the Virgin in the area of the Market Place, and then turn to see Dolphin House. This lavishly timbered house is one of the finest period properties in Diss.

SEE A PERFORMANCE

Diss Corn Hall
disscornhall.co.uk
St Nicolas Street, IP22 4LB
01379 652241
From music and dance to comedy, theatrical performances and films, Diss's Corn Hall is the place to head for an evening out. By day it hosts exhibitions featuring the work of local artists, runs workshops for learning new skills and manages the Diss

Museum which is housed in a building called The Shambles in the Market Place (open mid-Mar–Nov Wed and Thu afternoons, all day Fri and Sat, and Sun afternoons).

PLAY GOLF

Diss Golf Club

www.dissgolf.co.uk
Stuston Common, IP21 4AA
01379 641025 | Open daily including Bank Holidays

The heath and parkland course of the Diss Golf Club, which is located alongside the River Waveney, provides challenging golf for all standards of player. The narrow fairways are edged by trees and water features.

PLACES NEARBY

Children will jump at the chance to ride on the steam trains at Bressingham, which you'll find two and a bit miles away. Diss has a number of fine restaurants, and you'll be spoilt for choice, but if you fancy venturing a little further afield, then head for the Fox and Goose in Fressingfield, or the Crown in Burston.

Bressingham Steam Museum and Gardens

bressingham.co.uk
Low Road, Bressingham, IP22 2AB
01379 686900 | Open Mar–May and Sep–Oct daily 10.30–4.30; Jun–Aug 10.30–5.30

Alan Bloom is an internationally recognised nurseryman and a steam enthusiast, and has combined his interests to great effect at Bressingham. There are three miniature steam-hauled trains, including a 15-inch gauge called 'Waveney Valley Railway' running through two and a half miles of the wooded Waveney Valley.

The Dell Garden has 5,000 species of perennials and alpines; Foggy Bottom has wide vistas, pathways, trees, shrubs, conifers and winter colour (restricted opening). A steam roundabout is another attraction, as is the Steam Museum. There is also a museum of props and vehicles from *Dad's Army*. See the website for events are held throughout the year.

Fox and Goose Inn ❀❀
foxandgoose.net
Church Road, Fressingfield,
IP21 5PB | 01379 586247
The Fox and Goose Inn, housed in a timber-framed Tudor guildhall, has a wealth of character in its old beams and open fires, and the bar still serves real ales tapped straight from the barrel. Accomplished and creative European ideas pepper the kitchen's modern cooking, driven by Suffolk's abundant larder. The more formal evenings-only restaurant is upstairs, while downstairs there's a smaller dining room in the old lounge as well as the bar area.

The Crown
burstoncrown.com
Mill Road, Burston, IP22 5TW
01379 741257
Steve and Bev Kembery have transformed their 16th-century pub by the green into a cracking community pub, drawing locals in for top-notch ale and food, organising the village fete, hosting three beer festivals a year, and offering a weekly buskers' night and regular theme nights. Well worth finding.

▾ Diss Mere

Dunwich

Dunwich was an important port in Saxon and Norman times, exporting wool and grain to Europe and importing cloth and wine. It boasted a population of 5,000 and had at least three churches plus many monastic buildings, a mint, a large guildhall, alehouses, farmhouses and mills.

However, a fierce storm in 1328, which diverted the River Blyth northwards, effectively obliterated the settlement. The crashing North Sea breakers left a couple of solitary gravestones from the former Church of All Saints, near the

▼ The Dunwich coastline

cliff, and the crumbling walls of the Greyfriars friary as the only evidence of the medieval town lost beneath the waves.

The sea was the making and breaking of Dunwich. It was the sea that provided the reason for its existence, supporting its industries of shipbuilding and fishing, and bringing its most famous figure, St Felix of Burgundy, to preach Christianity to the pagans of East Anglia in the seventh century.

And it was the sea that silted up the harbour in a terrible storm in 1286, leading to its inevitable decline. Ever since, the sea has been reclaiming Dunwich, a process that continues at the rate of around one yard each year.

The Roman town here extended a mile beyond the present coastline. Half of this had disappeared by the time of the Norman Conquest, but the worst was yet to come. The remains of the last church tumbled over the cliffs as recently as 1920; Dunwich Museum has a series of dramatic photographs showing it collapsing year by year.

According to local legend, you can still hear the bells of the sunken churches pealing beneath the sea on a stormy night. A pioneering underwater survey has recently mapped the lost areas, and confirmed that many of the larger stone structures are still standing.

Just south of Dunwich is Dunwich Heath belonging to the National Trust. Beyond is the Minsmere RSPB Nature Reserve (see page 238), an area of marshes and lagoons that attracts many wading birds.

VISIT THE MUSEUM

Dunwich Museum

dunwichmuseum.org.uk

St James Street, Dunwich, IP17 3DT

01728 648796 | Open Mar Sat–Sun daily 2–4.30; Apr–Sep 11.30–4.30; Oct 12–4

The Dunwich Museum tells the fascinating story of this once bustling medieval seaport through narratives, including a series of dramatic photographs, showing it falling into the sea over the centuries. A scale model also features.

GET OUTDOORS

Dunwich Heath

nationaltrust.org.uk/dunwichheath

Saxmundham, IP17 3DJ

01728 648501 | Open daily, tea room open Mar–Nov

Dunwich Heath is run by the National Trust and is a quiet and peaceful place full of birds and other wildlife. Designated routes make it ideal for leisurely coastal walks. From July to September it is especially colourful with its carpet of purple heather and bushes of yellow gorse.

EAT AND DRINK

The Ship at Dunwich

shipatdunwich.co.uk

Saint James Street, IP17 3DT

01728 648219

Two minutes' stroll from the beach, the Ship at Dunwich is a well-loved old smugglers' inn overlooking the salt marshes and sea, and is popular with walkers and birders visiting the nearby reserves. The Ship keeps Dunwich on the map with hearty meals and ales from Adnams, Woodforde's and St Peter's – to name just a few. Its delightful unspoiled public bar offers nautical bric-a-brac, a wood-burning stove in a huge fireplace, flagged floors and simple wooden furnishings. It is locally renowned for its fish and chips. Look for the ancient fig tree in the garden, and take note of the inn's three annual beer festivals in spring, summer and autumn.

Duxford

Duxford is a small village a few miles south of Cambridgeshire and is best known as the airfield home of RAF Duxford during the Battle of Britain. In the centre of the village are cottages that sit snugly with Georgian country houses, two somewhat stately medieval churches, St Peter and St John the Baptist, and a gorgeous chapel, but it is the Imperial War Museum Duxford on the former RAF site that most people head for when visiting the village. The museum is well signposted and easy to find just off the main road from Essex into Cambridge. It's the largest aviation and war museum in the country, so you can't miss it.

VISIT THE MUSEUM

Imperial War Museum Duxford

See highlight panel overleaf

EAT AND DRINK

Duxford Lodge Hotel

duxfordlodgehotel.co.uk
Ickleton Road, CB22 4RT
01223 836444

Just a few minutes from the famous airfield and its museum, Edwardian Duxford Lodge Hotel is steeped in wartime history, having played host in the 1940s to stars and big names such as Bing Crosby, Winston Churchill and Douglas Bader. Its Le Paradis restaurant is a soothing, pastel-hued venue where crisp white linen, comfy chairs and smartly turned-out staff add an old-style charm to proceedings. The European-influenced food maintains a healthy attachment to familiar ideas – chicken liver and foie gras pâté for example, followed by loin of pork with black pudding mash, and apple and cider jus. To finish, there are comforting old friends such as sticky toffee pudding with toffee sauce. Accommodation at Duxford Lodge includes 15 comfortable and smartly furnished ensuite rooms.

Top 10 museums

- **Bressingham Steam Museum and Gardens**, Bressingham, page 118
- **Dunwich Museum**, Dunwich, page 122
- **Fitzwilliam Museum**, Cambridge, page 93
- **Gainsborough's House**, Sudbury, page 257
- **Imperial War Museum Duxford**, Duxford, page 124
- **Moyse's Hall Museum**, Bury St Edmunds, page 77
- **National Horseracing Museum**, Newmarket, page 196
- **Norfolk and Suffolk Aviation Museum**, Flixton, page 74
- **RNLI Henry Blogg Museum**, Cromer, page 104
- **Time and Tide Museum**, Great Yarmouth, page 143

Imperial War Museum Duxford

iwm.org.uk
CB22 4QR | 01223 835000
Open mid-Mar–mid-Oct daily 10–6; mid-Oct–mid-Mar 10–4

This remarkable museum tells the story of the impact aviation had on the nature of war, on people's lives and on the history of the region. Duxford is Britain's best-preserved World War II fighter station, and has seven impressive hangars – some with listed building status – filled with an extraordinary collection of aircraft and vehicles. Here you can see around 200 aircraft, naval vessels and military vehicles, plus sections dedicated to the Parachute Regiment and the Royal Anglian Regiment. Books and photographs help tell the story of Britain at war. If you are lucky, you may catch an air show; they are a regular feature among the special events.

▼ Imperial War Museum Duxford

The John Barleycorn
johnbarleycorn.co.uk
3 Moorfield Road, CB2 4PP
01223 832699
This thatched and whitewashed former coach house was built in 1660 and took the name John Barleycorn in the mid-19th century. During World War II, it was a favourite watering hole for the brave young airmen of Douglas Bader's Duxford Wing. Step through the door into the softly lit bar with a rustic mix of country furniture, large brick fireplace, old tiled floor, cushioned pews and hop-adorned low beams. It's a cosy place in which to enjoy a hearty home-cooked meal, washed down with a refreshing pint of Greene King IPA or Abbot Ale. Summer alfresco eating can be enjoyed on the flower-festooned rear patio.

East Bergholt

East Bergholt in Suffolk is famously the birthplace of 19th-century landscape painter John Constable. His childhood home, East Bergholt House, is no longer there but a plaque on railings marks the spot where it once stood; you can find it a few minutes' walk from the village's Church of St Mary the Virgin. Constable moved to London to join the Royal Academy, but he is said to have returned to East Bergholt every summer to draw fresh inspiration from the bucolic scenery of meadows, valleys, rivers and farmland.

Flatford Mill, which was owned by Constable's wealthy father, Willy Lott's Cottage and the Bridge Cottage were all painted by Constable and can be visited in the village. You can take a tour of these sites and enjoy some of the best walks you could wish for in the beautiful unspoiled countryside of the Dedham Vale.

The village has fine examples of half-timbered and thatched cottages and magnificent churches, reflecting its heyday during the 14th century when this part of East Anglia was one of the richest parts of England and the base of the wool industry.
See also Beautiful Dedham Vale (page 110)

Easton

see **Framlingham**, page 136

▲ Ely Cathedral

Ely

You will be bowled over by Ely. It has a real sense of harmony, with its vast cathedral, one of the most beautiful buildings you're ever likely to see, towering over the rustic cottages and elegant homes that surround it. Ely's history is awesome.

It has its origins in the foundation of an abbey in 673 on the Isle of Ely, which was under the protection of Saint Ethelreda. Destroyed by Danish invaders in 870 and then not rebuilt for over a century, the site was one of the last places in England to hold out against the rule of William the Conqueror.

The stunning cathedral is known as the Ship of the Fens for the distant views of the 170-foot-tall Octagon that dominates the surrounding low-lying wetlands. Oliver Cromwell lived in Ely for several years after inheriting the position of local tax collector. His former home dates from the 16th century and is now used as the tourist information office and a museum, with rooms displayed as they would have been in Cromwell's time.

Today, Ely has some attractive Georgian buildings and a large park that, together with the cathedral and its history, make this an appealing place to visit.

TAKE IN SOME HISTORY

Ely Cathedral

cathedral.ely.anglican.org

CB7 4DL | 01353 667735

Open summer daily 7–6.30; winter daily 7–6.30 (Sun to 5.30)

The present cathedral dates from 1083 and is a magnificent example of Romanesque architecture. You can take a tour of the cathedral, including the Octagon Lantern Tower, and visit the museum of stained glass inside. Choral music is a big attraction at the cathedral; there are concerts throughout the year and you can hear Evensong every day at 5.30 (4 on a Sunday).

VISIT THE MUSEUMS

Ely Museum

elymuseum.org.uk
The Old Gaol, Market Street, CB7 4LS | 01353 666655
Open summer Mon–Sat 10.30–5, Sun 1–5; winter Mon, Wed–Sat 10.30–4, Sun 1–4

Ely Museum is housed in a building dating from the 13th century that has been a private house, a tavern, a register office and, most famously, the Bishop's Gaol. It was sensitively renovated in 1997 and you can see much of the building's history, including prisoners' graffiti, hidden doorways and original planking on the walls. Telling the story of the area from prehistoric times to the 20th century, the museum is a history centre for the Isle of Ely and the Fens.

Oliver Cromwell's House

visitely.org.uk
29 St Mary's Street, CB7 4HF
01353 662062 | Open Apr–Oct daily 10–5; Nov–Mar Mon–Fri, Sun 11–4, Sat 10–5

Politician Oliver Cromwell (1599–1658) inherited this fine timber-framed house and local estates from a maternal uncle and moved here in 1636, along with his mother, sisters, wife and eight children. There are displays and period rooms dealing with his life, the English Civil War and domestic life in the 17th century, as well as the history of the Fens and the house itself, from its medieval origins to its role as an inn in the 19th century. Various special events are held during the year.

▾ Oliver Cromwell's House

Stained Glass Museum
stainedglassmuseum.com
The South Triforium, Ely Cathedral, CB7 4DL | 01353 660347
Open Easter–Oct Mon–Fri 10.30–5, Sat 10.30–5.30, Sun 12–6; Nov–Easter as above but Sun 12–4.30
It's fascinating to see stained glass up close, albeit in protective cabinets. Some 800 years of stained-glass history are illustrated in this unique museum inside Ely Cathedral, displaying over 100 panels of original windows rescued from Britain and abroad. The medieval section includes important loans from the Victoria and Albert Museum in London. There are also exhibits from Buckingham Palace and Windsor Castle, work by William Morris and John Piper, and changing exhibitions of contemporary work are held throughout the year.

PLAY GOLF

Ely City Golf Club
elygolf.co.uk
107 Cambridge Road, CB7 4HX
01353 662751 | Open daily including Bank Holidays
The slightly undulating parkland with water hazards formed by lakes and natural dykes ensure that the course at the Ely City Golf Club presents a challenge. There's a demanding par four fifth hole (467 yards), often into a headwind, and a testing par three second hole (160 yards) played over two ponds. The clubhouse offers meals.

EAT AND DRINK

Peacocks
peacockstearoom.co.uk
65 Waterside, CB7 4AU
01353 661100
The owners of Peacocks add a little extra to the traditional tea room experience with their homemade specialities. Light meals such as Norfolk ham salad and cakes are available all day, with both soup and a dish of the day offered. A treat are the freshly baked scones served with Cornish clotted cream. The choice of teas is remarkable, with 70 listed, so try something different – maybe the Chocolate Imperial from Paris.

PLACES NEARBY

The enthralling Wildfowl and Wetlands Trust's Welney Wetland Centre as well as Cambridge (see page 88) and the Wicken Fen National Nature Reserve (see page 279) are all within easy reach of Ely. En route you might like to take a refreshment stop at the Lazy Otter in the village of Stretham.

Welney Wetland Centre
wwt.org.uk
Hundred Foot Bank, Welney, PE14 9TN | 01353 860711 | Open Mar–Oct daily 9.30–5; Nov–Feb Mon–Wed 10–5, Thu–Sun 10–8
This important wetland site on the beautiful Ouse Washes, managed by the Wildfowl and Wetlands Trust, is famed for the breathtaking winter spectacle of wild ducks, geese and swans. Impressive

observation facilities, including hides and a heated main observatory, offer outstanding views of the huge numbers of wildfowl, which include Bewick's and whooper swans, wigeon, teal and shoveler. Floodlit evening swan feeds take place between November and February. In summer, the reserve is alive with over 40 per cent of all British wetland plant flowers. Butterflies, dragonflies and damselflies are in abundance, and the available summer walk gives visitors unique access to the wetland habitat.

The Lazy Otter
lazy-otter.com
Cambridge Road, Stretham, CB6 3LU | 01353 649780
A pub here has served fenland watermen for several centuries; today's incarnation is popular with leisure boaters on the River Ouse, which glides past the extensive beer garden. As well as overlooking the river, the garden has views over the rich farmland. Barley from these acres goes into a wide range of East Anglian beers, including the house ale from Milton Brewery. The pub hosts an annual beer festival.

Fakenham

The market town of Fakenham lies at the heart of Norfolk's flat open countryside and seems to be miles from anywhere. It's mentioned in the Domesday Book and was awarded its charter in 1250. It is best known locally for its racecourse. On race days people come from miles around and the town is bustling. There's a museum, too, dedicated to gas and local history, and a nature reserve and gardens at Pensthorpe which are worth a visit.

VISIT THE MUSEUM

Fakenham Museum of Gas and Local History
fakenhamgasmuseum.com
Hempton Road, NR21 7LA
01328 863150 | Open Jun–Sep Thu 10.30–3.30, Fri–Sat 10.30–1
Housed in a building that is the only surviving town gasworks in England, complete with all the apparatus needed to turn coal into gas, this museum offers a fascinating account of local social history. You can see original purifiers and condensers, and displays about heating, lighting and cooking through the decades. The town's gasworks closed in 1965.

GET OUTDOORS

Pensthorpe Wildlife and Gardens
www.pensthorpe.co.uk
Pensthorpe, NR21 0LN
01328 851465 | Open Jan–Feb daily 10–4; Mar–Dec 10–5
You can explore the beautiful lakes, nature trails and gardens designed by Chelsea Flower Show gold medalists at

Pensthorpe. Look out for the large collection of cranes in the Conservation Centre. There are purpose-built hides, daily bird feeds and warden-guided walks. Children can enjoy being detectives exploring the bug walks and discovering underwater wildlife.

GO TO THE RACES

Fakenham Racecourse
fakenhamracecourse.co.uk
The Racecourse, NR21 7NY
01328 862388
Race days at the Fakenham Racecourse are friendly affairs. It doesn't have a dress code so there's no stuffiness and everyone's welcome, including children. You can visit the paddocks and see the horses before they race. There are two restaurants and afternoon tea is available too.

EAT AND DRINK

The Blue Boar Inn
blueboar-norfolk.co.uk
Great Ryburgh, NR21 0DX
01328 829212
Just a few minutes' drive from Fakenham is the Blue Boar, a characterful listed inn. There's a lot to see here. Beyond the beer garden you'll find a round-towered medieval church which, according to legend, was once linked to the pub by a secret tunnel, while inside the pub there are quarry-tiled floors, beams and a vast inglenook. These are spread through a number of different floor levels, marking alterations to this popular local over the centuries. It was originally a coaching inn and was also used as a recruiting station during the Napoleonic Wars. All that's required of today's visitors is to enjoy the local Yetman's beers and the richly varied, Norfolk-based menu.

The Wensum Lodge Hotel
wensumlodge.co.uk
Bridge Street, NR21 9AY
01328 862100
Located in an idyllic spot by the River Wensum, just three minutes' walk from the centre of Fakenham, this lovely pub has a stream flowing through its garden and offers guests free fishing on the river. The building dates from around 1700 and was originally the grain store for the adjoining mill. The fine ales are complemented by home-cooked food prepared from locally supplied ingredients, with baguettes, jacket potatoes and an all-day breakfast on the light bites menu, with an à la carte menu for heartier fare. The hotel is an ideal base for cycling, birding, fishing and horseracing.

PLACES NEARBY

Just six miles or so from Fakenham is Thursford Green village, where you can visit the wonderful Thursford steam and mechanical collection and perjaps indulge in a behind-the-scenes tour and dine in the Old Forge Seafood Restaurant.

Thursford Collection
www.thursford.com
Thursford, NR21 0AS
01328 878477 | Open Apr–Sep Sun–Fri 12–5
The Thursford Collection is famous for being the world's largest collection of steam engines and mechanical organs. You can see Wurlitzer shows, silent movies, old-fashioned fairground carousels and static displays of both fairground and road engines, along with all kinds of related memorabilia. There are two behind-the-scenes tours: the first goes backstage, taking in dressing rooms, costume stores, and the wardrobe department; while the second visits the old forge and a re-creation of an engine yard of the 1940s. During November and December, people flock from miles around to the huge Christmas Spectacular shows and to take the children on Santa's Magical Journey. There's free entry to the shops between April and December and the Barn restaurant offers a full range of hot food and snacks.

The Old Forge Seafood Restaurant ⊛
seafoodnorthnorfolk.co.uk
Fakenham Road, Thursford, NR21 0BD | 01328 878345
This whitewashed former coaching station and forge used to be a resting place for pilgrims heading to Walsingham, and even merits a name-check in The Pilgrim's Progress (1678). A sympathetic refurbishment means that the beams, the York stone floor and walls, and even the original iron hooks where the horses were shod are in evidence in the cosy, buzzy restaurant. It's all about the seafood here – why not when you can get it in fresh every day from nearby Blakeney and Wells-next-the-Sea. Expect good, honest, rustic cooking, often with Spanish influences and using spices grown in the forge's garden.

Felbrigg
see **Cromer**, page 107

Felixstowe
Felixstowe, whose name means 'happy place', is a traditional Edwardian seaside resort on Suffolk's coast that continues to provide families with buckets of summer fun. Here, your children can ride bumper boats, go fishing for crabs and buy sticks of rock from kiosks on the pier, while older folk stroll along the promenade and drink tea at seafront cafes.

Yes, the character of Felixstowe, which is all rather genteel, hasn't changed much over the decades – the exception being its port. In the days of press gangs, Felixstowe was not a place to drop your guard. If you did so you risked spending the next few months or years sailing and fighting on the high seas. The town became a major port in 1886, and in recent years has grown to become Britain's largest container complex. A village has stood on the site since before the Norman Conquest. Its location made it a lynchpin in England's defences, most notably in 1667 when Dutch soldiers landed and failed to capture Landguard Fort.

During the late Victorian era, with the opening of the railway station, Felixstowe became a fashionable resort.

Today, despite the size of the port, Felixstowe retains its attractiveness. It has a long sand and shingle beach and extensive gardens line the promenade. Some of the gardens, such as those by the Spa Pavilion and Town Hall, have been listed on the English Heritage Register of Parks and Gardens of National Importance.

Just along the beach, Landguard Peninsula is a nature reserve with an historic fort and the Felixstowe Museum, and a passenger ferry links Felixstowe with Harwich in Essex, on the other side of the River Stour (sailing times vary according to the season and weather).

TAKE IN SOME HISTORY

Landguard Fort

landguardpartnership.org.uk
View Point Road, Landguard Peninsula, IP11 3TW | 01394 675900 Open Apr–Nov daily 10–5
Visit the site of the last seaborne invasion of England in 1667. There's a maze of rooms and bastion viewing platforms.

PLAY GOLF

Felixstowe Ferry Golf Club

felixstowegolf.co.uk
Ferry Road, IP11 9RY
01394 286834 | Open Mon–Fri, limited play at weekends and Bank Holidays
The Felixstowe Ferry Golf Club is the fifth oldest such club in England. It has a seaside links

▾ Landguard Fort

with pleasant views and easy walking and a nine-hole pay-and-play course.

EAT AND DRINK

The Regal Fish Bar and Restaurant

theregalrestaurant.com

Sea Road, IP11 2DH | 01394 273977

There's nothing quite like dining on the freshest fish and chips in a restaurant right on the seafront of a traditional town like Felixstowe. The Regal, housed in a glorious Victorian building looking out over the sea, where fish brought ashore just hours before is delivered daily, offers exactly that. Dine in the large restaurant or take away for chips by the sea – it's up to you.

Framlingham

You will adore the gorgeous Suffolk market town of Framlingham, or Fram as it's referred to by locals. Dominated in alarming fashion by its remarkably well-preserved fortifications that date from around the reign of King John (1166–1216), it is steeped in royal history. It was here at the castle, in 1553, that Mary Tudor gathered her supporters around her as she waited anxiously to learn whether she or Lady Jane Grey would be declared Queen.

Framlingham Castle is today in the care of English Heritage, and is one of the most important and beautiful medieval castles in the country. It simply oozes 800 years of history at every turn. Its unusual curtain wall, one of the earliest in England, is topped by 13 defensive towers. Unlike in other castles, it is possible to walk the full length of the battlements. Little remains of the interior of the castle, however, except a 17th-century poor house and medieval headstones.

A walk around the Framlingham – it is nice and compact, if a little steep in places – will show you attractive houses and shops that gather around the triangular Market Hill. In a county replete with glorious church architecture, the parish Church of St Michael is especially pleasing. The roof is resplendent with intricate fan tracery which conceals hammerbeams. There is also a splendid collection of 16th-century tombs belonging to members of the Howard family – John Howard (*c*.1425–85) was the first Duke of Norfolk – at the time when they owned the castle.

The town has many quaint buildings dating from the 17th, 18th and 19th centuries, the best examples of which can be found on Market Hill. Framlingham is surrounded by the villages of Sweffling, Kettleburgh, Earl Soham and Saxtead, and country lanes that are ideal for walking and cycling. It is an excellent base from which to explore an this part of Suffolk.

▲ Framlingham Castle

TAKE IN SOME HISTORY

Framlingham Castle

english-heritage.org.uk

IP8 9BT | 01728 724189

Open Apr–Jun and Sep–Oct daily 10–5; Jul–Aug 10–6; Nov–Mar Sat–Sun 10–4

The attractive, mellow-hued battlemented towers and walls of Framlingham Castle have had some notable owners. The Earl of Norfolk, Roger Bigod, built the castle somewhere between about 1189 and 1200 on the site of an earlier castle. The Bigods traditionally had tempestuous relationships with their kings – Hugh Bigod supported Henry II's eldest son when he rebelled against his father in 1173, Roger Bigod II held Framlingham against King John in 1216, and Roger Bigod IV refused to go to Flanders to fight for Edward I in 1297.

Framlingham Castle was also owned by the Mowbray family, one of whom was engaged to marry one of the unfortunate princes who 'disappeared' from the Tower of London, and the Howard family, members of which were Dukes of Norfolk in Henry VIII's time. It was at Framlingham that 'Bloody' Mary learned that she had become Queen of England in 1553. Later, Elizabeth I used the castle as a prison for priests who refused to accept the new Church of England.

Framlingham Castle has 13 towers, all connected by walls, and you can walk right round the castle. There are beautiful views over the mere. When the castle was no longer used as a ducal residence, it took on several different roles through the ensuing centuries, including

10 top castles

- **Baconsthorpe Castle**, page 58
- **Bungay Castle**, page 74
- **Burgh Castle**, page 148
- **Caister Castle**, page 84
- **Castle Acre**, page 265
- **Castle Rising Castle**, page 182
- **Framlingham Castle**, page 134
- **Norwich Castle**, page 215
- **Orford Castle**, page 231
- **Weeting Castle**, page 270

as a poor house – the buildings for which survive in the courtyard – a parish meeting place, dance hall, courtroom, drill hall and a fire station.

You can learn more about the castle's colourful past from the on-site exhibition, entitled Framlingham Castle: From Powerhouse to Poorhouse.

SEE A LOCAL CHURCH

St Michael the Archangel Church

Church Street, IP13 9BJ
01728 621082

Known affectionately as St Mike's, the Church of St Michael the Archangel is not far from the town centre, almost at the foot of the castle. You can see fabulous tombs and the 500-year-old nave roof, which is a masterpiece of carpentry. The hammerbeams are concealed behind timber vaulting. A masterpiece of a different kind is the ornate organ, built in 1674 by Thomas Thamar and still in use. Its case may be older, and is a rare survivor of the destruction of such organs ordered by Oliver Cromwell during the English Civil War.

This Perpendicular-style church was built by the third Duke of Norfolk, Thomas Howard, in 1550 as a family mausoleum, and it incorporates some remains of an earlier church. Look out for the capitals of the chancel arch which date from the 12th century. The church holds the tombs of the Howard family from before the Reformation. Some of the remains had to be moved to the church from Thetford Priory when Henry VIII dissolved the monasteries. They were joined by later family tombs of increasingly extravagant design, such as the gilded tomb of Henry Howard,

Earl of Surrey, who was beheaded, aged 30, in 1547.

EAT AND DRINK

The Station Hotel

thestationframlingham.com
Station Road, IP13 9EE
01728 723455

Built as part of the local railway in the 19th century, the Station Hotel has been a pub since the 1950s, outliving the railway which closed in 1962. Inside, you will find scrubbed tables and an eclectic mix of furniture. During the last decade it has established a fine reputation for its gutsy and earthy food, listed on the ever-changing blackboard menu. A typical lunch could be kedgeree, dinner might include pot-roasted rabbit and bean stew, or pan-fried mullet with linguine clam chowder. Many of the beers are brewed in Suffolk, and the pub hosts a beer festival in mid-July.

PLACES NEARBY

A five-minute drive away is the village of Cretingham, where locals will tell you the tale of a grisly murder at the vicarage in 1887. Today, it is a quiet, unassuming little place, with one of the area's finest golf courses. The quiet village of Easton is also close by; this was an estate up until the end of World War I when it was sold and divided into plots for new homes. Here, you'll find Easton Farm Park, one of the best places in the region for seeing rare breeds of farm animals. The village of Saxtead Green has the most gorgeous windmill imaginable.

Cretingham Golf Club

cretinghamgolfclub.co.uk
Cretingham, IP13 7BA
01728 685275 | Open daily

Cretingham Golf Club has a tree-lined parkland course with many water features, including the River Deben, which runs through it. The club house has a bar and restaurant area.

Easton Farm Park

eastonfarmpark.co.uk
Easton, IP13 0EQ | 01728 746475
Open see website for details

An award-winning farming museum and park, Easton Farm Park lies on the banks of the River Deben. There are plenty of breeds of farm animals, including Suffolk Punch horses, ponies, pigs, lambs and calves, goats, rabbits, guinea pigs and poultry. Children love to see the chicks hatching, and to join in the daily egg collecting, plus free hug-a-bunny and pony rides.

Saxtead Green Post Mill

english-heritage.org.uk
The Mill House, Saxtead Green, IP13 9QQ | 01728 685789
Open Apr–Sep Fri–Sat and Bank Holidays 12–5

With its massive sails silhouetted against the sky and its brilliant white round house that revolves on its base, you will adore the post corn windmill at Saxtead Green – it will bring a smile to your face the moment you set eyes on it. It dates from the late 1790s and is still in working order. You can climb the wooden stairs of this three-storey mill; each floor is full of fascinating machinery, such as millstones and the massive oak brake wheel. At the top you can see the windshaft, on which the sails and their fantail are fixed. The mill is classed as an Ancient Monument and is cared for by English Heritage. An audio tour explains the workings of the mill.

Grantchester

Grantchester, on the outskirts of Cambridge, conjures up images of jolly young men and winsome girls enjoying picnics next to the river, which flows gently between flower-strewn meadows. Bicycles are propped up against trees and poetry is in the air. Except that Grantchester is an altogether busier place today than as portrayed in the poems of Rupert Brooke (1887–1915), who was a student at King's College before World War I. His 1912 poem 'The Old Vicarage, Grantchester', in which he recalls happy days in the idyllic English surroundings of Cambridgeshire, immortalised a particular view of 'Englishness'. Brooke lived at the Orchard for a couple of years, and then next door at the Old Vicarage, the present home of author Jeffery Archer and his wife Mary.

Within walking distance of Cambridge, Grantchester is a lovely village of black-and-white half-timbered buildings, thatched cottages, a pretty church and meadows. The village is a favourite among both tourists and students who travel upstream from Cambridge by punt to eat a picnic in the meadows or at the tea gardens called the Orchard, as they have done since the 19th century.

EAT AND DRINK

Orchard Tea Garden

orchard-grantchester.com
45–47 Mill Way, CB3 9ND
01223 551125 | Open Mar–Oct daily 9.30–5.30; Nov–Feb 10–4.30

The tradition of serving afternoon tea at the Orchard began in 1897, when a group of students punted up the river and asked for refreshments. It soon became a regular thing. Among the famous people who have taken tea there are James Mason, Norman Hartnell, Emma Thompson, John Cleese, Peter Cook, Stephen Fry, Hugh Laurie, Griff Rhys-Jones, King George VI, Prince Charles and Clive James. Poets Ted Hughes and Sylvia Plath often walked to Grantchester from their city centre home for tea in the 1950s. The Rupert Brooke Society runs a small and informative museum in the grounds of the Orchard (opening times vary).

PLACES NEARBY

Head off to see the beautiful Anglesey Abbey, Gardens and Lode Mill (see page 99), Duxford (see page 123) and the delights of Cambridge (see page 88), which are 10 minutes or so away by car, and the enchanting Wicken Fen National Nature Reserve (see page 279).

Great Bircham

Great Bircham, together with the villages of Bircham Tofts and Bircham Newton, make up a community that sprawls over several miles of the flat north Norfolk countryside. It is best known for its windmill, which you can see for miles around.

GET INDUSTRIAL

Bircham Windmill

birchamwindmill.co.uk

PE31 6SJ | 01485 578393

Open 27 Mar–Sep, 10–5

This gorgeous, moody, grey tarred-brick windmill with huge white sails and a white cap is one of the last remaining purpose-built windmills in Norfolk. If you visit on a windy day, you'll see the sails turning at an alarming speed. It's a spectacular sight. There are five floors, which you can climb and, when the sails are turning, you can see the milling machinery working.

Next to the windmill is a bakery – simply follow the aroma of freshly baked. There's also a tea room, built on the site of the granary, which along with 17 blends of tea, also serves light lunches, scones and cakes.

You could make a trip to the windmill a day out as it stands in a complex with ponies, sheep, chickens and guinea pigs for children, a lovely garden to wander around and, at weekends, workshops where local craftspeople demonstrate their skills.

EAT AND DRINK

The Kings Head Hotel

the-kings-head-bircham.co.uk

Bircham, PE31 6RJ,

01485 578265

There's a new smartly appointed open-plan bar and lounge – think bright colours, patterned rugs on a wooden floor and tub chairs – at the Kings Head, where you can enjoy a drink, perhaps your choice from the 60-strong selection of gins, before moving through to the contemporary, spacious restaurant. The kitchen doesn't stray far from base to source its materials and uses them to good effect, with a versatile menu that embraces traditional fare and more modern concepts.

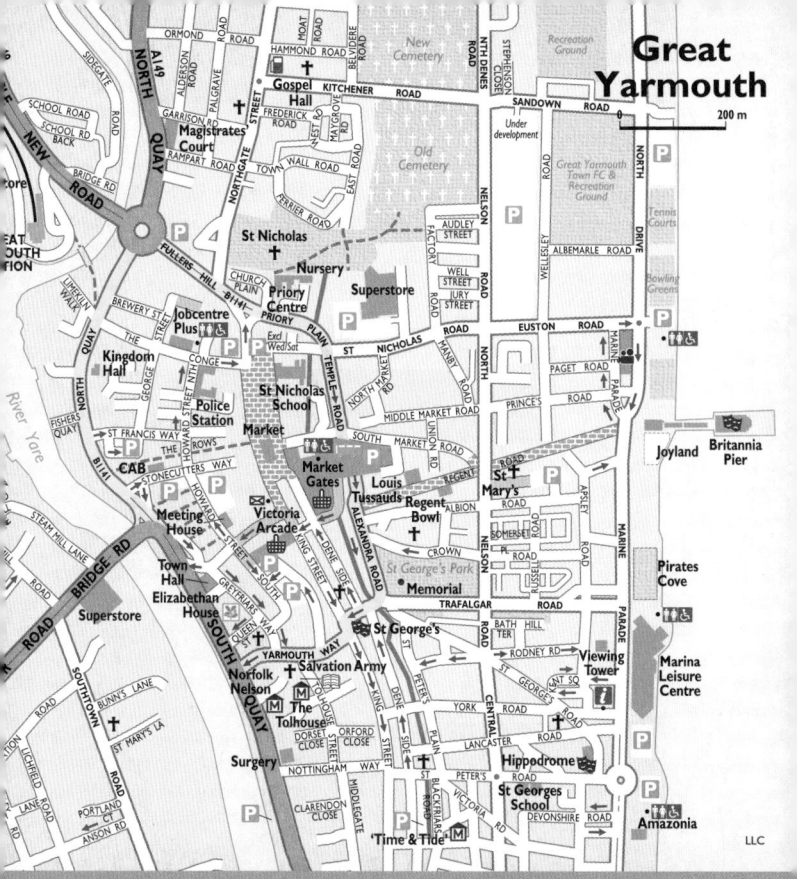

Great Yarmouth

Great Yarmouth – classic seaside resort

From modern theme parks and amusements set in gardens to miles of golden sands that hug the promenade, Great Yarmouth in Norfolk is every inch a modern seaside resort; in fact, it's the largest in East Anglia.

You'll find family attractions from carousels to one-armed bandits, from end-of-the-pier shows to zoos, spas, trendy cafes and gardens to keep everyone amused for hours, even interactive amusements for techno-savvy teenagers.

Great Yarmouth has been a prosperous seaside resort since 1760 when George II was on the throne. It has seen wars, flooding, the collapse of its fishing industry and the heyday of the music hall, and it had one of the first electric tramway systems in England. Today, it celebrates its heritage as one of the country's foremost maritime centres and Victorian seaside resorts while embracing the 21st century with aplomb.

Ancient peninsula

Great Yarmouth, or simply Yarmouth to locals, occupies a strategic location on the Norfolk coast, which has ensured its prosperity since Roman and Norman times. Remains of early settlers and their large communities can still be seen here today. Like the River Alde to the south, the Yare heads for the sea only to be deflected to the south by a narrow spit of land. It was on this peninsula that the port of Yarmouth developed over millennia – with, as was fashionable, its buildings facing away from the sea.

For centuries Yarmouth's prosperity grew, resting mainly on the vast shoals of herring in the North Sea. Merchants from all over Europe and Scandinavia would come to the medieval Free Herring Fair, which was held in the town and lasted 40 days from Michaelmas 29 September) to Martinmas (11 November). Before World War I, more than 1,000 fishing boats plied their trade from Yarmouth, but overfishing eventually took its toll and the port turned to gas and oil.

You can see reminders of Yarmouth's one-time immense fishing industry. A few houses still stand that were once part of the 'Rows' – small passageways running inland from the

▼ Great Yarmouth harbour

quayside lined with fishermens' houses. The Rows were so narrow that a special horse-drawn vehicle, known as a troll cart and only 3ft wide, was developed for moving goods in the town. Today, you can visit the Old Merchant's House, owned by English Heritage, which has been converted into a museum. Yarmouth's Time and Tide Museum, housed in a converted fish-curing works, also celebrates the town's maritime history.

Wide boulevards

Yarmouth today is an elegant place of wide boulevards and handsome buildings. Contemporary architecture sits comfortably with Tudor and Victorian merchants' houses and mansions, especially around the trendy quayside area and along the promenade. Now the buildings face the sea. Yarmouth 'turned round' in the 19th century when it became fashionable for Victorian families to visit the seaside, and the ever-resilient town was able to exploit its beach.

The beach and promenade remain the highlight for many visitors. Dominating the scene are Yarmouth's two piers, the Wellington Pier, which opened in 1853 (see page 145), hotly followed five years later by the Britannia Pier, where evening

band performances drew record numbers of people (see page 145). The late 1800s through to the turn of the century was a particularly prosperous time for Yarmouth, and musical and theatrical evenings were the highlight of most noble families' week.

Landmark piers

Both piers are landmarks. The Wellington Pier, and the Winter Gardens that forms part of its complex, has been turned into a huge family entertainment centre with bowling alleys and interactive gadgetry, while on the Britannia Pier you can still catch a show; comedies are popular, as are magic and dance shows. It also has two amusements arcades where you can challenge a one-armed bandit, before heading off for a spot of rifle shooting, bingo or hopping aboard the ghost train. You can buy multicoloured rock and enjoy doughnuts. Yes, it's good old family seaside fun.

Along Marine Parade, between the piers, you'll find the multi-million-pound Sea Life Centre (see page 144) with one of the few underwater viewing tunnels in the country, along with the Pirate's Cove Adventure Golf and Amazonia World of Reptiles. Opposite is the Hippodrome (see page 145), which has been thrilling audiences with its circus and water shows for decades. The building dates from 1903 and is one of only a handful of surviving purpose-built circus venues in the world, and the only one in England.

Market Gates shopping mall, off Temple Road, and Victoria Arcade near the Town Hall provide a vast selection of shops between them. High street names sit next to tiny specialist shops selling designer goodies. In the centre of town, the Market Place, which is thought to have been a place of trading since before the town was granted a charter in 1208, is a wide open space full of trees and benches – plus stalls six days a week. Here, and throughout the town, you will find stylish restaurants, pubs and pavement cafes to make your visit to Yarmouth complete.

◂ The Pleasure Beach

VISIT THE MUSEUMS

Elizabethan House Museum

nationaltrust.org.uk/elizabethanhousemuseum
4 South Quay, NR30 2QH
01493 855746 | Open Mar–Oct daily 10–4 (times vary)

This super museum, housed in a 16th-century quayside building, tells the story of everyday folk who lived from Tudor through to Victorian times. You can see room sets, including the wooden-panelled Conspiracy Room (was this where Charles I's fate was sealed?) and the kitchen, which give you a glimpse of how people lived. You can dress the family in Tudor costumes too and discover Victorian life, upstairs and downstairs. Children can play in the toy room, while the adults relax in the delightful walled garden.

The Rows and Greyfriars' Cloister

english-heritage.org.uk
South Quay, NR30 2RQ
01493 857900 | Open Mar–Sep daily 12–5

Known as the Rows, these narrow passageways ran inland from the quayside and were lined with the homes of fishermen. Today, few of the 17th-century houses remain, but the Old Merchant's House, owned by English Heritage, has been converted into a museum, and is open to the public. These houses are unique to Great Yarmouth. Guided walking tours explain how the rich and poor lived in these properties through history. The tours also visit the remains of a Franciscan friary, Greyfriars' Cloister, which has some rare early wall-paintings.

Time and Tide Museum

museums.norfolk.gov.uk
Tower Curing Works, Blackfriars' Road, NR30 3BX | 01493 743943
Open Apr–Oct daily 9.30–4.30; Nov–Mar Mon–Fri 10–4, Sat–Sun 12–4

Full of interactive technology that will keep the whole family occupied for hours, the Time and Tide is an award-winning museum housed in a restored Grade II listed Victorian herring-curing factory. It's one of the best preserved such factories from the period. The museum tells Great Yarmouth's fascinating story, from prehistoric times right through to the present day. You can visit the original smokehouse and see displays about fishing, wrecks and rescue, seaside holidays, port and trade, and the world wars. It also brings to life the herring-curing industry and the lives of the people who worked along the coast.

Tolhouse Museum

museums.norfolk.gov.uk
Tolhouse Street, NR30 2SH
01493 743933 | Open Tue–Fri 10–4 (to 8 Thu), Sat–Sun 12–4

You can discover the fate of convicted thieves, smugglers, witches, pirates and murderers at a time when punishments included transportation or execution in this gruesome but fascinating museum. It's housed in one of the oldest prisons in the country, and tells the story of Great Yarmouth's criminals and punishment. With the free audio guide you can hear the gaoler and his prisoners describe their experiences. Other exhibits detail the history of this former 12th-century merchant's house that went on to become one of the town's most important civic buildings.

Yesterday's World
yesterdaysworld.co.uk
34 Marine Parade, NR30 2EN
01493 331148 | Open Mar–Nov daily 11–5 (times vary)
An award-winning museum, Yesterday's World brings history to life with exciting life-sized street scenes complete with houses and shops looking as they would have done centuries ago. Evocative sounds and smells add to the experience. See a life-sized Henry VIII and his six wives, Laurel and Hardy and Charlie Chaplin. At this museum you can step back into the past and enjoy an amazing journey through 125 years of British social history. See over 150,000 artifacts with virtual and interactive exhibits. This amazing collection, which dates from the 18th century right through to the recent past, is one of the best social history records in the country. You can also take a ride on a Victorian carousel, and sit in an Anderson shelter and experience a World War II air raid. Be sure to stop for a while in the museum's traditional tea room.

Great Yarmouth Potteries and Smoke House
greatyarmouthpotteries.co.uk
19 Trinity Place, NR30 3HA
01493 850585 | Open Mon–Fri 9.30–3, Sat–Sun appointments only
Try your hand at throwing a pot or just watch the demonstrations of experts on potters' wheels at this popular attraction. A fully working pottery, it takes visitors through each stage from working with liquid clay to painting and glazing a finished pot. Here, too, are a museum dedicated to herring smoking, a gallery of nautical oil paintings and sculptures, photographs of a bygone era in Great Yarmouth and a video that tells the history of the town.

MEET THE SEALIFE

Sea Life
sealife.co.uk
Marine Parade, NR30 3AG
01493 330631 | See website for opening details
See sharks and brightly coloured clownfish, jellyfish, lobsters, penguins and dwarf crocodiles at Sea Life, located right on the seafront. Many of the species are endangered and have been rescued, or have been bred as part of a conservation project. The centre supports conservation around the world, and is actively involved with seahorse breeding programmes and

rescuing seals and other creatures. There's an adoption scheme if you or your family want to become more involved in the life of a sea creature.

ENTERTAIN THE FAMILY

Hippodrome

hippodromecircus.co.uk
St George's Road, NR30 2EU
Box office open Mon–Sat 10–4 (8 on performance days) and Sun 10–7 during summer and Christmas seasons. Shows 2.30 and 7.30 (can vary)

Yarmouth's Hippodrome, which opened its doors for the first time in 1903, is an institution. Housed in the last remaining purpose-built circus building in England, and one of only a few left in the world, it has a programme of summer circus and water shows that are simply spectacular. In winter you may catch an opera or concert. There's a small museum, the Hippodrome Circus Museum, where you can see props and old photographs. Opening times are the same as for the box office.

Britannia Pier

britannia-pier.co.uk
Marine Parade, NR30 2EH
01493 842914 | Open daily

Two amusement arcades can be found along the length of Britannia Pier, with a host of traditional slot machines and more futuristic interactive attractions. You can try your hand at bowling, bingo and mini-karting, or hop aboard the ghost train, dodgems or carousel. There are plenty of places to eat; you can nibble on everything from burgers and doughnuts to shellfish. At the end of the pier, the historic theatre offers comedy and musical shows throughout the year.

10 famous people from Norfolk

- **Henry Blogg**, UK's most celebrated lifeboatman
- **James Blunt**, singer
- **Howard Carter**, archaeologist
- **Diana, Princess of Wales**
- **Stephen Fry**, comedian
- **Myleene Klass**, singer and model
- **Ruth Madoc**, actress
- **Admiral Horatio Lord Nelson**
- **Roger Taylor**, musician
- **Robert Walpole**, first British prime minister

Wellington Pier

wellington-pier.co.uk
Marine Parade, NR30 3JF
01493 845947 | Open daily

Along with the Britannia, the Wellington Pier is a landmark in Great Yarmouth and is a magnet for families looking for traditional seaside fun. There are amusements and simulator rides, slot machines and a family 10-lane, 10-pin bowling alley. Shops, an ice cream parlour, cafe and bar, among many other things, can be found along its length.

Merrivale Model Village
www.merrivalemodelvillage. co.uk
Marine Parade, NR30 3JG
01493 842097 | Open Mar–Nov daily 10 (closing times vary)
Merrivale Model Village offers an altogether different experience. Set in more than an acre of attractive landscaped gardens, complete with winding pathways, streams and waterfalls, and even a lake full of koi carp, this mini village is delightful. As you wander leisurely among its tiny houses it's hard to believe you are so close to the bustle of central Yarmouth. The village is built on a scale of 1:12. Among the models are a working fairground, a stone quarry, houses, shops and a garden railway. The Penny Arcade gives you the chance to play old amusements, while a traditional tea room provides a welcome break.

TAKE TO THE WATER

Lydia Eva
www.lydiaeva.org.uk
South Quay, NR30 2QJ
07866 924762 | Open May–Oct Tue–Sat 10–4, Sun 12–4
You can take a trip on this lovely old steam drifter, which was built in 1930 and became a floating museum dedicated to fishing when its working days were up. A heritage lottery grant meant that it could be restored. In recent times, it has been MCA-coded, which means that it can now go to sea with up to eight passengers on board. You can steer the craft or be a stoker. A trip on the *Lydia Eva* is a memorable experience.

PLAY GOLF

Great Yarmouth and Caister Golf Club
caistergolf.co.uk
Beach House, Caister-on-Sea, NR30 5TD | 01493 728699
Open daily including Bank Holidays
This traditional, classic links-style course offers play over tight and undulating fairways partly set among sand dunes. There's gorse and marram grass to negotiate. The greens are well drained and a challenge for golfers of all abilities.

EAT AND DRINK

Andover House ❁❁
andoverhouse.co.uk
28–30 Camperdown, NR30 3JB | 01493 843490
A touch of boutique styling has been sprinkled over the

white-painted Victorian terrace that is Andover House, and these days it's a rather cool hotel, restaurant and bar, with a spruce look of fashionable muted pastel tones and a distinct lack of chintz. There's a daily specials board in support of the à la carte menu. The cooking treads a modish path and there are plenty of global flavours on show.

Imperial Hotel
cafecrurestaurant.co.uk
North Drive, NR30 1EQ
01493 842000
The grand old Imperial Hotel on Great Yarmouth's seafront has been providing generations of visitors with what they want, and in the 21st century that means the contemporary style of the made-over Café Cru Restaurant. Daily-changing blackboard specials bolster a repertoire of unpretentious modern British dishes wrought from splendid local materials, while smart staff in black aprons lend a buzzy bistro vibe to proceedings. Local Morston mussels in white wine, garlic and parsley are a perennial favourite.

PLACES NEARBY

The Roman remains of Burgh Castle, one of a chain of castles built to protect East Anglia from invasion, along with the ruins of St Olave's Priory, are just a few miles away as are the seaside towns of Caister-on-Sea (see page 83) and Lowestoft (see page 189). There are golf courses at Caldecott Hall in Fritton and the Gorleston Golf Club in Gorleston-on-Sea. For refreshments try the

▼ Burgh Castle

Fisherman's Return in Winterton-on-Sea.

Burgh Castle
english-heritage.org.uk
NR31 9PZ | 0870 333 1181
Open at any reasonable time
This once imposing castle is one of the best preserved Roman structures in the country. Sections of its massive walls still stand and make an imposing sight overlooking the inland waterway known as Breydon Water. The castle was built in the third century AD by the Romans, and would have dominated the area along the Saxon Shore, a stretch of coast that extends from the Solent to the Wash. It was one of a chain of forts built of mortared flint covered with cut flint and tile.

St Olave's Priory
english-heritage.org.uk
0870 333 1181 | Open at any reasonable time
The remains of an Augustinian priory, St Olave's is best known for its intricately carved, and virtually complete, brick-vaulted undercroft dated to the 14th century. It was founded nearly 2,000 years after the death in 1030 of St Olave, the patron saint of Norway.

Caldecott Hall Golf and Leisure
caldecotthall.co.uk
Caldecott Hall, Beccles Road, Fritton, NR31 9EY | 01493 488488
Open daily
The sprawling complex of Caldecott Hall has a parkland links-style course with testing dog-leg fairways. Facilities include a driving range and practise green.

Gorleston Golf Club
www.gorlestongolfclub.co.uk
Warren Road, Gorleston-on-Sea, NR31 6JT | 01493 661911
Open daily including Bank Holidays
The Gorleston Golf Club has a clifftop course, the most easterly in the British Isles. One of the outstanding features of the course is the seventh hole, which was rescued from cliff erosion about 20 years ago. The green, only eight yards from the cliff edge, is at the mercy of the prevailing winds so club selection is critical. A well-stocked bar is available.

Fishermans Return
fishermansreturn.com
The Lane, Winterton-on-Sea, NR29 4BN | 01493 393305
This dog-friendly, 350-year-old brick-and-flint free house stands close to long beaches and National Trust land, making it the ideal spot to finish a walk. Guest ales support Woodforde's Norfolk Nog and Wherry behind the bar, while the menus range from popular favourites such as omelettes and filled jacket potatoes to sirloin steak and three-bean chilli. Look out for fish and seafood specials on the daily-changing blackboard, where freshly caught mackerel or sea bass may be on offer. Don't miss the beer festival on August Bank Holiday.

Gressenhall

see **Dereham**, page 117

Hadleigh

While Hadleigh cannot boast a great castle or manor house, it does have a high street lined with some of the most beautiful buildings imaginable. There are not many towns of such character left in England today, and its medieval charm and architectural styles, ranging from timber-framed to Georgian – some painted in Suffolk pink and others with ornamental plasterwork known as pargeting – are a great attraction for tourists. The town's historic assets are bolstered by its thriving business and community spirit, so spend some time exploring its wide range of interesting shops, pubs and restaurants.

Hadleigh was once the royal town for the ninth-century Danish King Guthrum, who took a liking to it and is now said to be buried in St Mary the Virgin church. Later it became one of the most important wool and market towns in England. By the 16th century, in Suffolk, only Ipswich and Bury St Edmunds were more prosperous than Hadleigh. This prosperous past has left a legacy of more than 240 listed buildings.

EAT AND DRINK

The Bildeston Crown
thebildestoncrown.com
104 High Street, Bildeston,
IP7 7EB | 01449 740510
The 15th-century Crown is one of those Suffolk pubs that reveals its antiquity in its black beams and less than perfect symmetry. Yesterday's old coaching inn has been updated to a 21st-century version of the genre – an ambitious restaurant, classy pub and chic hotel rolled into one. It has bags of character and has been given a contemporary sheen. There's a space to suit whatever your mood, so you might sit outside in the courtyard, relax into a deep leather armchair by the fireplace in the bar, or seek out one of the many areas where you can eat, which includes the spiffed-up Ingrams with its fine-dining finish. The provenance of what appears on the menu is rightly a big deal here; the owner is a farmer and chef-patron Chris Lee (who runs the place with wife Hayley) keeps it all as local as possible. Bildeston hamlet is a couple of miles outside Hadleigh.

The Hadleigh Ram
thehadleighram.co.uk
5 Market Place, IP7 5DL
01473 822880
With its seriously stylish grey and cream country cottage shaker-style décor, and a menu that shows the passion of executive chef Oliver Macmillan and his team, the Hadleigh Ram

is one of the newest restaurants and inns on the block. It has been created in one of Hadleigh's gorgeous old period buildings, complete with gnarled golden oak timbers dominating the space. Outside is a cosy courtyard for alfresco drinking and dining. There are two menus, plus a set Market Menu, Sunday lunch and special occasion collections. All are complemented by a fine wine list.

The White Hart
hadleighwhitehart.co.uk
46 Bridge Street, IP7 6DB
01473 822206
Housed in a 14th century former coaching inn, complete with sloping floorboards and blackened oak beams, low ceilings and the most characterful inglenook fireplace imaginable, the White Hart is the image of a quintessential English country pub. Dark wooden tables and artifacts adorning the walls complete the picture. Hosts Phil and Angie Woodend, who've been in the trade for decades, know their beer and when you order from the wide selection on offer – that includes Adnams Southwold Bitter – you can be assured it will served at the perfect temperature. Classic and hearty pub-style food is the deal here, all cooked by chef Phil who, when not cooking in the kitchen, can usually be found sourcing fresh produce at local markets.

PLACES NEARBY

Just a couple of miles outside Hadleigh is the Brett Vale Golf Club in the village of Raydon. Its course takes you through a nature reserve and on lakeside walks, affording views over Dedham Vale (see page 110). Nearby, too, are Ipswich (see page 168) and Lavenham (see page 184).

Brett Vale Golf Club
brettvalegolf.co.uk
Noakes Road, Raydon, IP7 5LR
01473 310718 | Open daily including Bank Holidays
Brett Vale Golf Club has excellent fairways that demand an accurate tee and good approach shots. Some of the holes are affected by crosswinds, but once in the valley it is much more sheltered. Although short, the course is testing and interesting for all levels of golfer.

Haverhill

Haverhill lies almost on the Suffolk border where Essex meets Cambridgeshire, and although it can trace its roots back to Saxon times and was even mentioned in the Domesday Book of 1086, it has few historic monuments today. A fire swept through the town in 1667. In fact, it is now a sprawling town with a number of industrial areas that provide work for its large and growing population. It has plenty of amenities – everything from community halls to gyms, schools to eateries – including a particularly good golf club that welcomes visitors. Haverhill's original expansion was largely the result of families moving here from London when their homes were destroyed in World War II.

PLAY GOLF

Haverhill Golf Club

club-noticeboard.co.uk
Coupals Road, CB9 7UW
01440 761951 | Open daily including Bank Holidays

An 18-hole course lying across two valleys in pleasant parkland sets the Haverhill Golf Club apart. The front nine with undulating fairways is complemented by a saucer-shaped back nine, bisected by the River Stour, presenting a challenge to golfers of all standards.

Heacham

Just a 10-minute drive away along the Wash estuary from Hunstanton is the quiet Norfolk village of Heacham. It's an unassuming place so it might come as a surprise to learn that one of its most famous residents was John Smith who, in 1614, married Pocahontas, the Native American best known for protecting English settlers in Jamestown, Virginia. Her image is depicted on road signs throughout the village. Heacham is known for its huge skies, brilliant sunsets, peaceful beaches and fields of lavender.

ENTERTAIN THE FAMILY

Norfolk Lavender

norfolk-lavender.co.uk
Caley Mill, PE31 7JE | 01485 570384
Open Apr–Oct daily 9–5 and Nov–Mar 9–4

Norfolk Lavender is England's premier lavender farm, and home to the National Collection of Lavender. There are plants for sale and tours are available, including a tour of the distillery, from May to August. A lavender festival is held here every July. Facilities include an animal rare breeds centre, a play barn and farm shop, along with a new ceramics cafe where you can choose an item of pottery to paint and have it fired in the kiln to take home.

PLAY GOLF

Heacham Manor Golf

heacham-manor.co.uk
Hunstanton Rd, PE31 7JX
01485 536030 | Open daily including Bank Holidays

The championship-length course at Heacham Manor has been designed to incorporate the natural features of the surrounding landscape. With two rivers and four lakes to negotiate, it varies between links and parkland styles with views of the Wash. It's a long course, but with a number of teeing areas on each hole it is playable for all handicaps.

EAT AND DRINK

Heacham Manor Hotel
heacham-manor.co.uk
Hunstanton Road, PE31 7JX
01485 536030
Originally built as an Elizabethan manor, the Heacham Manor has been brought smartly up-to-date and its airy conservatory-style Mulberry restaurant is reason enough to pay a visit. The kitchen's output is simple, staunchly seasonal and driven by a sincere belief in local sourcing – salt marsh lamb comes from Wells-next-the-Sea, and the locally landed fish and seafood rack up very few food miles on their way to the table.

Holkham

Holkham is a quiet village on the Norfolk coast in the heart of the Holkham National Nature Reserve. Around 9,600 acres of pine-covered sand dunes, salt marshes and marshland provide habitats for a wide variety of flora and fauna. This area is north Norfolk's largest and most diverse nature reserve, and one of its most tranquil.

The reserve is known for its wildfowl and migrant birds, including thousands of pink-footed geese, and salt marsh plants such as sea lavender and sea aster. The sand dunes here were planted with Corsican pines in the late 19th century in an attempt to protect reclaimed farmland from wind-blown sand, and the trees have integrated into a landscape of wide windswept sands backed by a bank of dark green foliage.

The village is home to Holkham Hall, one of the country's finest estates, where you can easily spend a day looking around the hall, its gardens and the lovely Bygones Museum. A superb Palladian mansion, Holkham Hall is the home of the Coke family and the Earls of Leicester. It was built by Thomas Coke, first Earl of Leicester, between 1734 and 1764. It is said he was so inspired by Italian Renaissance architecture that he had the mansion built in a similar style. It remains largely unchanged today, a striking sight in rural north Norfolk.

Two local craftsmen spent 20 years sculpting the alabaster interior of the Marble Hall, copying classical Roman interiors. 'Capability' Brown landscaped some of the 3,000 acres of grounds, home to a large herd of fallow deer, and created the mile-long lake. The evergreen oaks that flourish here were originally brought from Italy. There is free daytime access to the walking and cycling routes in the park.Thomas William Coke (1754–1842), nephew of the hall's creator, devoted his

▲ Holkham beach

efforts to improving the estate and is renowned in agricultural circles as 'Coke of Norfolk'. He is credited along with Charles 'Turnip' Townshend of nearby Raynham Hall for devising the four-crop rotation system, which vastly improved farming productivity. He also served as a Norfolk MP for 50 years.

Holkham village serves mainly as an access point to the park and hall, and for Lady Anne's Drive, the estate road crossing the salt marshes to Holkham Beach.

Holkham Hall

holkham.co.uk
NR23 1AB | 01328 710227 | Open Mar–Oct hall Sun, Mon and Thu 12–4, museum & gardens daily 10–5

Holkham Hall is a testament to Thomas Coke's ambition and style. At the turn of the 17th century, the land on which the hall now stands was little more than desolate heathland. When Coke told his friends where he planned to build his home, many reacted with horror. That the designs for Coke's new house were inspired by buildings he had admired in the warm and gentle climate of Italy made his choice of location even stranger.

Today, as you enjoy the lawns and shade of abundant oaks and beeches, it is difficult to imagine that it was once an uncultivated heath. Some of the trees were planted as early as 1712 in anticipation of the splendid park that was to follow. You may picnic next to the peaceful lake or wander through acres of landscaped gardens and parklands. Or you may prefer to admire architect William Kent's great obelisk.

At the centre of all this is the resplendent hall itself, offering you the chance to see 2,000 years of fine art amassed by Coke. Holkham is one of the finest examples of Palladian revival architecture in England, with room after room of glittering splendour. Everywhere you'll see evidence of Kent's outstanding talent, especially in the exquisitely carved scrolls, shells, cherubs and flowers on the ceilings, the walls and the furnishings.

The Bygones Museum is housed in a stable block and has a remarkable collection of old vehicles and carriages belonging to the estate, plus a collection of more than 4,000 household items ranging from Victorian mechanical toys to tools, pots and pans.

Look out for the flint Church of St Withburga standing about half a mile from the hall towards the coast. It dates, in part, from the 13th century.

Holt

The historic Anglo-Saxon town of Holt is the thriving hub of north Norfolk and effortlessly manages to retain the charming atmosphere of a small country town. If you stroll down its main street you will see one elegant Georgian house after another. That's because in 1708 the town was all but obliterated in a massive fire that saw its fine medieval homes burned to the ground. The townsfolk received donations from all over England to help with its reconstruction.

Today, Holt is surrounded by the parkland of the Holt Country Park where once a racecourse brought members of the nobility to compete at race meetings for the 'Town Plate'. Now the 104 acres are covered in mature woodlands. There are more than 30 different species of tree here, including Scots pine, silver birch and oak. It is a sustainable working woodland.

The visitor centre provides lists of the flora and fauna you can see in the park. If you are lucky you might catch glimpses of red deer, muntjac deer or red fox at dawn or dusk, grey squirrels and large numbers of butterflies, including the red and white admiral, painted lady and purple hairstreak.

EAT AND DRINK

The Lawns Wine Bar

lawnsatholt.co.uk
26 Station Road, NR25 6BS
01263 713390

Fresh, seasonal local produce and a relaxed modern brasserie are at the heart of the appeal of this smart Georgian town house restaurant, bar and hotel in the centre of town. The fashionably decked-out restaurant – dark wood tables and leather high-backed chairs– smart bar area, bright conservatory and terrace overlooking the garden, provide plenty of choice.

Watermark Wine Bar & Restaurant

appleyard-holt.com
9 Appleyard, NR25 6BN
01263 710790

This is a light-filled, pleasant venue with double-doors opening on to a courtyard garden, where you can eat in the shade of a venerable copper beech. An upbeat, friendly atmosphere prevails, and the seasonally based menus are supplemented by daily blackboard specials, offering an extensive choice of bistro fare.

Wiveton Bell

www.wivetonbell.co.uk
The Green, Blakeney Road,
NR25 7TL | 01263 740101

There's a lively, cheerful atmosphere at the Bell, an 18th-century pub on the village green not far from north Norfolk's salt marshes, an Area of Outstanding Natural Beauty. Tables are bare wood, the seating is upholstered chairs and wooden pews, plain walls are hung with artwork, and the young staff are upbeat and proactive. The wide-ranging menus at the Wiveton Bell might feature chicken balti curry with mango chutney, an onion bhaji and basmati rice. Due deference is paid to seasonality: local asparagus, for instance, served with a soft-poached egg and hollandaise, and Brancaster mussels, steamed with white wine, shallots and cream.

PLACES NEARBY

Saxthorpe is just six miles or so from Holt and from here, signposted from its main crossroads, you can find Mannington Hall. It's open by appointment only, but you can visit the garden most days in the summer months. For country inn dining, you could head to the Kings Head in Letheringsett, or the Pigs in Edgefield.

Mannington Hall and Gardens
manningtongardens.co.uk
Saxthorpe, NR11 7BB
01263 584175 | Gardens open Jun–Aug Wed–Fri 11–5, May–Sep 12–5; Hall open by prior appointment only

Mannington Hall is a handsome 18th-century moated manor house that belonged to Horatio Nelson, the British Admiral best known for his part in the Napoleonic Wars, in particular the Battle of Trafalgar where he died in 1805. It is the focal point in an extraordinary garden, which contains a beautiful heritage rose garden, divided into several areas, each representing a period of the rose's historical development. In all there are more than 1,000 different varieties of roses here.

Around the corner of the house, a yellow rose climbs vigorously near a mauve

▼ Flint buildings at Holt

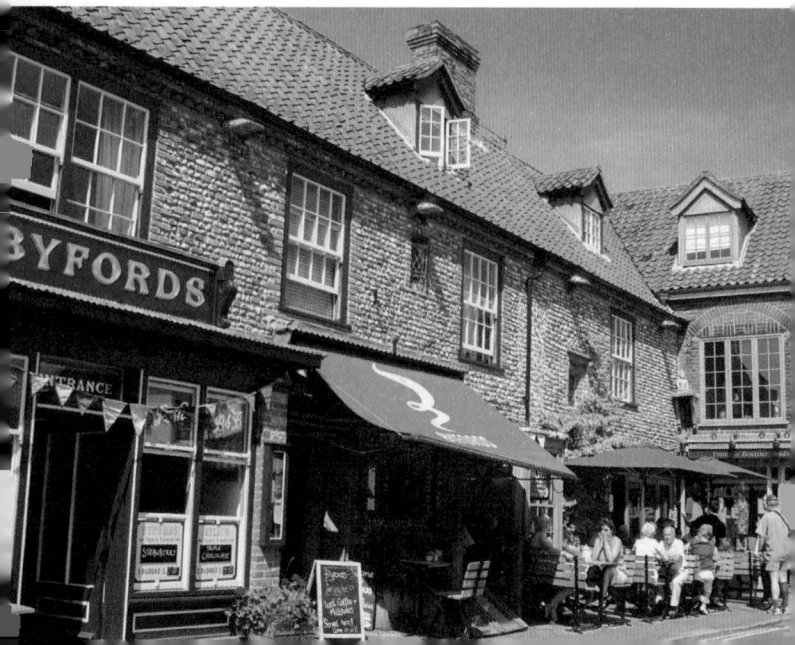

wistaria, while other low-growing shrubs brighten up the gravel with their pink and white flowers in early summer. Within the moat, sweetly scented herbs are planted to mirror the intricate pattern of the hall's dining-room ceiling.

The medieval garden has turf seats and some very old roses. Other formal areas of Mannington Hall include a tranquil 17th-century knot garden. You can also see lakes and a ruined church, which stands among unusual trees, including specimens of *Acer palmatum*,which are well over 100 years old. Music and theatre events are a regular feature at Mannington Hall.

The Kings Head

kingsheadnorfolk.co.uk
Holt Road, Letheringsett,
NR25 7AR | 01263 712691

Chris Coubrough's thriving Norfolk-based Flying Kiwi Inns snapped up this rather grand, manor-like building and revamped it in impressive style. Expect an elegant, rustic-chic feel throughout the rambling dining areas that radiate from the central bar, with rugs on terracotta tiles, squashy sofas and leather chairs fronting blazing winter log fires, feature bookcases, warm heritage hues, and an eclectic mix of old dining tables. The atmosphere is informal, the beer is East Anglian-brewed – try a pint of Adnams – and the food modern British and prepared from top-notch ingredients supplied by local farmers, fishermen and artisan producers; the pub has its own herd of Dexter cows. This gastro-pub has superb alfresco areas, including an excellent children's garden and a gravelled front terrace with posh benches and brollies.

The Pigs

www.thepigs.org.uk
Norwich Road, Edgefield,
NR24 2RL | 01263 587634

Bought by three ambitious co-owners in 2006, this 17th-century country inn on the edge of a lovely village has been transformed into a thriving local that celebrates all things Norfolk, both on the plate and in the glass. The lovely tranquil setting at the fringe of the village allows for a peaceful garden, while locals barter their fresh fruit and vegetables over the bar. An impressively versatile menu emerges from the kitchen, utilising forgotten cuts of locally sourced meat and produce from the pub's adjoining allotment. If it's genuine 'nose to tail' dining you're looking for, the honey, Colman's mustard and marmalade glazed pork ribs, followed by the slow-cooked belly of pork with smoky bacon beans, apple chutney, black pudding and crackling should fit the bill. Tapas-style starters called 'Iffits' also include devilled whitebait with gentleman's relish and lemon, thyme and garlic chicken wings. A children's cookery school has proved popular.

Horsey

In 1938 a devastating combination of high tides and storms hit Horsey. The sea surged inland, flooding buildings and fields, and forcing people to evacuate their homes. It was four months before the water subsided and the villagers were able to resume normal life, although it took another five years before the damaging effects of salt water on the fields was finally overcome and crops could be grown again.

Horsey is barely three feet above sea level and, as you walk around the reed-fringed mere and stroll along its many drainage channels, you will appreciate the wildness of this part of Norfolk and how vulnerable it is to the sea. The village and surrounding area are now in the care of the National Trust.

The village's most famous feature is the Horsey windpump, built to pump water from the surrounding farmland. It dates from the middle of the 19th century. Today, it is fully restored and you can go inside to the top.

Nearby, All Saints' Church dates from the 13th century and has an attractive thatched nave. Go inside and look for the stained-glass window in the south chancel commemorating Catherine Ursula Rising, who died in 1890. She is shown painting in her drawing room at nearby Horsey Hall.

▼ Horsey Gap

GET INDUSTRIAL

Horsey Windpump

nationaltrust.org.uk/horseywindpump
Horsey Mere, NR29 4ED
01263 740241 | Open Apr–Sep daily 10–5; Oct–Mar Wed–Sun and Bank Holidays

You can climb the five floors of this lovely old traditional windmill-like windpump built 200 years ago to drain the area, and see its inner workings, such as the drive shaft and giant cogs. From the top, there are panoramic views over Horsey Mere and the surrounding countryside. Grade II listed, the building features red-brick walls and a handsome weatherboarded cap in the shape of a boat.

It was rebuilt in 1912 by Dan England, a noted Norfolk millwright, and was in full working order when it was struck by lightning in 1940. It has since been fully restored and is now owned by the National Trust.

The windpump stands in an idyllic and remote spot on the edge of the Norfolk Broads overlooking Horsey Mere and marshes, noted for their wild birds and insects. The whole area is regarded as being internationally important for the conservation of a number of natural habitats found here. Wait long enough and you'll see hundreds of wigeon in winter, along with teal, shoveler, pochard, gadwall, goldeneye and tufted duck. Bitterns may be seen at any time of year. Look for stonechats, yellow wagtails and

grasshopper warblers if you head towards the dunes. You might also spot two rare warblers – Cetti's and Savi's. The former is a newcomer, and the latter is returning to areas where it was once common. A great way to appreciate the pump's setting is to take a walk around Horsey Mere along the signposted footpath.

Hoveton

The Norfolk village of Hoveton lies immediately opposite Wroxham on the River Bure and is a popular sailing and boating centre, buzzing with nautical activity. Hoveton is dominated by two churches, St Peter and St John, and has many upmarket houses, including the elegant 19th-century Hoveton Hall which, although not open to the public, stands in gardens where visitors are welcome (opening times can vary). See **The Norfolk Broads**, page 203

ENTERTAIN THE FAMILY

BeWILDerwood
see opposite

VISIT A MUSEUM

RAF Air Defence Radar Museum
radarmuseum.co.uk
RRH Neatishead, NR12 8YB
01692 631485 | Open Apr–Oct Tue & Thu and Bank Holiday Mondays 10–5, second Sat each month all year
This multi-award-winning museum is run by volunteers, most of whom worked at RAF Neatishead. It is housed in an original 1942 Radar Operations building and features themed exhibits, including the Battle of Britain Room, 1942 Ground Controlled Interception Room, Radar Engineering, Military Communications Systems and the Cold War Operations Room. You can see a display dedicated to the Royal Observer Corps, to Space Defence, Bloodhound Missiles and Original Mobile Radar Vehicles. The newest addition to the museum is the RAF Coltishall Memorial Room.

EAT AND DRINK

The Old Barn Restaurant
wroxhambarns.co.uk
Wroxham Barns, Tunstead Road, NR12 8QU | 01603 777106
The comfortable Old Barn Restaurant is set in extensive parkland within a complex known as Wroxham Barns. Here you can see a collection of 18th-century barns that have been reborn as small shops and working craft galleries – the sort of place where you'll want to wander, shop, sit and drink in the scenery. The restaurant serves breakfast, lovely light lunches, sandwiches, scones and cakes.

BeWILDerwood

bewilderwood.co.uk
Horning Road, NR12 8JE | 01692 633033 | Open Feb half term–Oct half term 10–5.30

BeWILDerwood is an award-winning wild and imaginative adventure park with magical treehouses, zip wires, jungle bridges, boat trips and storytelling. The setting for the book *A Boggle at BeWILDerwood* by local children's author Tom Blofeld, it's a wonderful, mystical land of brave adventurous creatures you may never see anywhere else in the world. Parents are encouraged to play alongside their children, which makes for an exciting day out for the whole family.

Hunstanton

Lying on the north Norfolk coast, Hunstanton is the only East Anglian seaside resort to face west. As such, it is known for its dramatic sunsets. The town is one of two halves: the old part where ancient red and white chalk limestone rocks offer a fabulously colourful backdrop to its beach, and a village steeped in history and legend; and the newer area of Hunstanton that dates from its life as a fashionable Victorian seaside resort.

You can see the ruins of a chapel and a lighthouse in Old Hunstanton. It is said that St Edmund, who went on to become King of East Anglia (see page 75), was shipwrecked in AD 855, and was so grateful for being spared a watery death in the Wash that he built a chapel in thanks. The 13th-century ruins still stand today, looking out across grey stormy seas. A later lighthouse, now privately owned, has become a symbol of Hunstanton, although it is no longer used as a beacon. The light was extinguished and was never lit again following its decommission in the 1920s. The newer part of the town dates from the mid-1840s and has an essentially Victorian atmosphere, with handsome hotels built in mock-Tudor style using the warm-coloured local limestone known as carrstone. They line the well-tended esplanade gardens next to the sea.

The resort was developed by Henry Styleman Le Strange of Hunstanton Hall, who promoted the idea of a railway line between the town and King's Lynn to attract visitors. Members of the Le Strange family have been squires and landlords here for more than 800 years. They laid claim to the beach and all that is in the sea for as far as a horseman can hurl a spear at low tide. The family still holds the title of Lord High Admiral of the Wash.

Today, the town offers a range of attractions including a Sea Life Sanctuary and a 400-seater theatre, along with vast expanses of white sandy beaches, walks along Peddars Way and birding aplenty.

MEET THE SEALIFE

Hunstanton Sea Life Sanctuary
sealife.co.uk
Southern Promenade, PE36 5BH
01485 533576 | Open daily 10–4
With over 35 displays, the highlight of this attraction is an underwater tunnel for close encounters with tropical sharks. There are otters, penguins, seals and many deep-sea creatures. One of the exhibits most popular with young children is Clownfish Kingdom. It also has an outdoor pirate ship play area.

▸ Hunstanton beach and cliffs

Top 10 attractions for kids

- **Africa Alive!** Kessingland, page 63
- **Amazona Zoo,** Cromer, page 107
- **Banham Zoo**, Banham, page 59
- **BeWILDerwood**, Hoveton page 161
- **Brancaster Activity Centre**, Brancaster Staithe, page 69
- **Dinosaur Adventure Park**, Lenwade, page 225
- **Gressenhall Farm and Workhouse**, Gressenhall, page 117
- **Merrivale Model Village**, Great Yarmouth, page 146
- **Pleasurewood Hills**, nr Lowestoft, page 191
- **West Stow Anglo-Saxon Village**, West Stow, page 80

PLAY GOLF

Hunstanton Golf Club
hunstantongolfclub.com
Golf Course Road, PE36 6JQ
01485 532811 | Open daily including Bank Holidays
A championship links course first established in 1891 and set among some of the best natural golfing country in East Anglia, the Hunstanton Golf Club has many bunkers and fast greens to play to your handicap – then you only have the strong wind to contend with. Good playing conditions all year round. A restaurant and well-stocked bar is available.

Searles Resort Golf Course
searles.co.uk
South Beach Road, PE36 5BB
01485 536010 | Open daily including Bank Holidays
The nine-hole par 34 course of the Searles Resort Golf Club is designed in a links style and provides generous fairways with good greens. There are good views of Hunstanton and the surrounding countryside. The course offers a challenge for all standards of golfers. The resort also includes plenty of activities for the whole family.

EAT AND DRINK

The Ancient Mariner Inn
traditionalinns.co.uk
Golf Course Road, Old Hunstanton, PE36 6JJ | 01485 536390
Summer evenings can be spectacular here when the sun sets across the sands of the Wash, and the light matches the colour of the real ales enjoyed by drinkers in the peaceful gardens of the Ancient Mariner Inn. Up to seven beers may be on tap at any one time. Equally enticing is the menu of modern pub classics such as fish pie or vegetarian Wellington. Daily specials boost the choice. The appealing flint-and-brick inn is creatively incorporated into the stable block of a Victorian hotel, the stylish rooms of which are popular with visitors to the beautiful Norfolk Coast Area of Outstanding Natural Beauty. Live music is hosted on the last Friday of every month.

Caley Hall Hotel ❁
caleyhallhotel.co.uk
Old Hunstanton Road,
PE36 6HH | 01485 533486
At the core of Caley Hall, a 10-minute walk from Hunstanton's unspoiled beach, is a 17th-century manor, with the restaurant in an attractive, spacious former stable block. Decor includes high-backed leather-look seats at wooden tables, a tartan-patterned carpet and a vaulted ceiling. The kitchen goes out of its way to find fresh local produce and puts together a short, interesting menu with a handful of dishes per course.

The Neptune Restaurant with Rooms ❁❁❁
theneptune.co.uk
85 Old Hunstanton Road,
PE36 6HZ | 01485 532122
Norfolk is home to some fantastic ingredients – the bounty of the sea and fertile land – and here at Kevin and Jacki Mangeolles' place you are perfectly placed to sample the best of everything. Their restaurant with rooms resides within an 18th-century coaching

▼ Beach huts at Hunstanton

inn close to the sea, with creepers climbing the red-brick walls. Once you're over the threshold, all is light and bright, with a touch of New England beachcomber style in its white tongue-and-groove panels, Lloyd Loom furniture, photographs of the coast, and model boats. And what arrives on your plate from the kitchen is perfectly balanced.

PLACES NEARBY

Within easy reach of Hunstanton is Snettisham Park, where you can enjoy a deer safari, among many other attractions. Stop for a while at the nearby King William IV Country Inn and Restaurant, the Rose and Crown or the Gin Trap Inn for a spot of refreshment, or pop into Thornham for the Orange Tree or the Lifeboat Inn, celebrity chef Marco Pierre White's former smugglers' inn turned upmarket gastro restaurant.

Snettisham Park
snettishampark.co.uk
PE31 7NQ | 01485 542425
Open Farm/safari Mar–Oct.
Contact park for tearoom and visitor centre times
Along with its hugely popular deer safari, which takes you on a 45-minute ride to see its herd of red deer, Snettisham Park offers farming activities such as bottle feeding the lambs, collecting eggs and feeding the calves. Children can enjoy pony rides and meeting the baby animals. There are special shows and walking trails, plus a visitor centre selling local produce and tea room. Evening safaris also take place during the summer months.

The King William IV Country Inn and Restaurant
thekingwilliamsedgeford.co.uk
Heacham Road, Sedgeford,
PE36 5LU | 01485 571765
Tucked away in the village of Sedgeford, this free house has been an inn for 175 years. Made cosy by winter log fires, it has four dining areas plus a covered alfresco terrace where you can enjoy a local crab salad in the summer months. You'll find five real ales on tap, and extensive menus, including gluten-free and vegetarian. Events include quiz Mondays, curry Tuesdays and piano Fridays.

The Rose and Crown
roseandcrownsnettisham.co.uk
Old Church Road, Snettisham,
PE31 7LX | 01485 541382
Brim-full with period atmosphere, the 14th-century Rose and Crown is all rambling nooks and crannies, low-beamed ceilings, wobbly floors and log fires, but it has brought in summery colours and a hint of beachcomber-chic to keep in step with the times. The kitchen has also shifted up a gear, serving time-honoured pub classics done right as well as unfussy contemporary ideas that celebrate the Norfolk larder. A children's menu is available too.

The Gin Trap Inn
gintrapinn.co.uk
6 High Street, Ringstead,
PE36 5JU | 01485 525264
The 17th-century Gin Trap is an irresistible pit stop. It balances all the virtues of a well-run pub – genuine hospitality, local ales and good food – in both the rustic bar with its bare bricks, gnarled beams and wood-burning stove in a walk-in fireplace, and in the smart candlelit restaurant and conservatory with its linen-clad tables. The kitchen buys its materials from local farmers and producers, and shows off its prowess with confidence.

Marco Pierre White, The Lifeboat Inn
lifeboatinnthornham.com
Ship Lane, Thornham, PE36 6LT
01485 512236
This rambling, 16th-century smugglers' inn, situated on the edge of a vast expanse of salt marsh, is a short stroll from sweeping beaches, renowned bird reserves and bracing coastal path walks. The ramble of old rooms retain their original character, boasting low-beamed ceilings, rug-strewn tiled floors, low doors, half-panelled walls, log-burning fires, and an array of rustic furniture – from carved oak tables to antique settles and pews. Antique oil lamps are suspended from the ceiling and a wealth of nautical bric-a-brac enhances the charm. The adjoining conservatory is renowned for its ancient vine and there's a walled patio garden. Food ranges from sausage and caramelised onion sandwiches, and starters like potted duck and salt and pepper calamari with lemon mayonnaise, to traditional fish and chips and braised lamb shank with roasted root vegetables and red wine jus. It's perfectly placed for visiting Sandringham and Nelson's birthplace at Burnham Thorpe.

The Orange Tree
theorangetreethornham.co.uk
High Street, Thornham, PE36 6LY
01485 512213
Standing in the centre of the village opposite the church, this family-run pub was once a smugglers' haunt. The 400-year-old whitewashed inn has evolved over the years into the stylish country pub it is today. Chef Philip Milner makes the most of freshly landed local seafood, and most of the meat is sourced from the nearby Sandringham Estate. Traditional beef Wellington gets the celebrity treatment with wild mushroom crepe, spinach and horseradish purée, smoked garlic and potato rosti and salted caramel pastry. Meanwhile, dishes on the bar classics menu could include Moroccan lemon, feta and chickpea burger, or free-range chicken and wild mushroom pie. Look to the board for the daily selection of sandwiches.

Ipswich

Suffolk's county town covers a large area and has masses of historic charm in its pedestrianised centre not far from its harbour on the River Orwell. One of England's oldest towns, Ipswich was originally founded as the Anglo-Saxon trading port of Gippeswic in the Kingdom of East Anglia around AD 600, and curiously retains much of its original street plan.

You'll find the centre easy to navigate, and do take a walk to the attractive harbour area, Neptune Marina Quay, which now has swish apartments and wine bars.

In the town centre, you'll see some fine examples of period houses and churches surrounded by modern offices and shops. Ancient House is one of the most beautiful. A Grade I listed mansion in one of Ipswich's main shopping streets, the Buttermarket, the Ancient House was built in the 15th century and has a facade decorated with elaborate pargeting (decorative plasterwork) and wood carvings. Four panels depict Europe, Asia, America and Africa, giving a glimpse of social history since Australia hadn't been 'discovered' when the house was built.

Other impressive places to look out for include the Cornhill, which is surrounded by Victorian buildings, including the Town

▼ Ipswich waterfront

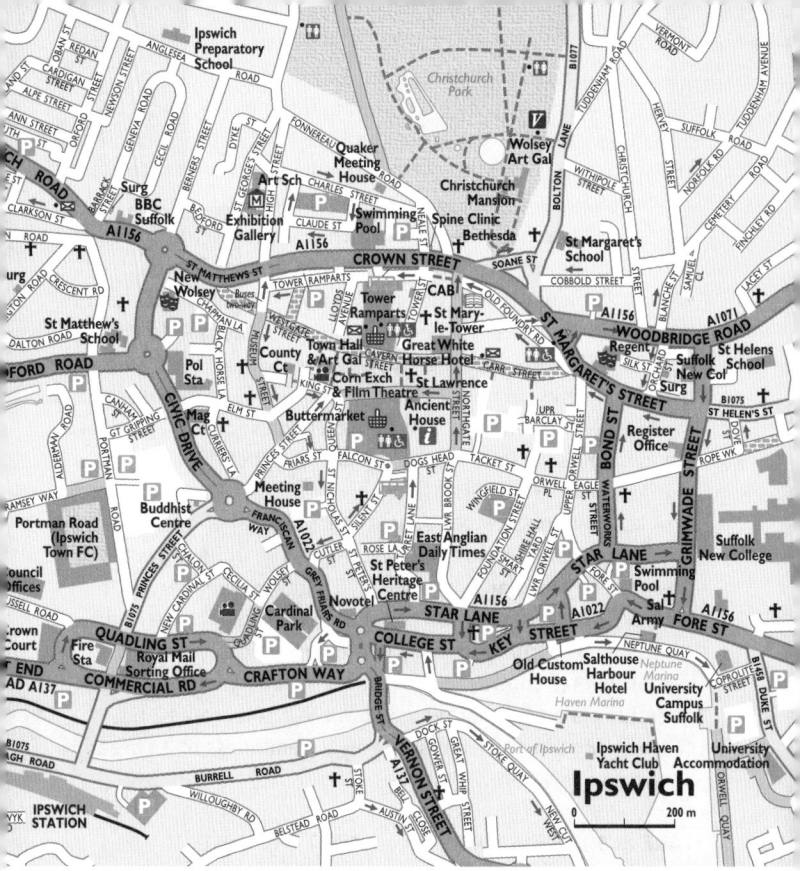
Ipswich Preparatory School
Christchurch Park
Wolsey Art Gal
Quaker Meeting House
Christchurch Mansion
Surg
BBC Suffolk
Art Sch
Exhibition Gallery
Swimming Pool
Spine Clinic
Bethesda
St Margaret's School
CROWN STREET
New Wolsey
CAB
Tower Ramparts
St Mary-le-Tower
WOODBRIDGE ROAD
ST MARGARET'S STREET
St Matthew's School
Town Hall & Art Gal
Great White Horse Hotel
Regent
Suffolk New Col
St Helens School
Pol Sta
County Ct
Corn Exch & Film Theatre
St Lawrence
Surg
CIVIC DRIVE
Mag Ct
Buttermarket
Ancient House
Register Office
BOND STREET
Meeting House
Buddhist Centre
Portman Road (Ipswich Town FC)
East Anglian Daily Times
Suffolk New College
GRIMWADE STREET
STAR LANE
Swimming Pool
St Peter's Heritage Centre
Novotel
Cardinal Park
Sal Army
FORE ST
QUADLING ST
Fire Sta
Royal Mail Sorting Office
COLLEGE ST
KEY STREET
Old Custom House
Salthouse Harbour Hotel
Neptune Marina
University Campus Suffolk
COMMERCIAL RD
CRAFTON WAY
Haven Marina
Port of Ipswich
Ipswich Haven Yacht Club
University Accommodation
VERNON STREET
BURRELL ROAD
IPSWICH STATION
Ipswich
200 m

Hall, and which was once the setting for markets, fairs and executions. In 1555, the so-called Ipswich Martyrs were burned at the stake here for their Protestant beliefs.

There are ruins of Ipswich's 13th-century Blackfriars friary, and many churches, the finest of which is St Mary le Tower, and a 16th-century college founded by Cardinal Thomas Wolsey. Look out for the beautiful timber-framed house on the corner of Silent Street. There's a plaque on the wall to Wolsey (c.1475–1530), the son of an Ipswich butcher, who became Lord Chancellor of England under Henry VIII but who was eventually charged with high treason and executed. Two doors along, another plaque marks the birthplace of the author V S Pritchett (1900–97).

A building in stark contrast is the Willis Faber and Dumas headquarters. A remarkable black-glass structure, it was designed by Norman Foster in 1975. Not far from here is the Wolsey Theatre, one of the finest drama venues in the region.

Ipswich is a bustling place of modern offices, shops and homes, sports centres, chic restaurants and gastro-pubs, riverside walks and gardens, and while it celebrates 21st-century living in its own distinct style, reminders of its great past are everywhere.

TAKE IN SOME HISTORY

Christchurch Mansion

cimuseums.org.uk

Soane Street, IP4 2BE

01473 433554 | Open Tue–Sun 10–5

Christchurch Mansion is a beautiful Tudor property built in 1548 on the site of an Augustinian priory and set in a park. You can see period rooms, including a Tudor kitchen, Georgian saloon and Victorian chambers. An art gallery has changing exhibitions, and is the venue for the Suffolk Artists' Gallery with its collection of paintings by John Constable (see page 110) – the largest collection outside London – and works by Thomas Gainsborough who was born in Sudbury in 1727 (see page 256).

VISIT THE MUSEUM

Ipswich Museum

cimuseums.org.uk

High St, IP1 3QH | 01473 433551

Open Tue–Sat 10–5

The Ipswich Museum is a fascinating place and includes a full-sized reproduction of a woolly mammoth, based on a skeleton discovered in Suffolk, in its natural history gallery. It's accompanied by a giraffe, a rhino and a group of gorillas, all mounted in their original Victorian cases. The museum has sections on Suffolk wildlife, Suffolk geology, Roman Suffolk and Anglo-Saxon Ipswich, plus one of the best bird collections in the country. An after-hours tour telling the story of the museum is available.

▲ Ipswich town centre

LOOK OUT FOR GRANDMA

On the corner of Princes Street and Queen Street, close to the Buttermarket, is a gorgeous statue of 'Grandma', one of the best-known cartoon characters of Carl Giles (1916–95) who drew cartoons for the *Daily Express* for decades, starting in the 1940s. Carl Giles worked in Ipswich and lived to see his creation unveiled as a statue.

GO TO THE THEATRE

Wolsey Theatre
wolseytheatre.co.uk
Civic Drive, IP1 2AS | 01473 295900
The Wolsey Theatre has a whole host of performances, from cheeky comedies and musicals to thought-provoking dramas, opera and dance. A popular highlight is its 'An audience with...' series, and its Christmas panto. Top names in television and film have appeared at the Wolsey.

PLAY GOLF

If you are a golfer you will be spoilt for choice in Ipswich. Three of its best courses are listed here.

Alnesbourne Priory Golf Course
priory-park.com
Priory Park, IP10 0JT
01473 727393 | Open daily including Bank Holidays
A fabulous outlook facing due south across the River Orwell is one of the many features of this course et in woodland. It has holes running among trees with some fairways requiring straight shots.

Ipswich Golf Club
ipswichgolfclub.com
Bucklesham Rd, Purdis Heath, IP3 8UQ | 01473 728941
Open daily except Bank Holidays
Many golfers are surprised when they hear that Ipswich

Top 10 performance venues

- **ADC Theatre**, Cambridge, page 96
- **Diss Corn Hall**, Diss, page 117
- **Hippodrome**, Great Yarmouth, page 145
- **Norwich Theatre Royal**, Norwich, page 220
- **Pavilion Theatre**, Cromer, page 106
- **Quay Theatre**, Sudbury, page 256
- **Sheringham Little Theatre**, Sheringham, page 239
- **Snape Maltings**, Aldeburgh, page 57
- **Theatre Royal**, Bury St Edmunds, page 78
- **Wolsey Theatre**, Ipswich, page 168

has, at Purdis Heath, a first-class course. In some ways it resembles some of Surrey's better courses; it has beautiful heathland with two lakes and easy walking. The nine-hole course is available on a pay-and-play basis.

Rushmere Golf Club

club-noticeboard.co.uk/rushmere
Rushmere Heath, IP4 5QQ
01473 725648 | Open daily except Bank Holidays

The heathland course of the Rushmere Golf Club has gorse and prevailing winds. It is challenging and a good test of golf. The clubhouse features a large bar area and a lounge that overlooks the putting green.

EAT AND DRINK

The Fat Cat

fatcatipswich.co.uk
288 Spring Road, IP4 5NL
01473 726524

Good beer and conversation are the two main ingredients in this no-frills free house. The Fat Cat is a top spot for beer aficionados, with a friendly atmosphere in two homely bars and a raft of real ales served in tip-top condition from the taproom behind the bar. The head-scratching choice – up to 22 beers every day – come from Dark Star, Elgood's, Green Jack and a host of local microbreweries. Soak up the beer with a range of simple bar snacks such as beef and Guinness pasties, sausage rolls, pork pies and baguettes.

Kesgrave Hall ◎

kesgravehall.com
Hall Road, Kesgrave, IP5 2PU
01473 333741

A buzzy bistro is at the culinary heart of Kesgrave Hall, a Georgian mansion in thick woodland in the Kesgrave district of Ipswich. Inside, a makeover has reinvented the place as a stylish boutique hotel with a pared-back modern look comprising oak floors, pine tables, leather chairs and muted shades of cream and sage. Outdoors, there's a spacious terrace with a retractable awning that keeps the place busy and you dry whatever the weather might bring.

Mariners
marinersipswich.co.uk
Neptune Quay, IP4 1AX
01473 289748
Moored alongside Neptune Quay, close to the town centre, this floating French brasserie on an old gunboat is a quirky destination in which to enjoy some good Gallic cuisine. The vessel might date back to 1899, when it was launched in Belgium, but inside it's still shipshape and has its original brass and woodwork. Go up on deck for an alfresco lunch in the sun, but wherever you choose to eat, look forward to good, honest French food confidently presented.

Salthouse Harbour Hotel
salthouseharbour.co.uk
1 Neptune Quay, IP4 1AX
01473 226789
Smack on the waterfront overlooking the marina, Salthouse Harbour is a converted warehouse reinvented as a design-led contemporary boutique hotel. Ablaze with vivid colours and with its rich red-brick walls hung with an eclectic collection of striking modern art and installations and eye-catching kitsch curiosities, the Eaterie rather undersells itself with such a self-effacing name. It is an expansive, well-thought-out space kept ticking over by a switched-on young service team. The name of the game is clearly to combine good quality, local and seasonal ingredients with lively contemporary treatments to produce a Mediterranean-accented menu with broad appeal.

The Ship Inn
Church Lane, Leavington
IP10 0LQ | 01473 659573
Overlooking the River Orwell at Ipswich's Levington Marina, the timbers of this 13th-century inn could be impregnated with the salt of the sea. The Ship stands within sight of the Suffolk marshes, where the hulks of beached sailing vessels were broken up for their precious beams. Families are welcome to enjoy the estuary views outside from the front seats or rear patio as the interior – full of maritime lamps, compasses and nautical keepsakes – is deemed as unsafe for children. The sophisticated menu changes daily and focuses on executing a select number of dishes well. These might include pan-fried sardines with tomato and coriander salsa, and confit of duck leg with red wine-braised cabbage and sweet potato fries.

PLACES NEARBY

Heading out of Ipswich on the road to Hadleigh you will come to one of the prettiest villages in this part of Suffolk. Hintlesham is quiet, leafy and probably best known locally for its superb 16th-century Grade I listed mansion, Hintlesham Hall, now a country house hotel and restaurant with a championship golf course in its parkland. Other eateries worth checking out are the Compasses at Shotley, the Swan Inn at Monks Eleigh and the Moon and Mushroom Inn at Swilland. In the nearby hamlet of Lindsey, take a slight detour to visit St James's Chapel, while in Witnesham you could enjoy a round of golf at the Fynn Valley Golf Club.

The Compasses
Ipswich Road, Shotley,
IP9 2QR | 01473 328332
On the spectacular Shotley peninsula, bordered by the rivers Orwell and Stour, this traditional 17th-century country pub offers a simple, good-value menu. There's nothing self-consciously primped and styled about its interior or its food offerings; it prides itself on not being a gastro-pub but offering good value and plenty of choice. There's a separate children's menu and some good vegetarian choices.

Fynn Valley Golf Club
www.fynn-valley.co.uk
Witnesham, IP6 9JA | 01473 785267
Open daily including Bank Holidays
The course of the Fynn Valley Golf Club is beautiful; opened in 1991, it has been created among parkland alongside a protected river valley. The course has matured into an excellent test of golf enhanced by just under100 bunkers, three water features and protected greens that have tricky slopes and contours.

Hintlesham Hall Hotel ❀❀
hintleshamhall.com
George Street, Hintlesham,
IP8 3NS | 01473 652334
Built in the 16th century with a pink-painted facade that was added in 1720, Hintlesham Hall is one of the most elegant properties imaginable. It stands in acres of grounds, quietly secluded from peering eyes by huge mature trees. The hall had long been a private residence when it was acquired by the celebrated chef Robert Carrier (1923–2006) who transformed it in 1971 into a prestigious country house hotel. Today, it is owned by hotelier Ruth Watson.

Hintlesham Hall remains a hotel of considerable charm – traditional, luxurious and grand. There are three dining rooms and the pick of the bunch is The Salon. The cooking of head chef Alan Ford is not so rooted in the past as the surroundings, but neither does it chase every modern fad and fashion. You might start with cider-braised pork belly, apple and leek terrine served with a golden sultana and apple relish, before moving on to breast of local Gressingham duck with a sweet potato and tarragon cake and wild mushroom sauce. Regional ingredients get a good showing on the menu. To finish, iced pistachio parfait is accompanied by spiced roasted plums, and the cheeses hail from Britain and France.

Hintlesham Golf Club
www.hintleshamgolfclub.com
IP8 3JG | 01473 652761
Open daily including Bank Holidays
The magnificent championship course of the Hintlesham Golf Club blends harmoniously with the ancient parkland surrounding it. Opened in 1991 but seeded two years beforehand, this parkland course has reached a level maturity that is rivalled in the area only by a few ancient courses. The course's signature holes are the 4th and 17th, both featuring water at inconvenient intervals.

St James's Chapel
english-heritage.org.uk
Rose Green, Lindsey, IP7 6QA
0870 333 1181 | Open daily 10–4
Built mainly in the 13th century, this tiny thatched, flint-and-stone chapel incorporates some earlier work. Although little documentation survives, it is thought the chapel served a castle that once stood in Lindsey, the remains of which are located nearby.

The Swan Inn ❀❀
monkseleigh.com
The Street, Monks Eleigh,
IP7 7AU | 01449 741391
The pretty village of Monks Eleigh is home to this attractive 16th-century thatched pub. It matters not if you're after a pint of local real ale, a bar snack or a full-on feed: flexibility is the name of the game. Old beamed ceilings and oak floors await, plus some intelligently unfussy bistro-style cooking, which can be taken in any part of the building, including the smart bar. Sound judgement from the kitchen allows the main ingredient (often local) to shine through in the likes of coarse pork rillette with green tomato chutney, or chilled Suffolk asparagus with parmesan flakes and balsamic dressing.

Moon and Mushroom Inn
themoonandmushroom.co.uk
High Road, Swilland, IP6 9LR
01473 785320
The delightful sight of several firkins of East Anglian beer behind the bar welcomes drinkers to this 400-year-old free house in the Suffolk countryside. Diners, too, relish the prospect of indulging in home-cooked specials such as wild rabbit pie or mushroom steamed pudding with four-mushroom sauce. The pub was reputedly a staging post for the despatch of convicts to Australia, and the records at Ipswich Assizes do indeed show that a previous landlord was deported for stealing two ducks and a pig. Today's guests are able to linger longer in the colourful cottagey interior or the fragrant rose garden.

▲ The Custom's House, King's Lynn

King's Lynn

King's Lynn, known to locals simply as Lynn, its original name, is an architectural dream, with almost every period represented, ranging from St Nicholas' Chapel – built between 1145 and 1420 to picturesque Burkitt Court almshouses – built in 1909 in memory of a Lynn corn merchant. You can take a stroll to see this living heritage – it makes for a great day out.

King's Lynn was an unassuming little place until it caught the eye of the Bishop of Norwich and then Henry VIII. Strategically placed on one of the most important waterways in medieval England, the town had a huge amount of trade passing through it. It exported corn from Lincolnshire, lead from Derbyshire, salt from Norfolk and Lincolnshire and, most importantly, wool from the East Midlands.

On top of this, it imported dried cod from Iceland and timber, pitch and resin from the Baltic, as well as Flemish and Italian cloths. With all these revenues, Lynn became a wealthy place, and Herbert de Losinga, the first Bishop of Norwich, decided he wanted it for himself. It became known as Bishop's Lynn, and

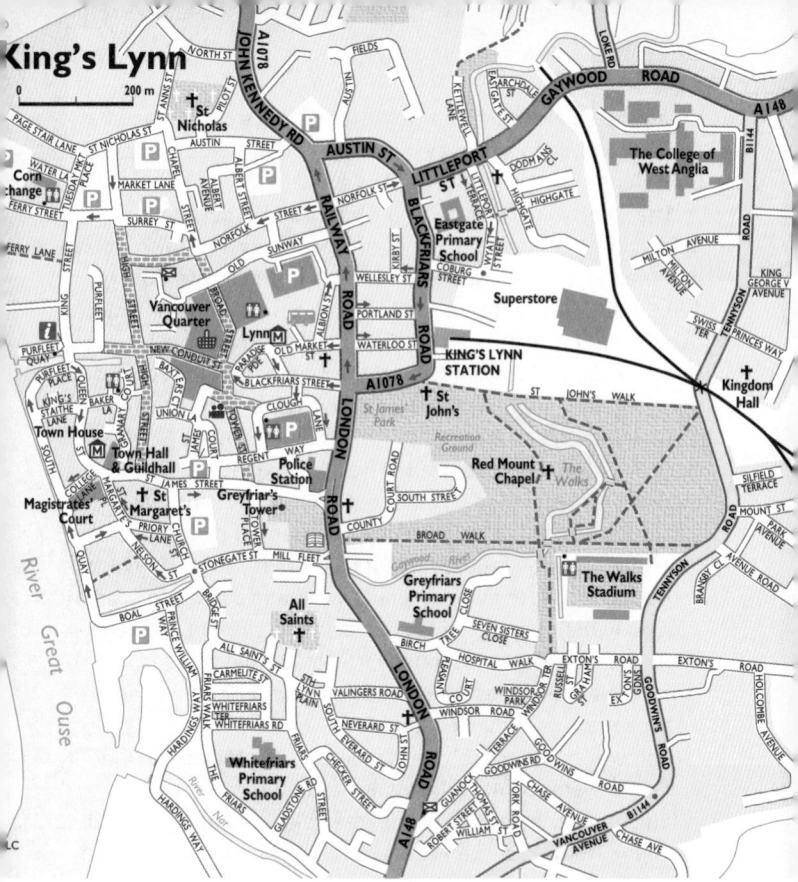

so it remained until the 1530s, when Henry VIII squashed its ecclesiastical association and named it King's Lynn. The change in name meant little to Lynn's merchants, who remained prosperous and continued to build their grand houses and churches, many of which can still be seen today.

Look out for the 14th-century Greyfriars Tower, once part of a Franciscan friary, and the churches and guildhalls of the market places. Despite the attentions of postwar planners, Lynn retains great character. It grew around not one but two market places, each close to the river and each with a noble medieval church and guildhall. Saturday Market's church, St Margaret's, is famous for its elaborate 14th-century brasses, baroque pulpit and 18th-century organ case, while the square's Trinity Guildhall with its 15th-century chequered flintwork – which was extended in 1624 and 1895 in the same style – is always admired. To the north is Tuesday Market with St Nicholas' Chapel and St George's Guildhall, another 15th-century edifice and the largest surviving medieval guildhall in England – now used as a theatre and arts centre. Between the two, on the quay, is the graceful old Custom House, containing the tourist information centre. Historic Lynn's civic treasures can be admired in a display that is part of the Tales of the Old Gaol House exhibit next to the Town Hall.

The refurbished warehouses along South Quay make for pleasant waterside strolling. Of the museums, the Town House in Queen Street displays Lynn's history and daily life from the 12th to the 20th centuries, and there is a museum of the old fishing quarter at True's Yard. Foremost among the exhibits at the refurbished Lynn Museum is the enigmatic 4,000-year-old upturned tree stump discovered preserved in shifting sands near Holme Beach in 1998, still with portions of the honeysuckle-stem rope used to haul it into place. Quickly dubbed Seahenge, the endangered Bronze Age relic was excavated amid huge controversy, but many of the original protestors may be relieved that it has at least stayed in Norfolk.

Across the Ouse at West Lynn, a dramatic change in scenery occurs, with flat arable fields of black soil, straight drainage ditches and scattered, isolated farmsteads and villages. This is the reclaimed landscape of the Fens bordering the Wash, a vast square-mouthed estuary between Norfolk and Lincolnshire. The coast here is mainly inaccessible, but the 13.5-mile Peter Scott Walk, named after the naturalist and wildlife painter who lived in the area, takes you along the old sea bank from West Lynn to his former lighthouse home near Sutton Bridge in Lincolnshire.

VISIT THE MUSEUMS AND CHURCHES

St Margaret's Church

stmargaretskingslynn.org.uk
St Margaret's Place, PE30 5DL
01553 772858

The Norman towers of this great church, which is almost of cathedral size and impact, dominate the west end of the building and, indeed, the skyline of King's Lynn. Between the two towers are a huge west window and a grand porch. Set into the southwest tower is an unusual 17th-century clock that tells the phases of the moon and the state of the tides on the Great Ouse. Look out for the words written round its face, 'Lynn High Tide'. St Margaret's was enlarged in the 13th century. Disaster struck on 8 September 1741 when a gale brought the spire of the southwest tower crashing down, destroying the lantern of a central tower and doing huge damage to the body of the church. The rebuilding work was completed in 1744, in the Gothic style, an unusual form to use at this time.

Inside, there are differing architectural features from its eventful history. And you can see two of the largest and most impressive brasses in Britain – the earliest is to Adam de Walsoken, who died in 1349, and the other is to Robert Braunche, who died in 1364. Both men were town mayors.

Take a look at the stalls and their misericords; they date from the late 14th century, as does the screenwork behind them. There are also screens with excellent woodwork from the 15th and 16th centuries. The beautiful wooden pulpit is Georgian and the eagle lectern is a rare brass example from the 16th century. The sumptuous reredos dates from 1899. It's well worth dedicating at least an hour to St Margaret's while you are in Lynn.

St Nicholas' Chapel

stnicholaskingslynn.org.uk
St Nicholas' Street, PE30 1QT

Although St Nicholas' is a large and imposing building, it served as a chapel for nearby St Margaret's for decades. It was rebuilt in grand style in the 15th century, and its south porch is an outstanding example of Perpendicular architecture. This is covered in a wealth of rich and complex carving, including a row of statue niches. Look out for the elegant spire built in the late 1800s to the designs of Sir George Gilbert Scott. Also striking from the outside is the enormous west window. The spacious interior is dominated by its superb wooden roof, lined with angels. The font was presented to the church in 1627 by Bishop Harsnett. The church has many tombs and memorials, one of the most noticeable being that to Benjamin Keene, made in 1757 by Scottish architect Robert Adam. It resembles a huge stone sugar bowl on top of an even larger stone cube.

Town House Museum

maritimeheritageeast.org.uk
46 Queen Street, PE30 5DQ
01553 773450 | Open Feb–Apr Mon–Sat 10–4; May–Oct 10–5

This charming museum is set in a 19th-century town house. Explore everyday life in King's Lynn through the ages in a series of carefully reconstructed rooms from medieval times to the 1950s. Enjoy collections of historic toys and costumes, and take the air in the delightful garden. Dotted around the displays are colourful games and activities that will certainly keep the children amused.

▼ The Guildhall, King's Lynn

Lynn Museum
museums.norfolk.gov.uk
Market Street, PE30 1NL
01553 775001 | Open Tue–Sat 10–5
Following a £1.2 million redevelopment, this charming museum tells the story of west Norfolk, and is home to Seahenge, the astonishing Bronze Age timber circle. A whole gallery is devoted to these unique 4,000-year-old timbers, and includes a life-sized replica of the circle, which was discovered off the coast of Hunstanton in the late 1990s. Original timbers are also displayed. The main gallery narrates the history of the area from the Iron Age to the 20th century. The museum also features the Iron Age gold coin hoard from Sedgeford, a display of pilgrims' badges and the beautiful 19th-century fairground gallopers made by Savages of Lynn.

SMELL THE FLOWERS

African Violet Centre
africanvioletandgardencentre.com
Terrington St Clement, PE34 4PL
01553 828374 | Open Mon–Sat 9–5, Sun 10–5
A warm and friendly welcome awaits you at the African Violet Centre. As well as providing an insight into the care and gorwth of African Violets, it is a major plant specialist, and the Centre offers a wide variety of plants for any enthusiast. It is also the winner of many Chelsea Gold Medals. The Courtyard Cafe features a children's play area.

PLAY GOLF

Eagles Golf Centre
www.eaglesgolfonline.co.uk
39 School Road, Tilney All Saints, PE34 4RS | 01553 827147 | Open daily including Bank Holidays
The parkland course of the Eagles Golf Centre has a variety of trees and shrubs lining the fairways. A large area of water comes into play on several of the holes.

King's Lynn Golf Club
club-noticeboard.co.uk
Castle Rising, PE31 6BD
01553 631654 | Open daily including Bank Holidays
At nearby King's Lynn Golf Club, the course is set among silver birch and fir woodland and benefits from well-drained sandy soil.

EAT AND DRINK

Bank House Hotel ◎
thebankhouse.co.uk
King's Staithe Square, PE30 1RD
01553 660492
Stylishly revamped to inject a hit of eclectic modern boutique style, this Georgian town house hotel with a slick modern brasserie-style restaurant lies in the heart of King's Lynn's historic quarter, on the River Ouse quayside. Bank House was Gurney's Bank in the 18th century (Gurney's was later absorbed by Barclays), and its former counting-house rooms have become the bar, which serves a fine spread of local ales and excellent wines, and the dining rooms.

The Stuart House Hotel, Bar and Restaurant
stuarthousehotel.co.uk
35 Goodwins Road, PE30 5QX
01553 772169
In a central but nevertheless quiet location, this hotel and bar is one of the town's favoured eating and drinking places. Top-notch East Anglian ales and traditional snacks are served in the bar, and there's a separate restaurant menu. Daily specials, like everything else, are home cooked from fresh local produce. Events include regular live music, murder mystery dinners and a July beer festival.

PLACES NEARBY

The historic of village of Castle Rising is about a five-minute drive from the outskirts of King's Lynn and is well worth a visit. It is famous for having been a 'rotten' parliamentary borough because of its small population, though it had a notable MP in Robert Walpole, Britain's first prime minister from 1721 to 1742; the Reform Act of 1832 put an end to its status. But the village is best known for its dramatic castle, one of the finest 12th-century hall-keep castle ruins in the country. Walpole's home, Houghton Hall, is close by, too.

If you fancy a round of golf, you could head for the Middleton Hall Golf Club in the nearby village of Middleton, while for refreshment you could try the Hare Arms at Stow Bardolph or Congham Hall Country House Hotel in Grimston.

▼ Castle Rising

Castle Rising

english-heritage.org.uk
PE31 6AH | 01553 631330
Open Apr–Nov daily 10–6; Nov–Mar Wed–Sun 10–4

This castle has seen battles and a royal resident. In 1327 Edward II was horribly murdered on the orders of his wife, Queen Isabella, and her lover, Roger Mortimer. At this time, Edward's heir, Edward III, was only 15 years old, and Mortimer and Isabella were able to rule England together by manipulating the young king. This state of affairs continued for three years until Edward III began to take matters into his own hands. Learning of the roles of his mother and Mortimer in the death of his father, Edward had Mortimer tried for treason and hanged in 1330. Isabella was spared trial but banished to live in the wilds of Norfolk in Castle Rising.

The village is inland but at one time it was on the coast. As late as the 18th century, paintings of the castle show ships in the background. Look out for the massive Norman earthworks that surround the castle, and the mighty, square keep built between 1138 and 1140. Several rooms remain in excellent condition.

Houghton Hall

houghtonhall.com
King's Lynn, PE31 6UE
01485 528569 | Open mid-May–Sep & Bank Holidays Wed–Sun 1–5

Robert Walpole, first Earl of Orford, was born in 1676. While he was First Lord of the Treasury and Chancellor, his brother-in-law and ally, Charles, second Viscount Townshend, was Secretary of State, and between them they wielded a formidable amount of power. When the relationship between these powerful men began to break down, Townshend was infuriated by Walpole's decision to build himself a glittering new palace at Houghton, a mere 10 miles from Townshend's ancestral seat of Raynham Hall. By the time Walpole became prime minister, he had managed to engineer Townshend's resignation from the government, and Townshend retired to Raynham in bitter defeat. When Walpole began lavishly entertaining his influential friends, Townshend left the area altogether.

Walpole built up a fine collection of Old Masters, as well as vast collections of furniture and sculpture. After his death in 1745, his feckless grandson sold most of the pictures to Catherine the Great, and they now grace the walls of the Hermitage Museum in St Petersburg. In 1797, Houghton passed to the Cholmondeley family, but it was not until 1913 that this magnificent palace became their permanent home.

Building at Houghton Hall was started in 1721 on the site of two earlier houses. The village of Houghton was demolished, and its inhabitants relocated outside the park gates; it then became known as New Houghton. It was not unusual in the 18th century for villages to be moved to suit their landlords. Walpole's house was originally designed by Colen Campbell, but James Gibbs added the cupola-like domes at each corner, and suggested that the main building material should be hard-wearing yellow sandstone brought by sea from Whitby.

Walpole left the entire interior design to William Kent, who added marble fireplaces, carved woodwork, many of the murals and much of the furniture. Kent's masterpiece is the cube-shaped 'stone hall', which has a plaster ceiling frieze and reliefs over the fireplace and door.

Middleton Hall Golf Club
middletonhallgolfclub.com
Hall Orchards, Middleton, PE32 1RY
01553 841800 | Open daily including Bank Holidays
The natural undulations and mature specimen trees at the Middleton Hall Golf Club offer a most attractive environment. The architecturally designed course provides a challenge for the competent golfer. There is also a covered floodlit driving range and short game facilities.

Congham Hall Country House Hotel ❀❀
conghamhallhotel.co.uk
Lynn Road, Grimston, PE32 1AH
01485 600250
With its pastoral location close to Sandringham House, acres of peaceful grounds including a magnificent herb garden hosting a whopping 400 varieties, plus a swish spa, a visit to Congham is a genuine treat. The pretty Georgian house is done out handsomely, and has long been a destination dining address in the county. French windows lead onto a terrace from the newly refurbished dining room, and tables are dressed in their best whites. The kitchen makes excellent use of the garden and the wider locale to deliver some well-crafted, classically minded cooking with an English flavour.

The Hare Arms
theharearms.co.uk
Lynn Road, Stow Bardolph, PE34 3HT | 01366 382229
Named after the Hare family, who have lived at Stow Hall since 1553, this ivy-clad pub has been run for the past 37 years by Trish and David McManus. No music drowns the conversation in the L-shaped bar and adjoining conservatory, which are both full of fascinating bygones the landlords have collected along the way. A large bar food menu is always available, which is supplemented by daily specials. The restaurant has a separate vegetarian menu with a good choice of dishes. Expect to see peacocks in the garden.

Lavenham

Don't be a bit surprised to find a film crew at work when you visit Lavenham. This impossibly gorgeous Suffolk town is one of the best-preserved medieval towns in England and regularly provides the backdrop to historical dramas on television and in films. During the 15th and 16th centuries it grew rich on the wool trade, exporting cloth to Europe and Asia. At one time its people paid more in taxes than the people of Lincoln and York.

Merchants and clothiers built the half-timbered houses that still attract visitors today. Many tea rooms, restaurants and souvenir shops have opened to meet the demands of tourists. At times, when coaches clog the High Street, you can't help but think that Lavenham is just too pretty for its own good. It's like an open-air museum of medieval architecture.

When the wool trade declined, nothing took its place, with the result that the town centre retains its medieval street plan, a network of lanes fanning out from the market square, dominated by the spectacular 16th-century Guildhall of Corpus Christi. Entire streets, such as Water Street, are lined with crooked, half-timbered houses, delicately colour-washed in ochre, mustard and Suffolk pink. Look out, too, for the pargeting (decorative plasterwork) such as the Tudor rose and fleur-de-lis on the facade of the Swan Inn. Lavenham has had a few famous residents. The artist John Constable attended the

▼ Little Hall, Lavenham

Old Grammar School in Barn Street. One of his friends was Jane Taylor, who wrote the nursery rhyme 'Twinkle, Twinkle Little Star' (1806) and who lived at nearby Shilling Grange. But the biggest name in Lavenham's history has been that of the de Vere family. Aubrey de Vere was granted the manor by his brother-in-law William the Conqueror. Four centuries later, John de Vere, 13th Earl of Oxford, led Henry VII's victorious army at the Battle of Bosworth in 1485. This was the final battle of the Wars of the Roses and it was in thanks for his safe return that local merchants built the parish church of St Peter and St Paul. One of the largest parish churches in England, its 141 foot flint tower dominates the skyline. With its rich Gothic tracery, coffered roof, graceful arches, columns and aisles, it is also one of the finest examples of the Perpendicular style.

VISIT THE MUSEUM

The Guildhall of Corpus Christi

nationaltrust.org.uk/lavenham
Market Place, CO10 9QZ
01787 247646 | Open Mar Wed–Sun 11–4; Apr–Oct daily 11–5; Nov Sat–Sun 11–4

The Guildhall of Corpus Christi is one of the finest timber-framed buildings in Britain. It was built around 1530 by the prosperous Corpus Christi Guild, for religious rather than commercial reasons. The hall now houses a local history museum telling the story of Lavenham's cloth trade riches in the 15th and 16th centuries. You can also see the walled garden with its 19th-century lock-up and mortuary.

EAT AND DRINK

The Great House Restaurant and Hotel ◎◎

greathouse.co.uk
Market Place, CO10 9QZ
01787 247431

Opposite the 16th-century timber-framed Guildhall, owned by the National Trust, the Great House is itself pretty ancient behind its Georgian facade, though its dining room has been given a thoroughly modern look. It's a calm and soothing room, decorated in soft tones, with a dark wood floor and comfortable upholstered chairs at white-clothed tables set with flowers and sparkling glasses. The cooking has its roots in the great French repertoire, but that's not to say there aren't some more global influences at play as well. There's a new patio for warm days.

The Swan ◎◎

theswanatlavenham.co.uk
High Street, CO10 9QA
01787 247477

The historic market town of Lavenham grew fat on the wool trade in Tudor times, and that is precisely how long the Swan has been feeding all-comers. The textbook 15th-century timber-framed inn is a tangle of sagging timbers both inside and

▲ The Swan at Lavenham

out – even its ancient brick floors are constructed of ballast from the wool ships that made the town's fortune – and there are oak panels, inglenook fireplaces, and cosy nooks and crannies which have hosted many a boozy session for World War II pilots who came in from Lavenham airfield to let off steam. It's hard to imagine a more evocative setting for a repertoire of crowd-pleasing pub classics; or you could trade up to the atmospheric Gallery restaurant and tuck into modern British dishes beneath soaring barn-style rafters and the impressive minstrels' gallery.

PLACES NEARBY

The equally gorgeous architecture found in the village of Kersey, and at Melford Hall and Kentwell Hall in Long Melford (see below), is worth adding to your schedule when exploring this part of Suffolk. Both villages are little more than a 10-minute drive from beautiful Lavenham.

Long Melford

Long Melford takes its name from its layout: lots of gorgeous pink- and yellow-washed period country houses and shops dotted along a long, straight, three-mile stretch of road, and a mill ford crossing. You can wander along this road, Hall Street, where you'll find chic tea emporia, designer fashion studios, art and fine food galleries and showrooms full to bursting with antiques. Long Melford is big on antiques, and featured prominently in the television series *Lovejoy*.

Two of the country's most magnificent country estates can be found in Long Melford, just a couple of miles apart. You could easily spend a day or more in Long Melford, visiting not only Hall Street, but also the delightfully romantic moated Kentwell Hall and the impressive red-brick pile of the Hyde Parker family, Melford Hall. The estates are easy to find – at the end of Hall Street is an expansive village green and their entrances can be found ahead and to the right.

TAKE IN SOME HISTORY

Kentwell Hall

kentwell.co.uk

CO10 9BA | 01787 310207

Open Mar–Sep 11–5

Kentwell Hall is a moated red-brick Tudor country house with stunning gardens, woodland walks and a rare breeds farm. You approach the house along a mile-long lime-tree-lined driveway that culminates in a spectacular view of the property and its front courtyard.

Restoration started here in 1971 and still continues today, with new features being added all the time. You can see the living areas of the house, such as the drawing room and the great hall, the kitchens, bakery and dairy.

In the Domesday Book, the manor of Kentwell was valued at £4 and owned by Frodo, brother of the first Abbot of Bury St Edmund's. The manor of Kentwell has been sold several times during its long history. It remained in Frodo's family until it passed to a family that took the name of the manor itself – the de Kentwells.

By 1250, it was in the hands of Henry III, who granted it to his half-brother, Sir William de Valence. The Hall was owned briefly by the 14th-century poet John Gower, and eventually came to Sir William Clopton through his mother Katharine Mylde in 1403. William's son, John (1423–97), seems to have been responsible for the earliest parts of the existing complex.

One of the highlights of Kentwell Hall is its now legendary re-creations of

▾ Kentwell Hall

everyday life in Tudor times. Actors and members of the public – you can apply to take part – dress in Tudor costumes and tell of their lives as members of the noble family, musicians, farm workers, dairymaids, blacksmiths, bakers or cooks. The hall also hosts 1940s Britain days. No visit to Kentwell would be complete without admiring the grounds. The rare-breeds farm is well worth a visit too.

Melford Hall

nationaltrust.org.uk/melfordhall
CO10 9AA | 01787 379228
Open Easter week 1.30–5; Apr and Oct Sat–Sun 1.30–5; May–Sep Wed–Sun

Melford Hall has changed little externally since 1578 when Elizabeth I was entertained here, and retains its original panelled banqueting hall. It was first the home of monks, and then the Hyde Parker family from 1786 to the present day. It is run on a day-to-day basis by the National Trust.

You can see the Regency library, Victorian bedrooms, extensive collections of furniture and porcelain, and a small display of items connected with Beatrix Potter, who was related to the family, including the original Jemima Puddleduck given to a child of the family by Beatrix herself.

The garden contains some spectacular specimen trees and a banqueting house and there is an attractive walk through the park. Special events are held throughout the year, including the annual Beatrix Potter Fun Day in July.

EAT AND DRINK

The Black Lion Hotel ❁❁

blacklionhotel.net
Church Walk, The Green, CO10 9DN
01787 312356

Overlooking Long Melford's village green, and with Melford Hall and Kentwell Hall minutes away, the Georgian Black is an inviting prospect. Expect full-flavoured modern British dishes with plenty of flair and imagination. You could keep things casual in the lovely bar, where there's a real fire, a water bowl for Rover and views across the green, or sit in the more formal restaurant with its deep green walls, antiques and oil paintings, opening onto a Victorian walled garden.

▸ PLACES NEARBY

The George ❁❁

thecavendishgeorge.co.uk
The Green, Cavendish, CO10 8BA
01787 280248

This 16th-century whitewashed inn is Grade II listed, and better described as a restaurant. The George's interior is dominated by wood, from the bare tables to the heavy beams that lend the place its character. The reassuring buzz of kitchen activity in the background reminds you what the main priority is. A Mediterranean-inflected repertoire of modern British dishes is on offer.

Lowestoft

The busy seaside resort of Lowestoft is Britain's most easterly town, and as such the first place in the country to catch the morning sun. You'll find it is significantly less kiss-me-quick than Great Yarmouth to its north, and it has a more stately feel about it.

The main street is a pretty enough place, lined with merchants' houses dating from the time when Lowestoft was a busy, although less frenetic than some, fishing harbour. There are major shop chains, schools and more informal eateries too. Away from the centre, the town's streets were once flanked by breweries, small industries and cottages, many occupied by labourers who worked on the farms that surrounded the town before development took over and farmland became covered in shiny new housing estates.

Evidence suggests that Lowestoft has been inhabited for around 700,000 years, and saw communities evolve during the Neolithic, Bronze and Iron Ages right through to Roman and Saxon times. Since the 14th century, when this small harbourside village began its expansion, Lowestoft has evolved into a major fishing port, which was later steadily replaced by light industry and North Sea oil and gas exploitation as its fisheries saw a decline. One of its major industries was the production of soft-paste porcelain, which became highly desirable and which, today, is extremely rare and valuable.

From Victorian times, Lowestoft benefited from its miles of golden beaches and quickly became a fashionable seaside resort. Today, people still flock to its beaches – the best ones are near the two piers, the South Pier and the Claremont.

Lowestoft's inner harbour, a scenic area known as Lake Lothing, plugs into Oulton Broad and the River Waveney, the most southeasterly point of the Norfolk Broads, which makes it a popular point of embarkation for holiday trips on the waterways.

If literature and art are your passions, you'll be interested to know that Thomas Nashe, the English poet and dramatist, was born here in 1567, as was composer Benjamin Britten in 1913 (see page 52). Oulton Broad is the place to which Norfolk author George Borrow (1803–81) returned following his travels, and where he wrote many of his books. He died here in 1881. And nearby Blundeston was the birthplace of Dickens' David Copperfield.

VISIT THE MUSEUMS

East Anglia Transport Museum

eatm.org.uk
Chapel Road, Carlton Colville, NR33 8BL | 01502 518459 | Open Apr–Sep Thu 1–5, Sun 11–5, plus school holidays and Bank Holidays
Motor, steam and electrical vehicles are exhibited in this fascinating museum, all of which have seen service around the country over many decades. A highlight is the reconstructed 1930s street scene, which is used as a setting for working vehicles. You can ride by tram, trolley bus and narrow gauge railway within the museum complex. There's a woodland picnic area served by trams.

Maritime Museum

lowestoftmaritimemuseum.org.uk
Sparrows Nest Gardens, Whapload Road, NR32 1XG | 01502 561963
Open Apr–Nov daily 10–5
Housed in a gorgeous flint cottage which, according to the plaque above the door, was restored in 1828, this museum was founded in 1958 by a group of enthusiasts and has steadily expanded. The cottage, the museum's permanent home, has since been sympathetically extended to make space for all the exhibits. It focuses on maritime history: themed exhibits trace the history of Lowestoft and its connections with the sea, displaying ancient and modern fishing boats, commercial boats, fishing gear, shipwrights' tools, and lifeboats, a wheelhouse, steam drifter cabin and a fish market, with models, charts and other memorabilia. It has a new audio-visual room and an art gallery too.

ENTERTAIN THE FAMILY

Claremont Pier

claremontpier.co.uk
Wellington Esplanade, NR33 0QN
01502 573533
The Claremont Pier was originally built in Victorian times when it was almost obligatory for all seaside resorts to have at least one pier, but a few gales over the years have meant that sections have been replaced. Today, it has a plethora of attractions to suit all tastes, from the Fun Palace amusement arcade and Palace Casino to a contemporary wood strip roller-skating rink known as Rollers. There are a couple of bars and a music venue.

South Pier

thesouthpier.co.uk
Royal Thoroughfare, NR33 0AE
01502 512793
If you fancy a spot of 10-pin bowling followed by a fish and chip supper, then you should visit Lowestoft's South Pier. On this historic pier, where once a reading room and bandstand attracted Victorian visitors, you'll find entertainment for the family, including modern and traditional coin machines and video games.

Pleasurewood Hills

See highlight panel opposite

Pleasurewood Hills

pleasurewoodhills.com
Leisure Way, Corton, NR32 5DZ
01502 586000 | Open Mar–mid-Jul days vary 10–5; mid-Jul–Sep daily 10–6; Oct–Nov days vary 10–4

Set in 50 acres of coastal parkland, Pleasurewood Hills has all the ingredients for a great family day out. There are thrills for the bravest adventurers, such as the Wipeout, which claims to be the most extreme rollercoaster in the East of England. There are rides for younger children and shows with sealions, parrots, acrobats as well as the Magic Circus spectacular. When the action gets too much, take a leisurely ride on the alpine chairlift or jump aboard one of two railways that weave their way through the park.

HIT THE BEACH

Lowestoft's beaches are golden and sandy, and those around the Claremont Pier have a Blue Flag accreditation.

PLAY GOLF

Rookery Park Golf Club
rookeryparkgolfclub.co.uk
Beccles Road, Carlton Colville, NR33 8HJ | 01502 509190
Open daily including Bank Holidays
Mature trees line the parkland courses and follow a route over gently undulating ground.

EAT AND DRINK

The Crooked Barn Restaurant ◎◎
ivyhousecountryhotel.co.uk
Ivy House Country Hotel, Ivy Lane, Oulton Broad, NR33 8HY
01502 501353
This glorious thatched barn was built around 1800, and comes complete with creaking floorboards and a welter of skew-whiff heavy beams. Views over pretty gardens and ornamental ponds are a draw, and on summer days you can sit in the courtyard. The culinary stock-in-trade is modern British and European dishes made with predominantly local prime ingredients, making a virtue of their simplicity and freshness.

Flying Fifteens
19a The Esplanade, NR33 0QG
01502 581188
These popular tea rooms offer full waitress service. All the food is home-cooked using the best ingredients, and chips are banned from the menu. Specialities include locally smoked salmon, local oak smoked ham and, on Saturdays,

▾ South Beach

fresh Cromer crab. There are no set meals, just a good choice of sandwiches, soup and omelettes, baguettes and cakes. There are over 40 loose-leaf teas from around the world too. The name Flying Fifteens comes from a 15 foot-long sailing boat designed by Uffa Fox in the 1940s.

PLACES NEARBY

Somerleyton Hall in the pretty village of the same name is nearby (see page 241), as is the popular Africa Alive! wildlife park (see page 63). Both Beccles (see page 61) and the lively Great Yarmouth (see page 139) are short journeys away. Heading out towards Great Yarmouth you'll find the Pettitts Animal Adventure Park in the village of Reedham, a pretty little place on the banks of the River Yare. Trains cross the Yare on the mighty swing bridge.

Pettitts Animal Adventure Park
pettittsadventurepark.co.uk
Reedham, NR13 3UA
01493 700094 | Open Apr–Oct daily 10–5

Aimed at younger children, the lovely Pettitts Animal Adventure Park is three parks in one. Rides include a railway and roller coaster. Its adventure play area has a mini-golf course, ball pond and tea room. Young children will love the entertainment provided by clowns, puppets and live musicians. Among the animals you can see here are small horses, wallabies, birds of prey, goats, alpacas and reindeer.

Madingley

see **Cambridge**, page 99

Mildenhall

If you've got aircraft enthusiasts in the family they're in for a splendid time in the Breckland town of Mildenhall. The massive Royal Air Force bases, RAF Mildenhall and RAF Lakenheath used by the United States Air Force, can be found in this small market town. While the bases are, understandably, off limits, there's an observation area at RAF Lakenheath, plus you will almost certainly see F-15 fighter bombers and other military planes on manoeuvres in the skies.

During World War II, RAF Mildenhall was one of a number of Suffolk airfields used by the Allied forces. Others included Lavenham, Eye and Mendlesham. Wellington bombers from Mildenhall engaged the German Navy within a day of war being declared. Throughout the war they continued to attack German targets as well as providing cover for Allied troops during the D-Day landings in Normandy and the evacuation of Dunkirk. In all, some 200 aircraft from Mildenhall were lost and 1,900 men killed in action during the war. The American presence at Mildenhall began in 1950 and it is now the gateway to Britain for more than 100,000 military personnel each year.

Mildenhall revolves around its market place, in the centre of which stands an elaborate hexagonal market cross dating from the 16th century. Here, the community, which is today very much a mix of military and non-military, gathers every Friday for the town's large market, as it has done for around 600 years. From here you can take the short walk to the Mildenhall Museum, which tells the story of the town.

Mildenhall's other claim to fame is the Mildenhall Treasure, the most significant hoard of Roman silverware ever discovered in Britain. The story of its discovery is almost as remarkable as the treasure itself. In January 1943, farmer Gordon Butcher was ploughing at West Row when he found a metal bowl buried in the ground. He showed it to his boss, Sydney Ford, who happened to collect antiques. Curiosity got the better of the pair and between them they dug up 34 pieces of blackened silverware, including plates, spoons, goblets and bowls, and a great dish almost 2 feet in diameter, richly decorated with scenes from Roman mythology. Ford took the objects home, cleaned them up and kept them on his mantelpiece for three years until eventually someone persuaded him to take them to the police. In 1946, the hoard was declared treasure trove and given to the British Museum. Ford and Butcher received a reward.

VISIT THE MUSEUM

Mildenhall Museum
mildenhallmuseum.co.uk
King Street, IP28 7EX
01638 716970 | Open Wed–Thu and Sat 2–4.30, Fri 10.30–4.30
This bright and fresh museum housed in two flint cottages contains a replica set of the Mildenhall Treasure, including bowls, ladles and the great dish (all the originals are in the British Museum). The museum also has galleries devoted to local history, ecology and RAF Mildenhall.

SEE A LOCAL CHURCH

St Mary Church
High Street, IP28 7EA
01638 711930
The grandeur of the impressive Church of St Mary reflects Mildenhall's prosperous history. A Grade I listed church, it was rebuilt between the 13th and 15th centuries on the site of a previous chapel. Look out for its many architectural features; in fact, its distinguished medieval craftsmanship makes it one of the great churches of East Anglia.

The tall 15th-century west tower and the huge decorated east window are the features that strike most people first. The two-storey north porch of about 1420 makes a fittingly grand entrance to the church, with its fine stone vault and roof bosses. Inside, you'll see even more remarkable and extravagant roofs above the nave and both aisles, which are embellished with throngs of carved angels and biblical figures. The nave roof, especially, is a remarkable survival: unable to reach the immensely high carved angels to destroy them with their bare hands, the puritan iconoclasts tried to shoot them to pieces instead. Many of the figures are still peppered with gunshot.

PLAY GOLF

West Suffolk Golf Centre
westsuffolkgolfcentre.co.uk
New Drove, Beck Row, IP28 8RN
01638 718972 | Open daily including Bank Holidays
This course has been gradually improved to provide a chance to play an inland course in all weather conditions. Situated on the edge of the Breckland, the dry nature of the course makes for easy walking among rare flora and fauna.

EAT AND DRINK

The Bull Inn
bullinn-bartonmills.com
The Street, Barton Mills, IP28 6AA | 01638 711001
The Bull has dropped the 'olde' from its name and gone back to its original moniker, which seems appropriate given the forward-thinking boutique approach that's going down here. There are designer bedrooms, a bar where you can drink a pint and eat some smart bar food, and a brasserie-style restaurant with a nifty menu that's big on local ingredients. The Bull Inn is easy to find on the outskirts of Mildenhall in the village of Barton Mills.

Newmarket

Where most English high streets are lined with conventional shops, in Newmarket you'll see cosy little places with the latest jodhpurs and breeches, or colourful jockey silks, on display in their windows, shoe shops selling a nice line in riding and stable boots, saddlers, farriers and bookmakers. Statues of horses stand outside shops. Souvenir shops are crammed with mugs and pictures depicting horses, and secondhand bookshops are full of books telling the story of horseracing. You almost expect the local Waitrose to sell horse feed.

Newmarket has been the capital of British horseracing since James I (1566–1625) built a palace in an acre of land, complete with extensive stables, and moved his summer court here in 1605. The town soon became a fashionable royal resort and the home of the sporting fraternity. Long before that, Queen Boudicca used to race her chariots across Newmarket Heath, but it was James I, followed by Charles I and Charles II, who sealed the town's fate as the top venue for the 'Sport of Kings'.

Look out for Palace House on your visit. It's an impressive red-brick property in the town centre and houses the tourist information centre and a museum, so you shouldn't miss it. In fact, the house is a wing of a much grander palace that Charles

II had built in the late 1660s, and is all that remains today. William Samwell (1628–76), a celebrated English architect, was commissioned to design the palace, said to have been one of the king's favourite homes. Further along Palace Street is a white house with shutters. This is where Nell Gwynne, one of the king's favourite mistresses, lived.

The National Horseracing Museum, which has a fascinating collection of riding clothes, rosettes, photographs and other memorabilia, tells the story of racing, and is one of many things to see on a visit to Newmarket. A 'must' is a visit to Warren Hill to see the famous gallops where the horses train each morning from dawn to around midday. The sight of dozens of horses galloping at speed in the early morning, when there's still dew on the grass and a light mist in the air, furnishes a memory that will last a lifetime.

One of the finest views of the town is from Newmarket Heath. Here you will see the Rowley Mile racecourse and the Millennium Grandstand. Not far from here is Queensberry House, headquarters of the British Bloodstock Agency, the National Stud and Tattersalls, the largest bloodstock auctioneers in Europe and the oldest in the world.
See **Horseracing at Newmarket,** page 33

▼ Racehorses training at Newmarket

VISIT THE MUSEUM

The National Horseracing Museum

nhrm.co.uk
99 High Street, CB8 8JH
01638 667333 | Open Mar–Dec Mon–Sat 10–5, Sun 10–4 including Bank Holidays; Jan–Mar Tue–Sat 10–4

This award-winning museum is packed with artifacts, paintings and photographs that tell the story of the people and horses involved in racing in Britain. Look out for the colourful racing silks worn by some of the world's greatest jockeys, including Frankie Dettori when he won every race on a seven-race card in one afternoon, and Francis Buckle (1766–1832), one of the first ever leading jockeys. You can see a valuable bronze statue of Kincsem, a thoroughbred who won all of her 54 races between 1876 and 1879, and the revolver Fred Archer (1857–86) used to shoot himself. Archer, perhaps the greatest jockey of all time who was 13-times champion jockey, was just 29. There's a hands-on gallery too, where you can have a go at riding on the horse simulator – horseracing is not as easy as it looks – and try on racing silks. You can also chat to the retired jockeys and trainers who work in the museum and are always happy to recite stories and tell of their experiences. The museum organizes mini bus tours to visit the gallops, a stable at dawn and Tattersalls the auctioneers.

PLAY GOLF

Links Golf Club

www.linksgolfclub.co.uk
Cambridge Road, CB8 0TG
01638 663000 | Open daily including Bank Holidays

With its gently undulating parkland setting surrounded

▼ Francis Buckle silks

▼ NHRM practical gallery

by racecourses, the Links is one of the most attractive golf clubs in the region. Its 18-hole par 72 course is also one of the most challenging for both beginners and experienced players. The club operates a reciprocal arrangement with 12 other clubs around the country, which formed in 1902, the year the Links opened, so if you are a member you can play here too.

EAT AND DRINK

Bedford Lodge Hotel ⊛⊛
bedfordlodgehotel.co.uk
Bury Road, CB8 7BX
01638 663175
A Georgian hunting lodge built for the Duke of Bedford in the 18th century, this place has been a hotel since the 1940s. Its position near the racing at Newmarket, England's centre of operations for the sport of kings since medieval times, means that no opportunity is lost in the decorative theming to celebrate the equestrian life, and if you've had a win at the races, there are plenty of ways of celebrating it, from spa treatments to a festive occasion in the Squires restaurant. An extensive menu of brasserie dishes spans the range from straightforward classics to more adventurous offerings. The fixed-price menus are particularly good value.

Bushel
Drapery Row, Rookery Centre, CB8 8EE
The Bushel is a glorious old building where, so the story goes, Charles II attended cock fights in the 17th century. It was tastefully refurbished not so long ago and now has a chic cream and caramel decor, completed by wooden floors and original wood beams.

▾ Frankie Dettori's silks

The Bushel once stood in a maze of tiny lanes not far from the High Street and Charles II's palace, and a mere stone's throw from his mistress's Nell Gwynne's house; today it is surrounded by the Rookery Centre with its modern shops. Nevertheless, it serves excellent real ales and nouvelle-pub lunches, and makes a welcome place for a break.

National Horseracing Museum Café
nhrm.co.uk
99 High Street, CB8 8JH
01638 667333
This lovely cafe is inside the museum, within a beautiful walled garden full of geraniums, and provides a respite from the bustle of Newmarket High Street. It serves breakfast and morning coffee through to lunches and afternoon tea, with dishes freshly prepared on the premises. Be sure to try its carrot cake – it's truly delicious.

The Rutland Arms Hotel ◎
bespokehotels.com
33 High Street, CB8 8NB
01638 664251
A coaching inn with plenty of period charm, the Rutland Arms is at the heart of the action in the racing hotspot of Newmarket. Runners and riders on the menu in the informal, green-carpeted Carriages dining room take in bistro classics, as well as one or two more modern dishes.

PLACES NEARBY

Both Wicken Fen National Nature Reserve (see page 279) and Anglesey Abbey and Lode Mill (see page 99) are within a short drive, as is the city of Cambridge (see page 88). For refreshments you could head for Tuddenham Mill, a gorgeous converted watermill in Tuddenham St Mary, the 14th-century Star Inn or the White Pheasant in Fordham, on the road to Ely. In nearby Worlington, you could play golf at the Royal Worlington and Newmarket Golf Club.

Tuddenham Mill ◎◎◎
tuddenhammill.co.uk
High Street, Tuddenham St Mary, IP28 6SQ | 01638 713552
One of the more striking hotel and dining venues in East Anglia is to be found at a converted watermill on the Suffolk–Cambridgeshire border, between Newmarket and Bury St Edmunds. Some conversions gently transmute the former function of a building, disguising it in the process, whereas at Tuddenham it has become a central feature, the gigantic waterwheel encased in glass in the first-floor restaurant, while inset window panels in the floor allow views of the water rushing by below. There are ducks and swans nesting on the River Kennett, and the view over open countryside from the terrace tables on a summer evening is of a well-nigh perfect English idyll.

Old gnarled beams dominate the interiors, but are offset with plain modern restaurant design, in the form of unclad black tables with black napkins, black-clad staff and smart, simple tableware. Paul Foster and his team source and forage locally and therefore seasonally, but there is also a willingness to bring less familiar ingredients and techniques to the menus.

The Star at Lidgate
lidgatestar.co.uk
The Street, CB8 9PP
01638 500275
This quintessential English pub dates back to the 14th century. An important meeting place for local residents, the pub is popular with Newmarket trainers on race days, and with dealers and agents from all over the world during bloodstock sales. Originally two cottages, the two traditionally furnished bars still fit the old-world bill with heavy oak beams, log fires, pine tables and antique furniture, but the dishes on the menu are a mix of Spanish and British. There's an extensive wine list, too, with a number of well-priced Riojas jostling for position alongside the real ales on tap.

The White Pheasant
whitepheasant.com
Fordham, CB7 5LQ | 01638 720414
This 18th-century building stands in a fenland village between Ely and Newmarket. In recent years its considerable appeal has been subtly enhanced by improvements that preserve its period charm. You can enjoy locally brewed ale, a glass of wine, homemade lemonade or strawberryade while perusing the menus. Food is taken seriously here, with quality, presentation and flavour taking top priority, using produce sourced as locally as possible.

Royal Worlington and Newmarket Golf Club
royalworlington.co.uk
Golf Links Road, IP28 8SD
01638 712216 | Open daily including Bank Holidays
The inland links course of the Royal Worlington and Newmarket Golf Club is renowned as one of the best nine-hole courses in the world. Well drained, it provides excellent winter playing conditions, as well as being a popular summer course.

Newton

Newton in Suffolk has a real community spirit. You can play golf on its huge 40-acre village green – it was turned into a proper nine-hole course around the time the club was formed over a century ago. Residents gather for special events in the pub, Saracens, which has benches overlooking the green and has acted as an impromptu golfers' club house for years. The Newton Green Golf Club now has a further course, which is more challenging for serious golfers. Newton, which lies near Sudbury (see page 256), is home to the ancient woodlands at Edwardstone Woods, a designated Site of Special Scientific Interest, and Alstrop Wood. Here, many species of trees thrive, some 500 years old, including hornbeam and wild cherry trees.

PLAY GOLF

Newton Green Golf Club
newtongreengolfclub.co.uk
Newton Green, CO10 0QN
01787 377217 | Open Mon, Wed, Sun and Bank Holidays, and Tue pm
The Newton Green Golf Club is one of the oldest in the region, founded in 1907. It has two flat courses that meander around a pond. The first nine holes are open with bunkers and trees, while the second nine holes are tight with ditches and gorse.

EAT AND DRINK

Saracens Bar and Eatery
saracensbarandeatery.co.uk
The Green, Sudbury Road
CO10 0QJ | 01787 379036
This gorgeous 14th-century former coaching inn is handsome in heritage colours, with benches outside and a seasonal plethora of hanging baskets full of flowers. It's just as pretty inside – think gnarled crooked wooden beams and stone fireplaces. Once known as the Saracen's Head, and now transformed into a swish gastro-pub renamed Saracens Bar and Eatery, it offers favourites like whitebait and Caesar salad to start, followed by hearty homemade beef lasagne, Stilton, mushroom and broccoli bake, or scampi. You could try one of its creamy desserts to round off your meal. A daily changing blackboard of specials adds to the choice.

PLACES NEARBY

The Case Restaurant with Rooms
thecaserestaurantwithrooms.co.uk
Further Street, Assington,
CO10 5LD | 01787 210483
Open lunch and dinner
Located in deepest Suffolk countryside, this great little property has bags of character. Dating back to about 1700, the whitewashed country inn used to be a private home but now there are beautiful bedrooms and a cosy restaurant to attract paying customers. It's a little like eating in someone's front room (in a nice way), with a wood-burning stove, dark wood tables and low ceiling beams.

Norfolk Broads

The protected Norfolk Broads
Moving silently between the swaying reedbeds of Barton Broad, it's hard to imagine that the tranquil landscape through which you are passing is anything but natural. No visit to Norfolk would be complete without a trip to the Broads National Park. This is a patchwork of interlinked streams, lakes and channels that wind sluggishly over the flat land to the east of Norwich.

▲ Thurne Windmill

Today, wildlife-watching is a popular and inspirational experience best enjoyed by visiting one of the many nature reserves. With such a diverse landscape, it is not surprising that other activities are also in demand here – fishing, sailing, windsurfing, rowing, canoeing, boating and walking – so striking the right balance in the provision of amenities, one that is sympathetic to the needs of the Broads rather than to the needs of visitors, is difficult and ongoing.

Natural or manmade?

Three major rivers – the Bure, Waveney and Yare – supply most of the water to the meres, ponds and marshes before entering the great tidal basin at Breydon Water and flowing into the sea at Great Yarmouth. Despite the fact that the Broads comprise one of England's best wilderness areas, most natural historians and archaeologists accept that their origin lies in

▼ Hickling Broad

ancient human activity. That is the great paradox of the Norfolk and Suffolk Broads. Like so many British landscapes, even this apparently untouched 'natural' landscape was once the scene of great human industry. Unlike any other national park, it was manmade around 500 years ago in an area of hollows that were the direct result of large-scale medieval peat extraction.

The extent of that extraction was deduced by meticulous examination of the records of St Benet's Abbey, a Benedictine monastery on the banks of the River Bure at Holme, near Ludham. The scanty flint-faced ruin of St Benet's, now dominated by the remains of an 18th-century red-brick tower mill just inside the gatehouse, is one of the most important historic monuments in the Broads, and more than likely dates back to the 9th century. The abbey was rebuilt and endowed with three manors by King Canute in 1020.

▼ St Benet's Abbey

▲ The Broads at Horsey

The abbey's records show that from the 12th century onwards large areas of Hoveton parish were set aside for peat digging, and in one year alone more than a million turves (blocks of peat used for fires) were cut. This industrial-scale extraction went on continuously for more than 200 years, and by the early 14th century, at the height of its importance, the cathedral priory at Norwich was using nearly 400,000 turves annually. The peat diggings were eventually joined to the main river systems when wildfowlers, fishermen and reed cutters dug channels to link them.

Water, water everywhere

But where did all the water come from? From the 13th century onwards there was a slight change in the relative levels of the land and the sea, and coastal and low-lying areas such as the Broads became increasingly at risk from flooding – not unlike the effects of global warming and the predicted rise in sea levels today. There were some cursory attempts to dredge peat from under the steadily rising waters, but by the 15th century peat digging was no longer practical and it was abandoned.

▲ Boathouses, Hickling Broad

Tithe maps from the 1840s show that the Broads once covered nearly 3,000 acres of open water. Since then, the shallow lakes formed from the peat diggings have gradually filled with dead and dying vegetation and sediment. The total area of open water today is less than half that during the 18th century, but there are still 125 miles of lock-free, navigable rivers and broads within the national park. The Broads, which cover 117 sq miles of Norfolk, and parts of Suffolk, became England's 11th national park in 1989. What they lack in crags, mountains and moorlands that characterise other national parks, the Broads make up for in their ever-changing waterscapes.

Today, the Broads are one of the most important wetland landscapes in Europe, and provide a home to many spectacular forms of plants and wildlife.

Mills, often mistakenly called windmills, punctuate the Broads' skyline, but in almost every case these are windpumps, built to drain water from the marshes. Wonderful examples can be seen at Berney Arms, Herringfleet, Turf Fen (How Hill), Boardman's Mill and Thurne Dyke. It makes you wonder if they attracted the same kind of outcry when they were erected as 21st-century wind turbines do today.

Navigating the Broads

There are few major centres of population within the National Park, but just beyond the boundaries lie the city of Norwich (see page 212) and the towns of Great Yarmouth (see page 139) and Lowestoft (see page 189). Here you are on dry land, but the best way to explore the Broads themselves, given that they hug the courses of many rivers, is by boat, for it is then that the illusion of remoteness is heightened and the prospect of seeing something rare and wonderful is enhanced by an approach that is slow and quiet. Indeed, the Broads have been important for sailing and boating since Victorian times, offering a unique navigation system for which special inland sailing craft – wherries – were developed. Wherries have featured on the Broads for centuries and their use in river trade was instrumental in making Norwich England's second city. The earliest wherry-type vessel was square rigged, but by the early 19th century, the wherry had become single-sailed, and better designed for the shallow waters of the Broads.

PLACES TO VISIT

There are many wonderful places in the Broads. Wroxham (see page 284), which has long been regarded as the region's capital, the pretty villages of Ludham, Hoveton and Ranworth (see page 234), and the nearby Broadland Wildlife Centre (see page 235) shouldn't be missed. Perhaps the place where its real spirit can best be captured is the thatched and gabled Edwardian house of How Hill.

Situated on the highest point of the national park, a mere 40 feet above the sea, How Hill was built by the Norwich architect Edward Boardman, and now serves as an environmental education centre and nature reserve run by the Broads Authority and the How Hill Trust. The views from the house take in the winding River Ant and the reedbeds of Reedham, Clayrack and Bisley, all watched over by the red-brick tower of the Turf Fen windpump.

▾ Broadlands Wildlife Centre

▾ Hickling

North Walsham

If you've ever worn clothing made from a light-weight material known as Walsham, you can thank the weavers of North Walsham. Along with its neighbour Worstead, which gave its name to a much heavier cloth used for winter clothing, the town became a thriving weaving centre in the 12th century when settlers from Flanders came to live here.

The town's prosperity grew and by the 14th century its people were able to build a magnificent church, complete with one of Norfolk's tallest towers, which became the centre of the community. Even today, North Walsham's Church of St Nicholas, although now in ruins, remains one of the largest parish churches in England and the town's landmark. You can see it for miles around.

As you wander around the streets of North Walsham, look out for the wayside stone near the water towers that tells how its people were involved in the Peasants' Revolt of 1381, and were defeated in the Battle of North Walsham, one of the last battles in a rebellion that saw peasants throughout England rise up against the authorities.

Nearby is Paston College. Horatio Nelson and his brother William were educated here in the 18th century when it was Paston Grammar School. Horatio was 12 when he left the school to begin his naval career.

EAT AND DRINK

Beechwood Hotel ❀❀

beechwood-hotel.co.uk
20 Cromer Road, NR28 0HD
01692 403231

This handsome creeper-clad Georgian hotel should exert a strong pull for murder and mystery fans, since Agatha Christie came here frequently when it was owned by family friends, and her framed letters are hung in the hallway. It is a lovely personal touch that sums up the exemplary attitude to service and attention to detail that is the hallmark of this charming small hotel. The elegantly traditional dining room is the setting for some well-crafted, contemporary cooking, delivered by a kitchen with a passion for sourcing top-grade Norfolk produce.

PLACES NEARBY

East Ruston Gardens

eastrustonoldvicarage.co.uk
East Rushton Old Vicarage, East Rushton, NR12 9HM
01692 650432 | Open Mar–Oct Wed–Sun and Bank Holidays 1–5.30

East Ruston Gardens lie a mile and a half from the Norfolk coast and promise an improbable horticultural tour. They are protected from the strong wind by belts of trees and dense hedges, and have all the ambience of the Mediterranean, the luxuriance of the tropics, the aridity of the

Arizona desert and, in a field spattered with cornflowers and poppies, the nostalgia of childhood.

Alan Gray bought the property in 1973 when the former vicarage had a look of desolation and the surrounding two acres were waist-high in weeds. He saw this as a blank canvas on which to create an oasis-like cordon around the Arts and Crafts brick-and-tile house.

Today, the gardens extend over 32 acres. Part of Alan Gray's vision was to maintain a high level of colour and interest, and to give the garden a sense of place by harnessing nearby landmarks; a porthole in a hedge neatly frames the Happisburgh lighthouse.

The extended season of colour is nowhere better exemplified than in a field and woodland garden, which is criss-crossed by meandering paths. Several thousand bulbs are planted each year to reinforce the already glorious display of snowdrops and aconites in February. Special areas include the Fern Garden and the Exotic Garden, which is awash with bedding plants, many no longer available commercially. Bananas and *Tetrapanax papyrifer 'Rex'* add structure with their large imposing foliage, and a tall fountain adds drama.

To protect the tender, rare and unusual plants the owners planted large shelterbelts of Monterey pine, Italian alder, the Mediterranean oak and many eucalypts which, as they have developed, have improved the micro-climate. More protection comes from mixed hedgerows, planted for their changing colours and textures and as habitats for birds.

These gardens are a delight. Regular garden events are held here, and Alan Gray gives demonstrations and tours.

▼ Decorated screens, St Nicholas Church in North Walsham

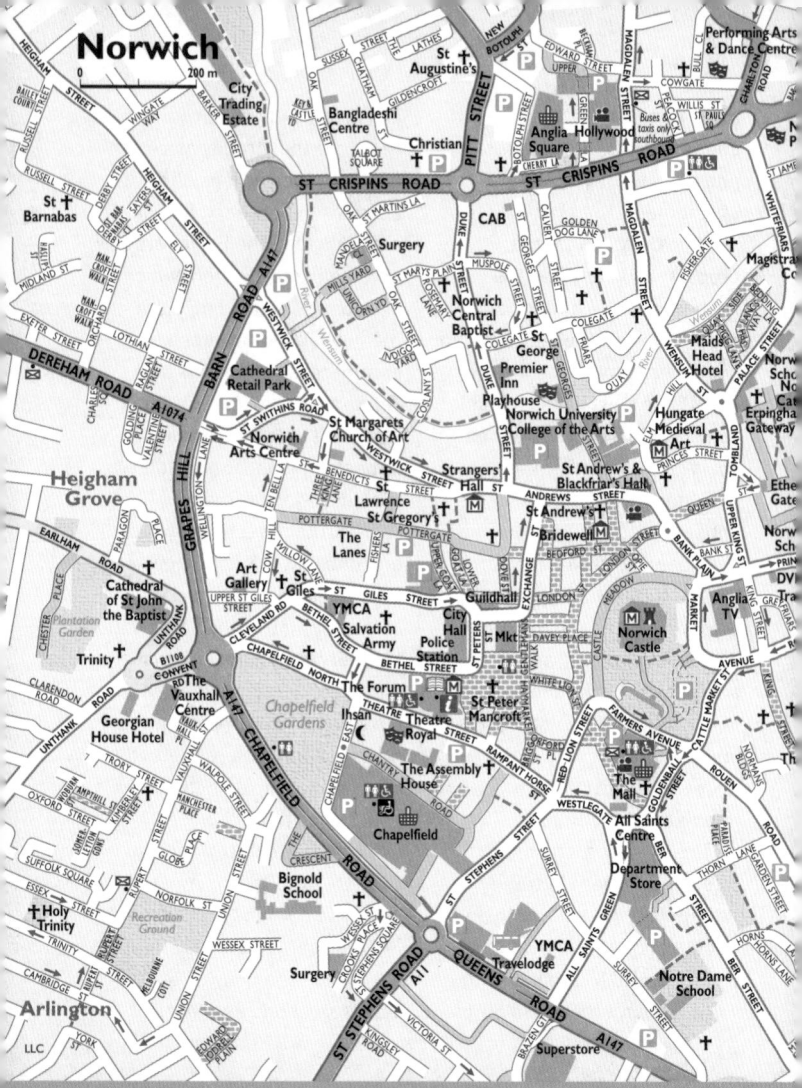

Norwich

When William the Conqueror arrived here in 1066 and decided that this was to be the place for one of the grandest palaces the country had ever seen, Norwich was already the largest city in England after London. Both the Romans and the Anglo-Saxons had developed the city which had its own mint and a thriving market.

Norwich Castle, which was to become one of William's favourite royal palaces, was a grand building. In fact, architecturally, it was one of the most ambitious buildings yet seen when work commenced in 1067. Its 12th-century massive stone keep symbolised the king's power and wealth at a time when buildings tended to be small and made entirely of wood.

▲ Norwich Cathedral

Today, Norwich Castle is the city's most iconic building and a great museum. Without doubt, it should be the first place on your list to visit while you're in Norwich.

Wealth and the wool trade

Nearly 30 years after work began on the castle, another of Norwich's iconic buildings was conceived. Norwich Cathedral is a magnificent structure which took over 150 years to build. Norwich had become the centre of the Norfolk wool trade and, as such, was supremely wealthy. This is reflected in the grandeur of the cathedral, considered one of the best-preserved, most complete Romanesque buildings in Europe.

▲ Elm Hill, Norwich

Don't miss the opportunity to marvel at the cathedral's wondrous architecture, including its tower and cloisters, which are the highest and largest, respectively, in England. It also has an extraordinary roof and some original wall-paintings. By the 14th century, the main part of the city was enclosed by thick walls, guarded by gates and towers, which meant that access could be restricted – anyone who entered had to pay a toll. By the 15th century, Norwich was the largest walled city in Europe; its 2.5-mile wall enclosed an area greater than that of the City of London. You can still see remains of the city walls dotted around today.

During the Middle Ages, the wealth derived from wool founded no less than 57 churches within the city walls; 31 still remain. This prompted the local saying that Norwich had a church for every week of the year, and a pub for every day.

Norwich's status continued to grow over the next few centuries until when, in 1845, the railway brought a direct link with London, bringing with it new opportunities. The city's printing and publishing industry – the Norwich Post was the first provincial newspaper published in England in 1701 – flourished, along with its brewing, clothing manufacture and structural engineering industries.

Certainly the overriding impression on visiting Norwich is that of taking a step back in time, in the most agreeable sense. It is a modern city, but the scope for a little self-indulgent time travel is good.

Norwich Castle

museums.norfolk.gov.uk
Castle Meadow, NR1 3JU | 01603 493625 | Open Jul–Sep Mon–Sat 10–5, Sun 1–5; Oct–Jun Mon–Sat 10–4.30, Sun 1–4.30

Norwich Castle was built between 1067 and 1075 as a royal palace for William the Conqueror, with its magnificent stone keep added in the 12th century. In the 14th century, the castle was the city gaol, and remained so for some 500 years. Take a minute to look at the castle mound; it is the largest in England.

Today the castle houses a fascinating museum with displays of art, archaeology, natural history, Lowestoft porcelain (see page 189), Norwich silver and a large collection of paintings, with special emphasis on the Norwich School of painters. A display of British ceramic teapots is a pleasant diversion.

You can take a guided tour of the dungeons and battlements, plus there's a programme of exhibitions, children's events, an art gallery and evening talks throughout the year.

▼ Norwich Castle

Norwich Cathedral

cathedral.org.uk
12 The Close, NR1 4DH | 01603 218300 | Open daily 7.30–6 (occasionally closed for special services)

The splendid Norman craftsmanship, and the sheer scale and sense of tranquillity of Norwich Cathedral, has attracted visitors and pilgrims here for nearly a millennium. It has the second highest spire and the largest monastic cloister in England. Inside, you'll see the 1,000 or so carved medieval roof bosses and the original wall-paintings in the Jesus Chapel and the presbytery. The soft cream Caen stone building remains a place for quiet reflection as well as for participation in daily services and the rich pageantry of the church's festivals. An education and visitor centre is now open.

PLACES TO SEE

Norwich has so much to offer the visitor, from amazing historic structures to contemporary theatre, fine dining, shopping and leisure activities. Look out for the Great Hospital built in 1249; St Andrew's and Blackfriars' halls dating back to the 14th century and forming the only English friary of that period to survive intact; and the 15th-century Guildhall and Dragon Hall that both host heritage events.

The Georgian Assembly House regularly hosts concerts and exhibitions, while the Forum is pure 21st century and buzzes with activity in its digital galleries and television studios. The University of East Anglia is based on the outskirts of Norwich. Meandering among all these buildings are little lanes and streets lined with designer boutiques and fashionable restaurants.

There are parks, colourful gardens, huge open spaces and riverside walks, while the Norfolk Broads, in the form of the River Wensum on which the city sits, tap a tentative finger at the very gates of Norwich.

TAKE IN SOME HISTORY

Norwich Castle

See highlight panel on page 215

Norwich Cathedral

See highlight panel opposite

10 country houses

- **Blickling Hall**, Norwich, page 108
- **Felbrigg Hall**, nr Norwich, page 107
- **Holkham Hall**, Holkham, page 154
- **Houghton Hall**, King's Lynn, page 182
- **Ickworth House**, Horringer, page 80
- **Kentwell Hall**, Long Melford, page 187
- **Mannington Hall**, Saxthorpe, page 156
- **Oxburgh Hall**, Oxborough, page 232
- **Sandringham House**, Sandringham, page 236
- **Somerleyton Hall**, Somerleyton, page 241

Norwich Cathedral cloisters

Dragon Hall

dragonhall.org
King Street, NR1 1QE
01603 663922 | Open Apr–Oct Tue–Thu 10–4, Sun 12–4

This dramatic medieval trading hall was built by a wealthy local merchant, Robert Toppes (1405–67), in 1427, around an earlier brick-and-flint house. He clearly had excellent taste and a seemingless bottomless purse. You can see where he would have once displayed and stored wool and cloth, probably timber too, and the spices that would have brought him his great wealth. Buyers would come to the hall to trade and this magnificent building was designed to impress them.

On the first floor is an outstanding Great Hall with a crown post roof and superb beams. There's a dragon carved into the wood, which gives the house its name. When Toppes died, the property was sold and partition walls were built inside to divide it into low-cost housing for the poor and shops. The roof was concealed within attic space, and remained hidden for hundreds of years, only to be rediscovered in the 1980s. Today, it is open to the public as a heritage building.

The Assembly House

assemblyhousenorwich.co.uk
Theatre Street, NR2 1RQ
01603 626402

The Assembly House is an elegant Georgian building designed in 1754 by architect Thomas Ivory and built as a venue for afternoon tea, dancing and assemblies for Norwich's elite. You can see high-ceilinged rooms painted in delicate shades of yellow and cream, still looking as they did in Regency times. Beautiful carvings can be seen on the ceilings and panelled walls. The gentry would have gathered in the Grand Hall and perhaps moved on to the Noverre Ballroom or the Music Room with its minstrels' gallery. You can tour the rooms or attend one of the many events or concerts.

VISIT THE MUSEUMS AND GALLERIES

Sainsbury Centre for Visual Arts

scva.ac.uk
University of East Anglia, NR4 7TJ
01603 593199 | Open Tue–Fri 10–6, Sat–Sun 10–5

Housed in a world-class building, designed by Norman Foster, on the edge of the University of East Anglia campus, this is an inspirational public museum exhibiting outstanding public art for free. You can see modern and world art in permanent collections, in addition to special exhibitions which change every few months. A library, conservatory display area and gallery cafe can be enjoyed here too. The centre opened in 1978 to house Sir Robert and Lady Sainsbury's collection of art by English artists; this has grown to include works by emerging European artists.

The Forum
theforumnorwich.co.uk
Millennium Plain, NR2 1TF
01603 727050
One of Norwich's newest and most contemporary buildings. Here, you can see an exhibition or visit the digital gallery or its vast Millennium Library. The complex is home to BBC East, which broadcasts television and radio programmes live, the tourist information office and food outlets.

Colman's Mustard Shop and Museum
mustardshopnorwich.co.uk
15 Royal Arcade, NR2 1NQ
01603 762142
Colman's has been making its world-famous mustard in Norwich for nearly 200 years. Housed in the glorious art-nouveau Royal Arcade, near Norwich market, the Colman's Mustard Shop and Museum is designed as a replica Victorian shop and tells the story of this local family and their products.

TAKE A PUNT

Norwich Punting Co
norwichpunting.co.uk
Friars Quay, NR3 1ES
07810 047845
A great way to learn about Norwich's history and see the city from an entirely new angle is to take a punt on the River Wensum. You'll see St James Mill, Cow Tower, the quayside, White Friars Bridge and Bishopsgate Bridge, plus a lot more, while listening to a commentary. Punts depart every 15 minutes from the punt station next to Friars Quay.

▾ Colman's Mustard Shop

SEE A PERFORMANCE

You'll be able to catch a family show, a comedy or pantomime, a musical or operatic performance or some serious drama, even a puppet show, at Norwich's theatres, which include the Norwich Theatre Royal, the Norwich Playhouse and the highly recommended Norwich Puppet Theatre.

Norwich Theatre Royal
theatreroyalnorwich.co.uk
Theatre Street, NR2 1RL
01603 630000

Norwich Playhouse
norwichplayhouse.co.uk
St Georges Street, NR3 1AB
01603 598598

Norwich Puppet Theatre
puppettheatre.co.uk
St James, Whitefriars, NR3 1TN
01603 629921

GO SHOPPING

Head for Norwich Lanes just off Guildhall Hill where you'll find shop after shop of stylish clothes, food and souvenirs. Upmarket goodies can be found in Jarrold department store in Exchange Street, and in the art-nouveau 1899 Royal Arcade, off Castle Street. Norwich Market with its 200 or so stalls opposite City Hall, is the place for bargains. Other shopping streets to make for include quaint Timber Hill, cobbled Elm Hill and the pedestrianised Gentleman's Walk, all in the city centre. Out of town is Magdalen Street with its quirky independent shops, the modern Riverside Retail Park and the contemporary Chapelfield Shopping Centre.

PLAY GOLF

Norwich has a number of excellent golf courses. There's the challenging parkland course with water features at many of the holes at the De Vere Dunston Hall club, and the Costessey Park Golf Course where the course lies in the Tud Valley, providing players with a number of holes that bring the river and manmade lakes into play. At Sprowston Manor, the course is set in 100 acres of parkland with an impressive collection of oak trees. The two courses at the Wensum Valley Hotel are set in 350 acres and designed to complement the natural landscape. Eaton Golf Club offers an undulating, tree-lined parkland course. At the Royal Norwich Golf Club, the parkland course has remained largely unchanged since 1924 and is a challenging test of golf.

Costessey Park Golf Course
costesseypark.com
Old Costessey, NR8 5AL
01603 746333

De Vere Dunston Hall
devere-hotels.co.uk
Ipswich Rd, NR14 8PQ
01508 470444

▸ The Royal Arcade

JEWELLERS
ABRAXAS JEWELLERS

Eaton Golf Club
eatongc.co.uk
Newmarket Road, NR4 6SF
01603 451686

Royal Norwich Golf Club
royalnorwichgolf.co.uk
Drayton High Road,
Hellesdon, NR6 5AH
01603 429928

Sprowston Manor
marriottsprowstonmanor.co.uk
Wroxham Road, NR7 8RP
01603 410871

Wensum Valley Hotel, Golf and Country Club
wensumvalleyhotel.co.uk
Beech Avenue, Taverham, NR8 6HP
01603 261012

EAT AND DRINK

Adam and Eve
adamandevenorwich.co.uk
17 Bishopsgate, NR3 1RZ
01603 667423
This enchanting, brick-and-flint inn sits beneath trees at the fringe of the grounds of the cathedral, the builders of which lodged at the pub, and has been licensed since 1249. It's a refreshing step back in time, free of electronic diversions while rich with local beers from Humpty Dumpty and Wolf breweries; spirits here include the ghosts of lingering, long-gone locals. Who can blame them when the food is as rewarding as the ales; visitors resting on a tour of Norwich's finest can expect no-nonsense quality pub classics like filled large Yorkshire pudding, trawlerman's pie, home-made curry or chilli. The hanging basket displays are stunning.

Best Western Annesley House Hotel ◎◎
bestwestern.co.uk
6 Newmarket Road,
Norwich, NR2 2LA
This Georgian and Grade II listed house is a pretty property a short walk from the centre of the city. It's got three acres of gardens to call its own, so really does feel like a little oasis. There are views over the garden from the conservatory restaurant, which has a decidedly contemporary finish with its wood-affect flooring, leather seats and darkwood tables. The kitchen matches the decor with its equally modish approach, which consists of sourcing good quality East Anglian ingredients and subjecting them to some fashionable Pan-European preparations. For example, hand-dived scallops, wrapped in smoky streaky bacon, are served with crisp pork belly, roast shallot purée and chicken jus.

Brummells Seafood Restaurant ◎
brummells.co.uk
7 Magdalen Street, NR3 1LE
01603 625555
In the oldest part of the city, Brummells shows its age with its beams, standing timbers and stone walls; candlelight adds a romantic glow to the

rustic interior in the evening; and a welcoming log fire burns in the winter. Seafood cooked to consistently high standards is the draw, and there are some meat dishes as well.

The Maids Head Hotel ◎
maidsheadhotel.co.uk
Tombland, NR3 1LB
01603 209955
This part-timbered, part-brick building opposite the cathedral has its roots in the 13th century, although nowadays it provides conference facilities as well as all the other amenities expected of a modern hotel. Its restaurant is in a splendid room, once a courtyard, now glassed over with a pitched roof. It's airy and spacious, with a terracotta floor and well-appointed dark wood tables. Well-presented, modern British dishes are the kitchen's stock in trade. A trendy starter like properly cooked scallops with pancetta crisps and cauliflower purée may be followed by something old-fashioned and hearty like a game pie – its meat tender, its pastry perfectly crisp, with a rich gravy and roasted root vegetables.

The Red Lion
redlion-eaton.co.uk
50 Eaton Street, Eaton, NR4 7LD
01603 454787
This heavily beamed 17th-century coaching inn has bags of character, thanks to its Dutch gable ends, panelled walls, suit of armour and inglenook fireplaces. The covered terrace enables customers to enjoy one of the real ales or sample a glass from the wine list outside during the summer months. The extensive menus include light meals and snacks.

Ribs of Beef
ribsofbeef.co.uk
24 Wensum Street, NR3 1HY
01603 619517
Originally an alehouse in the 18th century, between the 1960s and 1980s this building was used variously as an antiques shop, electrical store and fashion boutique before Roger and Anthea Cawdron relicensed it in 1985. They continue to welcome locals and holidaymakers cruising the Broads. The pub is valued for its comfy leather seats, range of cask ales, excellent wines and traditional English food using locally sourced produce. Breakfast is available until midday, while hearty choices like beef and ale stew, nut roast and wholetail scampi rub shoulders with sandwiches, burgers and jacket potatoes on the varied main menu. Sit outside on the jetty during the warmer months for fabulous river views.

Roger Hickman's Restaurant ◎◎◎
rogerhickmansrestaurant.com
79 Upper St Giles Street, NR2 1AB
01603 633522
Roger Hickman's name now hangs above the door of the

restaurant formerly known as Adlard's, a veteran of Norwich's gastronomic scene, where he once ran the kitchen as head chef. 'If it ain't broke don't fix it' seems to have been the approach since Hickman's return to his old stomping ground; in terms of style and ambience, at least, the place remains intimate, relaxed and with a touch of class thanks to its linen-swathed tables on stripped wooden floors, and clean-cut cream walls hung with colourful prints. On the culinary front, however, things have shifted gear into warp speed. Hickman has refined his already impressive technique still further and is now turning out finger-on-the-pulse cooking in a French-accented contemporary idiom.

St Giles House Hotel ◎◎
stgileshousehotel.com
41–45 St Giles Street, NR2 1JR
01603 275180
You could punctuate your perusal of Norwich city centre's retail opportunities with a pit stop in St Giles House for coffee, a massage, cocktails or something more gastronomically satisfying in the Bistro. This grand Edwardian pile is worth a gander in its own right – beyond its magnificent pillared facade is a palatial interior of marble floors, oak panelling and elaborate plaster ceilings, all sharpened with a slick contemporary makeover.

The Sugar Hut ◎
leelathaicuisine.co.uk/thesugarhut
4 Opie Street, NR1 3DN
01603 766755
Leelanooch Hongmo's expanding empire now incorporates four restaurants – this venue not far from the castle, plus two others in Norwich and one in Coltishall. The ethos throughout combines the famed courtesy of the Thai service approach with some impeccably authentic cookery. A yellow and blue colour scheme offsets the black-clad staff to a tee, and the food is as bracing and vibrant as can be.

Tatlers ◎
tatlersrestaurant.co.uk
21 Tombland, NR3 1RF
01603 766670
Hard by the cathedral in the Tombland district of the city, this converted Victorian town house is the very image of a modern restaurant, its three interlinked rooms decked in today's shabby chic, with unclothed tables and bare floors offset by striking modern artworks in bold primary colours. Expansive bay windows and high ceilings give the place an airy feel, and in the evenings especially it's filled with the happy buzz of Norwich's gastro-cognoscenti. Fashion-conscious combinations of seasonal ingredients orientate the brasserie-style menus, where truffled goats' cheese might appear with beetroot,

watercress purée and red onion jelly, as an overture to pork mini-ribs with chips, garnished with rocket and pomegranate salad.

PLACES NEARBY

Less than a 10-minute drive away in the tiny hamlet of Lenwade you'll find the Dinosaur Adventure Park, while on the outskirts of Norwich, near the airport, you'll come across the village of Horsham St Faith. Around the late 1930s, the village was home to RAF Horsham St Faith and is today home to the City of Norwich Aviation Museum. At Frettenham, you'll find the Hillside Animal Sanctuary, while at Weston Longville the challenging course of the Weston Park Golf Club. Refreshments stops are plentiful in the villages that surround Norwich.

Dinosaur Adventure Park
dinosauradventure.co.uk
Weston Park, NR9 5JW
01603 876310 | Open Jan–mid-Mar and mid-Oct–Dec daily 9.30–4; mid-Mar–mid-Jul and mid-Sep–mid-Oct 9.30–5; mid-Jul–mid-Sep 9.30–6
Visitors can help the ranger 'Track: T-Rex' on the Dinosaur Trail and meet giants from the past including the new spinosaurus. Then they can make friends with animals, from hedgehogs to wallabies, or examine bugs and snakes in the secret animal garden. There is also an adventure play area.

City of Norwich Aviation Museum
cnam.co.uk
Old Norwich Road, NR10 3JF
01603 893080 | Open Apr–Oct Tue–Sat 10–5, Sun and Bank Holidays 12–5; Nov–Mar, Wed and Sat 10–4, Sun 11–3
A massive Avro Vulcan bomber, veteran of the Falklands conflict, dominates the collection of military and civilian aircraft at this museum. There are several displays relating to the aeronautical history of Norfolk, including some on the role played by Norfolk-based RAF and USAAF planes during World War II, and a section dedicated to the operations of RAF Bomber Command's 100 Group. A Nimrod shows the development of electronic warfare into the 21st century.

Hillside Animal Sanctuary
hillside.org.uk
Hill Top Farm, Hall Lane, Frettenham, NR12 7LT
01603 736200 | Open Apr–May and Sep–Oct Sun–Thu 10–5; Jun–Aug Sun–Fri 10–5
You can come and see the heavy horses, ponies and donkeys as well as sheep, pigs, rabbits, ducks, hens, goats and many more rescued animals in their home in the beautiful north Norfolk countryside. The Hillside Animal Sanctuary has its own museum where you can relive the farming days of

yesteryear surrounded by an extensive collection of carts, wagons and farm machinery.

Weston Park Golf Club
weston-park.co.uk
Weston Longville, NR9 5JW
01603 872363 | Open daily including Bank Holidays
A challenging course set in 200-acres of magnificent, mature woodland and parkland.

The Lavender House ◎◎
thelavenderhouse.co.uk
39 The Street, Brundell, NR13 5AA
01603 712215
The exterior may be an archetypally English thatched 16th-century cottage, but the interior of Lavender House has been reworked with a pared-back modern look involving exposed brickwork, modern art, high-backed leather chairs and crisp linen-clad tables beneath its head-skimming oak-beamed ceilings. Chef-proprietor Richard Hughes is the driving force in the kitchen turning out what he defines as 'modern Norfolk' cuisine. This translates as plenty of local produce delivered in flavour-driven dishes.

Park Farm Hotel ◎
parkfarm-hotel.co.uk
Hethersett, NR9 3DL
01603 810264
The family-run hotel has been modified over the past half-century from a rather grand Georgian farmhouse into a modern spa hotel, still surrounded by 200 acres of open countryside not far from Norwich. A smart orangery-style restaurant overlooking the gardens is where the main dining action goes on, in an atmosphere of bright informality, enhanced by boldly coloured paintings. The kitchen does simple things extremely well, turning out a decent niçoise salad followed perhaps by five-spice pork belly, slow-roasted and served with chilli and soy egg noodles with stir-fried veg, or skate with wild mushrooms in red wine jus. The tiramisù is reassuringly doused in espresso and Tia Maria for a very moreish finish.

The Parson Woodforde
theparsonwoodforde.com
Church Street, Weston Longville, NR9 5JU | 01603 881675
Just a short drive from Norwich, in the village of Weston Longville, this pub started life as the Five Ringers back in 1845. Now it's a free house with a great selection of real ales and a restaurant. A range of local cask ales are on offer alongside a menu that showcases fantastic Norfolk produce in dishes such as a duo of braised lamb shank with a fruit terrine and horseradish mash with thyme.

Stower Grange ◎
stowergrange.co.uk
40 School Road, Drayton, NR8 6EF | 01603 860210
The creeper-covered former rectory a few miles outside

Norwich makes a relaxing rural retreat, and is decorated in classic country-house style, with a dining room done in restful pastel shades looking out through floor-to-ceiling windows onto the well-tended gardens. Menus offer a broad range of choice, from the Oriental mash-up that is Thai-spiced duck with mango and chilli chutney and duck wonton, to mains such as slow-cooked belly of Blythburgh pork with sweet potato fondant, spiced chick peas and preserved lemon purée, or roast hake with braised lentils, salsa verde and wilted spinach. It's good to see sharper flavours being celebrated in desserts like lemon sponge with lemon curd sauce and gooseberry ice cream.

Thailand Restaurant
thailandrestaurantnorwich.co.uk
9 Ring Road, Thorpe St Andrew, NR7 0XJ | 01603 700444
The name tells you all you need to know about the cultural orientation of this abidingly popular restaurant on the outskirts of Norwich (booking seems essential), with traditionally dressed staff serving a repertoire of classic dishes. The cooking is vibrantly and accurately seasoned and timed, and carefully presented.

10 non-fiction reads

- *George Crabbe: Selected Poems*, Penguin Classics
- *John Constable: Oil Sketches from the Victoria and Albert Museum* by Mark Evans, Victoria and Albert Museum
- *Constable* by Jonathan Clarkson, Phaidon Press
- *Henry Blogg of Cromer – The Greatest of the Lifeboatmen* by Cyril Jolly, Poppyland Publishing
- *The Anglo-Saxons* by James Campbell, Penguin Books
- *Lords and Communities in Early Medieval East Anglia* by Andrew Wareham, Boydell Press
- *Hidden Places of East Anglia* by Barbara Vesey, Travel Publishing
- *Military Airfields of Britain: East Anglia, Norfolk and Suffolk* by Ken Delve, The Crowood Press
- *East Anglia and its North Sea World in the Middle Ages* by David Bates and Robert Liddiard
- *Suffolk Airfields in the Second World War* by Graham Smith, Countryside Books

▲ Orford Castle

Orford

Orford is one of the oldest settlements on the River Alde and has a beautiful 12th-century castle built by Henry II to prove it. The castle is owned by English Heritage and is splendidly preserved, especially its unusual polygonal three-turreted castle keep which has survived almost intact and which has a spiral staircase inside each of the three immense towers. The details of the castle's construction are extensively recorded in royal documents.

The castle has a maze of passageways and small chambers to explore, with the Upper Hall housing the town's local history museum. As the story goes, the king had the castle built in 1165 as a defence against invaders and to control his East Anglian fishing and shipping interests, which included the then thriving medieval port of Orford. Orford was a prosperous place, due to its fishing and shipbuilding industries, but like so many towns up and down this coastline, its waters silted up. Boats also increased in size and access to the river through the silted creeks and the shifting shingle bar at the tip of the spit, which is today known as Orford Ness, became more difficult. By 1673 the fishing trade was struggling and then went into decline. In 1722, Daniel Defoe (1660–1731), described it as 'once a good town, but now decayed'.

Orford today is full of character and has a real sense of community. You'll feel the welcome the moment you arrive. You can admire its pretty brick-and-timber cottages, visit the many traditional craft workshops, and see the small-scale smokehouses and oyster beds. Look out for Butley Creek. It's signposted, but if you have difficulty locating it any local will tell you where it is. Here, the beds yield oysters so fine they have long been a delicacy on the menus of Suffolk restaurants. There's a smokehouse, here, too, founded by Richard Pinney, of Pinney's of Orford, where fishermen smoke trout and mackerel, kippers, eels and salmon over whole oak logs.

Orford village is now separated from the sea by the 10-mile Orford Ness, Europe's largest vegetated shingle spit, which runs parallel to the shore and gets longer every year. Its salt marshes, shingle ridges and lagoons make it an important location for breeding and passage birds and rare plants. Orford Ness and Havergate Island, an RSPB bird reserve in the River Ore and Suffolk's only island (accessible by pre-booked boat trips only), form the Orfordness–Havergate National Nature Reserve. The area is home to many bird and wildlife species. In spring and summer it shelters breeding avocets and terns, while in autumn and winter large numbers of ducks, wigeon, pintail and teal can be seen. Brown hares are also abundant here and can be viewed at close range; they are at their most active in early spring.

The spit has played a significant part in Orford's history. Its isolation made Orford Ness a perfect place for military testing and it became a secret Ministry of Defence site; over 70 years, major advances were made in the fields of radar, military photography, bombs and atomic weapons. Orford Ness's combination of wilderness and strange, derelict structures is oddly compelling and is what makes the spit such a special place, particularly with the knowledge that it was here in the 1930s, along with Bawdsey Manor near Felixstowe, that Sir

Robert Watson-Watt and a small team of scientists took the first steps in the development of the air-defence system, which became known as radar. Without the work carried out at Orford Ness, the outcome of the Battle of Britain and the whole course of World War II might have been very different.

You can cross over to Orford Ness by ferry from Orford Quay, and then orient yourself by the former telephone exchange. Take a look inside the building as there's a display that tells the history of Orford Ness and a large aerial photograph of the shingle spit.

Behind the building is an observation platform with views over the Stony Ditch creek and the strange pagoda-type structures of the Atomic Weapons Research Establishment (AWRE), which operated here at the height of the Cold War. A large grey building to the north, known as Cobra Mist, was a top-secret Anglo-American satellite research base alleged to have been involved in tracking UFOs. It now houses transmitters for the BBC World Service, which also uses the tall radio masts beyond.

The pagodas of Orford Ness, which dominate the skyline along with Orford's castle and its red-and-white lighthouse, are a chilling reminder of war. Their distinctive design was to contain any accidental explosions. Today, this is a quiet place. The buildings remain as permanent reminders of another age, and barn owls nest in the abandoned barracks. The National Trust took it over in 1993.

▾ The Oysterage, Orford

TAKE IN SOME HISTORY

Orford Castle

english-heritage.org.uk
IP12 2ND | 01394 450472
Open Mar–Nov daily 10–5, including Easter; Nov–Dec Sat–Sun 10–4; Jan–Mar Sat–Sun 10–4 (opening times can vary)

Dating from the 12th century, and remarkably well preserved, Orford Castle is a must-see attraction when exploring the Suffolk coast. Its rooms offer a real sense of what day-to-day life must have been like in a castle in medieval England.

Inside, there's a maze of passages that lead to the kitchen, a small chapel and bed chambers built within the turrets. You can explore the lower and upper halls with their displays of medieval seals, coins and regalia, and climb right up to the roof where there are fabulous views seaward to Orford Ness.

In the basement of the castle you can see a well, which would have been a vital source of water for its residents, including Henry II who had the castle built in 1165.

As the story goes, when Henry II came to the throne in 1154 he inherited a troubled kingdom from King Stephen. The barons, keen to accrue personal power, had manipulated tensions between Stephen and his rival for the throne, Matilda (Henry's mother). Hugh Bigod, Earl of Norfolk, was one such baron who had immense influence in East Anglia and owned most of its castles. In order to assert his authority, Henry II took castles belonging to Bigod and built Orford Castle to protect Orford's prosperous harbour.

Orford Castle was completed in two years, and comprised an unusual 21-sided keep surrounded by walls and defensive towers. Today, only the keep survives, but it is one of the most remarkable in England due to its design. It rises to some 90ft in height and has five storeys. If you stand outside and look up at its mighty creamy-grey walls, you can get a sense of how formidable this castle once was to potential invaders.

GET OUTDOORS

Orford Ness National Nature Reserve

nationaltrust.org.uk/orfordness
IP12 2NU | 01728 648024
Open Jul–Sep, access by National Trust ferry (sailings subject to weather, check website for times)

You can take the National Trust ferry across to visit some of the long-abandoned buildings in the Orford Ness National Nature Reserve and learn more about when this remote area was a secret Ministry of Defence site. A flat wilderness of salt marshes, shingle ridges and quiet creeks, Orford Ness is an important breeding ground for birds and other wildlife species, as well as home to a large number of rare plants. If you are lucky you may catch sight of a brown hare. In spring and summer look out for avocets and terns, and in autumn and winter ducks, wigeon, pintail and teal.

EAT AND DRINK

The Crown and Castle ❁❁

crownandcastle.co.uk

IP12 2LJ | 01394 450205

This award-winning restaurant and hotel stands on the site of an inn apparently built into the walls of Orford Castle eight centuries ago. Today, it is separated from the castle by a little lane. It's co-owned by Ruth Watson, television's hotel inspector and a renowned chef, so you can be sure it's a good bet for a meal or an overnight stay. The cosy, yet elegant Trinity Restaurant, complete with beams, unclothed wooden tables and comfortable burgundy-velvet cushioned chairs and benches, serves top quality food. The place is still an inn popular with the locals as well as being something of a foodie destination, with the daily-changing, Italian-accented menu majoring on modern, unpretentious and flavour-driven dishes that showcase the best the local area has to offer.

Oxborough

A wonderful detour when visiting towns such as Swaffham is Oxburgh Hall, the magnificent ancestral home of local barons the Bedingfelds in the village of Oxborough. As you follow the signs for the hall, look out for the remains of Oxborough's Church of St John, famous for housing in its surviving chapel two elaborate terracotta tombs of the Bedingfeld family.

Oxborough is also where a massive Bronze Age ceremonial dagger was unearthed in 1988. It is one of only five oversized daggers, or dirks, known to exist in Europe, and they are so similar that they could well have been made by the same person. It dates from *c.*1300–1400 BC and is so large (nearly 28 inches long) and heavy that there is doubt it was ever used as a dagger. The Oxborough Dirk is now on display in the British Museum in London.

TAKE IN SOME HISTORY

Oxburgh Hall

nationaltrust.org.uk

Oxborough, Nr Swaffham, PE33 9PS | 01366 328258 | Open house Mar–Nov, Sat–Wed 11–5; gardens Jan–Dec Sat–Wed 11–5

Oxburgh Hall is a glorious place to visit. It's a remarkably handsome house with a high gatehouse and surrounded by a wide moat. The outstanding feature of this 15th-century building is its 80-foot-high Tudor gatehouse, which has remained unaltered throughout the centuries. You can visit grand rooms, including the King's Room where Henry VII is said to have stayed in 1487, before climbing to the top for panoramic views. You can even crawl inside a genuine 16th-century priests' hole.

On display are many priceless treasures; in particular, rare needlework by Mary Queen of Scots and Bess of Hardwick. Outside, a parterre garden of French design complements the wide moat. Built by Sir Edmund Bedingfeld, a baron of Norfolk, in 1482 as a family home, Oxburgh Hall is now managed by the National Trust. Members of the family still live here today.

10 top delicacies

- Adnams Ales
- Brancaster mussels
- Colman's Mustard
- Cromer crab
- Nelson slices
- Norfolk ginger biscuits
- Orford oysters
- Samphire
- 'Stewkey blue' cockles
- Suffolk Gold cheese

Potter Heigham

Potter Heigham is a village standing in one of the most idyllic areas of Norfolk, the gateway to the Upper Thurne and focal point of the northerly Broads. It takes its name from a pottery that once stood here and the Saxon lord, Heacham, who founded the settlement. Potter Heigham is a popular and busy water resort, with a pretty medieval bridge over the River Thurne that runs through the village. The bridge dates from around 1385 and is regarded by experienced boatmen to be the most difficult to negotiate anywhere on the Broads. Its opening is so small that only cruisers can pass under it at low water.

If you enjoy walking, the long-distance footpath between Cromer and Great Yarmouth, known as Weavers' Way, passes right the village. Nearby is the beautifully preserved Church of St Nicholas. Its round tower dates from the 12th century, while part of its main structure dates from the 1300s.

Hickling Broad, the largest and wildest of the Norfolk Broads – used as a seaplane base during World War I – can be found at Potter Heigham. There's an abundance of nature trails and boardwalks around here, plus lots of sailing opportunities.

Birders will find equal pleasure in nearby Horsey Mere, a large triangular-shaped broad, with a nature reserve on the northern bank. The Ludham and Potter Heigham Marshes and the Heigham Holmes nature reserves are here too, though access is limited. You should be able to catch sight of marshland birds such as oystercatcher and snipe, and perhaps even the rare Norfolk hawker dragonfly was rare here.

Ranworth

Ranworth is one of the most picturesque villages in the Broads. A delightful place, it is located on the edge of Ranworth Broad, on Malthouse Broad, so called because of the old malt houses nearby. Ranworth Broad is a nature reserve divided from Malthouse Broad by a thick bank. The village itself is dominated by the 14th-century church, St Helen's, known as the 'Cathedral of the Broads' owing to its grandeur and height. The view from the tower repays the long climb up and is one of the finest in the area, extending over the gardens of the village to the Malthouse and Ranworth Broads, towards the dark-green wet woodlands of Ranworth Marshes, and the silvery, winding course of the Bure. The church itself – thatched until a fire in 1963 – contains one of the finest and best-preserved painted rood screens in the country and an illuminated songbook, both dating from the 15th century.

With ghostly monks and sightings of the devil carrying the spirit of a local military man on horseback, Ranworth lays claim to being the most haunted village on the Broads.

The ghost of a traitorous monk is also said to haunt St Benet's Abbey, a short way across the marshes and the River Bure. In the days immediately following the Norman Conquest, the monk betrayed his brethren to the soldiers of William the Conqueror in return for being made abbot. True to their word, the Normans appointed him abbot for life, then promptly nailed him to the abbey doors and skinned him alive as reward for his treachery. The Normans had no love for traitors, even Saxon ones. Today, the abbey is in ruins, but it remains a distinctive sight, with a windmill built into the walls of the gatehouse.

See **The Norfolk Broads,** page 203

GET OUTDOORS

Broadlands Wildlife Centre
www.norfolkwildlifetrust.org.uk
Ranworth Broad, NR13 6HY
01603 625540 | Open daily from 10 (closing times vary)

From Ranworth, the Broadlands Wildlife Centre can be reached along a nature trail through woods and marshes. The centre is housed in an attractive building which has a Norfolk reed-thatched roof and floats on pontoons on the edge of Ranworth Broad, giving superb views of the boat-free water. The upper gallery is a good place from which to observe the amazing diversity of wildlife on the Broads.

PLACES NEARBY

Visit the pretty villages of Hoveton (see page 160) and Wroxham (see page 284), both a short drive away.

Reedham

see **Lowestoft**, page 193

▼ Ranworth Broad

Sandringham

Sandringham is the Norfolk country retreat of Queen Elizabeth II, and stands in glorious countryside between King's Lynn and Hunstanton. The house was built in 1870 for the Prince and Princess of Wales, who later became King Edward VII and Queen Alexandra, and stands in formal grounds full to bursting with shrubs and trees. Along with the house and gardens, you can visit the museum, a visitor centre and the parish church attended by the Royal family when they're in Norfolk.

▼ Sandringham House

TAKE IN SOME HISTORY

Sandringham House

sandringhamestate.co.uk
PE35 6EN | 01485 545408
Open Apr–Jul and Aug–Sep daily 11–4.45; Oct–Nov 11–4

The sumptuous neo-Jacobean house has been handed down through the generations and is now a favourite holiday home of the Queen and her family. The main ground-floor rooms used by the royal family when in residence are open for the public to view. You can see the elaborate decor as it looked in Edwardian times, and personal items collected by members of the family over many decades.

VISIT THE MUSEUM

Sandringham House Museum

Open Apr–Jul and Aug–Sep daily 11–5; Oct–Nov 11–4

Sandringham's museum is housed in the former coach houses and stables block, and contains fascinating displays of royal memorabilia. A highlight, especially for motor enthusiasts, has to be the royal collection that includes the first car ever owned by a member of the monarchy, a 1900 Daimler Phaeton. There's a mighty fire engine too, a Merryweather from 1939, which was used by the estate's own fire brigade. Elsewhere, there are displays of personal items, such as gifts given to the Queen on state visits abroad, and Arts and Crafts tiles and plaques once used in the estate's dairy.

GO ROUND THE GARDENS

Sandringham House Gardens

Open Apr–Jul and Aug–Sep daily 10.30–5; Oct–Nov 10.30–4

Sixty acres of glorious grounds surround the house and offer beauty and colour throughout the seasons. In Edwardian times the gardens were laid out in a formal manner as was fashionable then; in more recent times this layout has been complemented with areas of lawns bordered by magnificent trees. In addition to the gardens, a further 600-acre country park surrounds the house. It is dotted with cottages and contains the visitor centre from where you can arrange a tractor tour of the park. There's information, too, on nature trails that criss-cross the park, a sculpture trail and a scenic drive. If shrubs and flowers are your passion, you'll love the plant centre.

SEE A LOCAL CHURCH

Church of St Mary Magdalene

Open Mar–Jul and Aug–Sep Mon–Sat 11–5, Sun 1–5; Oct–Nov Mon–Sat 11–4, Sun 1–4 (open only for services in winter)

St Mary Magdalene is the parish church of Sandringham village attended by the royal family. In its present form, the beautiful carrstone church dates back to the 1500s. You can see the silver altar, silver pulpit and 17th-century Spanish processional cross presented to Queen Alexandra, a 9th-century Greek font and priceless stained-glass windows.

Saxmundham

Saxmundham conjures up images of pretty Suffolk pink-and-pale-yellow-washed timber-framed cottages lining a bustling market place. In reality, Sax, as it's affectionately known by locals, is exactly that, albeit now surrounded by Victorian and more modern development.

This historic market town was mentioned in the Domesday Book of 1086, and achieved its market charter somewhere around 1272. It was once an important communications link between London and Great Yarmouth, and developed with the coming of the railways in the 19th century. Better communications brought industry and the need for housing. Saxmundham grew at a fast pace in Victorian times. Rows of small cottages and grand 19th-century statements of wealth were built, and can still be seen today.

Not far from Saxmundham, which is at the centre of the unspoiled Suffolk Heritage Coast, is Minsmere, one of the RSPB's most famous nature reserves. Here, you can see thousands of varieties of migrant and wading birds through the course of a year. For birders, Minsmere is a corner of heaven. It has been a reserve for over 50 years and pioneered the use of observation hides and management of wetland areas.

GET OUTDOORS

Minsmere RSPB Nature Reserve

rspb.org.uk

IP17 3BY | 01728 648281

Open daily dawn to dusk, visitor centre Feb–Oct 9–5; Nov–Jan 9–4

Set on the beautiful Suffolk coast between Southwold and Aldeburgh, the Minsmere reserve offers an enjoyable day out for all. Nature trails take you through a variety of habitats to the excellent hides. Spring is a time for birdsong, including nightingales and booming bitterns. In summer, you can watch breeding avocets and marsh harriers. Autumn is excellent for migrants, and in winter hundreds of wildfowl visit the reserve. Look out for otters and red deer.

The visitor centre has a well-stocked shop and licensed tea room, and you can find out more about the reserve. There is a programme of events throughout the year, including several for children and families. Self-guided activity booklets help families make the most of their visit.

EAT AND DRINK

Sibton White Horse Inn

sibtonwhitehorseinn.co.uk

Halesworth Road, Sibton, IP17 2JJ

01728 660337

There's not a pool table or bleeping one-armed bandit in sight at the White Horse, a textbook real pub in the quiet Suffolk village of Sibton, just a couple of miles or so from

Saxmundham. The food may be great, but the place hasn't gone all gastro. First and foremost it is the village inn where locals pop in for a pint and a chat. The setting is pure Tudor, as its raised gallery, blackened beams, huge inglenooks and ancient floors of recycled Roman tiles all attest. The kitchen deals in unpretentious modern dishes created with a passion that hauls in fish from the nearby Suffolk coast, and meat and game from local farms.

Saxtead Green

see **Framlingham**, page 136

Saxthorpe

see **Holt**, page 156

Sheringham

Sheringham is perched on the 'top' of Norfolk, right on the coast, and has the look of a much-loved seaside resort. The Victorian houses, mostly made of flint, lining the esplanade, the manicured gardens and the beach – complemented by the cries of seagulls as the small fleet of fishing boats unload their catch on the quayside – provide a classic scene.

Like many coastal towns in Norfolk, Sheringham grew wealthy because of fish. In its heyday, the town was a bustling place with several hundred boats providing southern England with crabs and lobsters. A good railway link to London meant the seafood could be easily transported to market. There're not so many fishing boats nowadays, but its seafood is still sought after and is a highlight on many a Norfolk restaurant's menu.

Sheringham has all the amenities, including a theatre, you would expect of a town with a modern community, its numbers bolstered by the visitors who flock here in summer. There's a super museum dedicated to the sea, steam trains on the Poppy Line and, in Upper Sheringham, the National Trust's Sheringham Park. Look out for nearby All Saints' Church. It has many fittings from the 15th century, including a well-preserved rood screen and bench ends, with quirky carvings including a baby in a shroud, a monkey and a mermaid.

Book lovers can delight in the presence of Peter's Bookshop, located on St Peter's Road (just round the corner from Sheringham Station). This antiquarian and secondhand wonderland is one of the best bookshops in East Anglia and it's very unlikely that you'll come away without a purchase.

VISIT THE MUSEUM

The Mo

sheringhammuseum.co.uk
Lifeboat Plain, NR26 8BG
01263 824482 | Open Mar–May and Oct–Nov Tue–Sat 10–4, Sun 12–4; Jun–Sep Mon–Sat 10–4, Sun 12–4

The Mo, Sheringham Museum, has a collection of lifeboats, fishing boats and seafaring memorabilia which are displayed in the Boat Hall in the ground floor galleries, plus there's a chance to experience a replica fisherman's cottage. The other galleries feature a range of changing displays as well as local history. A viewing tower provides fabulous views over the sea and town.

GO ROUND THE GARDENS

Sheringham Park

nationaltrust.org.uk/sheringham
Wood Farm, Upper Sheringham, NR26 8TL | 01263 820550
Open dawn to dusk, visitor centre and cafe open Jan–mid-Mar and Nov–Dec Sat–Sun 11–4; mid-Mar–Aug daily 10–5; Sep–Oct Thu–Mon 10–5

Sheringham Park is best known for its outstanding displays of rhododendrons and azaleas from mid-May to June. There are more than 80 species of them. The park is one of the finest examples of landscape design in the country and surrounds Sheringham Hall, which is privately owned and occupied. Look out for the gazebo and viewing towers in the gardens, from which you can get stunning views of the Norfolk coast.

TAKE A TRAIN RIDE

North Norfolk Railway (The Poppy Line)

www.nnrailway.co.uk
Sheringham Station, NR26 8RA
01263 820800 | Open Feb–Mar and Nov weekends; Apr–Oct daily, plus Santa Specials in Dec

North Norfolk Railway is a full-sized heritage steam railway network running between Sheringham and Holt, with an intermediate station at Weybourne. The route, affectionately known as the Poppy Line, runs for over five miles along the coast, and up through the heathland. En route are three genuine Victorian stations. Sheringham Station features a Railway Shop as well as a museum siginal box. At Holt Station, the William Marriott Railway Museum (open Mar to Oct) is housed in a replica goods shed and tells the story of the Midland and Great Northern Joint Railway from its birth.

GO TO THE THEATRE

Sheringham Little Theatre

sheringhamlittletheatre.com
Station Road, NR26 8RE
01263 822347

The Sheringham Little Theatre has a programme of drama, film, music and comedies throughout the year, including its summer repertory season (one of the last surviving examples in the country) and Christmas panto. The work of local artists is a feature in the foyer and the theatre runs regular stage skills courses.

PLAY GOLF

Sheringham Golf Club
www.sheringhamgolfclub.co.uk
Weybourne Road, NR26 8HG
01263 823488 | Open daily including Bank Holidays
The course at the Sheringham Golf Club is laid out along a rolling, gorse-clad cliff top from where the sea is visible on every hole.

EAT AND DRINK

Dales Country House Hotel
www.mackenziehotels.com
Lodge Hill, NR26 8TJ
01263 824555
Handy for a stopover if you've been ogling the spectacular rhododendrons and azaleas in Sheringham Park gardens next door – and you'll find that the grounds of the Dales Country House Hotel are no slouch either. Just a mile or so inland from Sheringham and the coast, the stepped-gabled Victorian house has heaps of period charm, although the cooking in Upchers restaurant takes a rather more contemporary European view of things. With the briny so near, fish and seafood are always going to be a good idea.

PLACES NEARBY

Barely a 10-minute drive away in Weybourne is the fabulous Muckleburgh Military Collection centre, where you can see working tanks and military vehicles.

The Muckleburgh Military Collection
muckleburgh.co.uk
Weybourne, NR25 7EG
01263 588210 | Open half-term in Feb, Apr–Oct daily 10–5
The Muckleburgh Military Collection is the largest privately owned military centre of its kind in Norfolk. Exhibits include restored and working tanks, armoured cars, trucks and artillery of World War II, and equipment and weapons from the Falklands and the Gulf War. There are live tank demonstrations most days during the school holidays, and even the chance to hop aboard for a ride in military vehicles and visit the restored shore defence gun pits. The centre incorporates the Museum of the Suffolk and Norfolk Yeomanry. A cafe children's play area and picnic area are available.

Somerleyton

The village of Somerleyton is famous for being the home of English engineer Christopher Cockerell (1910–99) when he invented the hovercraft – a commemorative column stands in the village centre – and for supplying bricks from its small brickworks for the construction of Liverpool Street Station in London. But today it may be even more famous for the lavish pile that is Somerleyton Hall. The village was once part of the Somerleyton Hall estate and there are gorgeous red-brick, thatched cottages all grouped together around the green. The scene is pure chocolate-box pretty, which, indeed, was the original idea: the cottages and their layout were designed to resemble a traditional idyllic village street scene but in reality they were the homes of people who worked at the hall. The village is named after a Viking, Sumarlithi, a non-aggressive invader who arrived in the 10th century and found the Norfolk countryside much to his liking. There's a real sense of calm and tranquillity in the village, which lies close to the River Waveney, a few miles northwest of Lowestoft in Suffolk.

TAKE IN SOME HISTORY

Somerleyton Hall

somerleyton.co.uk

NR32 5QQ | 0871 222 4244

Open hall and gardens Apr–Sep Thu and Sun 10–5 (plus mid-Jul–mid-Sep Wed)

Somerleyton Hall is one of the most lavish country houses in East Anglia, indeed in England. Beautiful architecture and antique furniture, trademark Crossley carpets, a distinct and pleasing 'lived-in' feel, and a yew maze of mind-boggling ingenuity provides huge appeal.

You can enjoy 12 acres of gardens and parkland, which feature a walled garden full of ornate greenhouses, old species of flowers and trees and a small museum of gardening memorabilia. For the youngsters there's an adventure playground, a mini-farmyard and a Viking fort, as well as pony treks. Within the grounds Fritton Lake offers boat trips and fishing.

Highlights of the hall include the lavishly wood-panelled entrance hall, a beautiful ballroom with sculpted marble features, a dining room and the library.

The hall dates back to 1240 when nobleman Peter Fitzosbert had a manor house built on the site, and over the course of the next few centuries it grew in size. In 1604, the house was bought by entrepreneur John Wentworth who turned it into a beautiful Tudor-Jacobean mansion.

Over the years it has had many owners, including Sir Thomas Allin (1612–85), an admiral who fought in the English Civil War, and Sir Samuel Morton Peto, an MP and wealthy businessman. Peto adored Italian architecture and gardens, and over the course of the next few years had extensive work done at Somerleyton Hall to transform it into the Anglo-Italian masterpiece standing in immaculately sculpted gardens you can see today.

The estate was later owned by Sir Francis Crossley (1817–72), an MP and famous carpet manufacturer, who was created a baronet for services to industry. Today, the estate is owned and lived in by the fourth Baron Somerleyton, Hugh Crossley.

EAT AND DRINK

The Duke's Head

dukesheadsomerleyton. co.uk
Slug's Lane, NR32 5QR
01502 733931

Owned by and overlooking the Somerleyton Estate, this spruced-up pub stands tucked away down Slug's Lane on the edge of the village. Renowned locally for its imaginative seasonal menus, which champion game and meats reared on the estate farms, it thrives as a gastro-pub and the rambling and very relaxed bar and dining areas fill early with diners in the know. Bare boards, beams and crackling log fires set the informal scene for savouring game terrine; pork belly with cider cream sauce; and white chocolate cheesecake from the dinner menu. There's an equally inviting brunch menu . Savour the views over a pint of Woodforde's Wherry in the garden in summer.

Top 10 rainy day attractions

- **Anglesey Abbey**, Lode, page 99
- **The Caister Castle Car Collection**, Caister, page 84
- **The Forum**, Norwich, page 219
- **Houghton Hall**, Houghton, page 161
- **Hunstanton Sea Life Sanctuary**, Hunstanton, page 162
- **The Muckleburgh Military Collection**, Weybourne, page 241
- **North Norfolk Railway (The Poppy Line)**, Sheringham Station, page 240
- **Norwich Castle**, Norwich, page 215
- **Oliver Cromwell's House**, Ely, page 138
- **The Thursford Collection**, Thursford, page 131

South Walsham

see **Wroxham**, page 285

Southwold

One of the most picturesque towns on the Suffolk coast, Southwold has an ancient pedigree dating to before the Domesday Book of 1086. Packed with interest for both historians and visitors, it is a genteel sort of place, not unlike a typical seaside resort of the 1920s and 1930s, and a great place to stay when exploring the Suffolk coastline.

There's none of the brashness of Suffolk's Felixstowe (see page 131) or neighbouring Norfolk's Great Yarmouth (see page 139). If you visualise rows of brightly coloured beach huts sitting in line next to the sandy beach, a pier devoid of amusement arcades that for decades has received paddle steamers, and beer from the Adnams brewery, the town's largest employer, delivered to pubs on horse-drawn drays, then you have the character of Southwold.

Southwold, which was granted a market charter 1489, sits on a virtual island surrounded by marshes, creeks and reedbeds between the River Blyth and the sea. Today, it's a seaside resort with centuries-old cottages, elegant Georgian houses, small quiet streets and peaceful greenswards, but this hasn't always been the case. In Saxon times it was one of East Anglia's busiest ports, later becoming an important medieval fishing harbour and in Victorian times it was a popular, if understated, place for weekend excursions.

Like so many towns on the east coast, Southwold faced the problem of silting, which brought about a decline in the importance of the harbour and the town's prosperity. And like Great Yarmouth, Southwold had to reinvent itself. Its revival took the form of a flourishing yet refined resort when, in Victorian times, it became fashionable to enjoy the seaside.

Today, the pier dominates Southwold's seafront. It was originally built between 1899 and 1900 and, at over an eighth of a mile long, could easily accommodate the sea-going paddle steamers that plied along the coast in late Victorian times. Even today you can hop aboard a restored paddle steamer, the *Waverley*, which berths at the pier.The town itself is dominated by a 100-foot-tall lighthouse, built in 1890, which was taken out of service in the 1930s. Also worth a visit is the small but impressive museum, and the 500-year-old Grade I listed Church of St Edmund, King and Martyr, one of four churches in the town. Elsewhere, pink-and blue-washed cottages and Georgian town houses, including Buckenham House, one of East Anglia's finest modern art galleries, sit around greens that have been left undeveloped to serve as firebreaks – a disastrous fire in 1659 destroyed much of the town.

VISIT THE MUSEUM

Southwold Museum

southwoldmuseum.org
9–11 Victoria Street, IP18 6HZ
01502 726097 | Open Good Fri–Oct 2–4 (Aug 10.30–12)

You'll love this superb little museum housed in a Dutch-style cottage complete with beams and nooks, which tells the story of Southwold's maritime past, its local archaeology, geology and natural history. Old paintings and photographs, models and wildlife exhibits, sit very comfortably with 21st-century interactive displays.

▸ Southwold beach

ANGELLEY

Southwold Pier

www.southwoldpier.co.uk
North Parade, IP18 6BN | 01502 722105 | Open May–Sep daily from 9; Sep–May from 10 (closing times vary)

This historic pier has a small pavilion which houses a quirky collection of modern penny arcade-style machines by English inventor and cartoonist Tim Hunkin. It's known as the Under the Pier Show, and will make you roar with laughter. Look out for the Water Clock Tower and the Quantum Tunnelling Telescope too. The tower's message is about water recycling and the telescope about what could occur in the North Sea – both are hilarious fun.

The pier has a small interactive family amusement arcade too, which the pier owners are proud to say has no gambling machines, along with a handful of shops selling upmarket souvenirs and organic produce. The Seaweed and Salt has a great collection of textiles and ceramics, while the Curlew has a range of hand-carved wooden birds. The Treasure Chest has Southwold keepsakes, including ornaments and a delicious range of jams, chutneys and fudges. Buckets and Spades is a magnet for children with everything they'll need for the beach.The pier has three eateries that will surely tempt your tastebuds. The Beach Café serves the freshest fish and chips and is famed throughout East Anglia; the Clockhouse offers light meals; and the à la carte Boardwalk Restaurant (booking recommended) has a menu that offers a fusion of tastes.

Buckenham House
buckenhamgalleries.co.uk
81 High Street, IP18 6DS
01502 725418 | Open Mon–Tue and Fri–Sat 10–5, Sun 12–4, and Bank Holidays 10–5
Buckenham House is one of the most elegant Georgian houses in Southwold – and you'll find it's one of its most intriguing. Externally it looks every inch a Georgian town house, but step inside and you'll see it's pure 16th century. It was built by a wealthy Tudor merchant. Today, it houses the Buckenham Galleries, one of the finest contemporary art galleries in the region with an eclectic mix of paintings, ceramics, glass work and sculptures. Its permanent exhibition features the work of artists engaged by the gallery, with the emphasis on displaying different styles and mediums. You'll be sure to find something that catches your eye. In addition, it hosts further exhibitions by invited artists throughout the year. The gallery occupies the ground and first floor, and the cellar has been transformed into a cosy coffee house serving lavish cream cakes.

SEE A LOCAL CHURCH

St Edmund, King and Martyr Church
Bartholomew Green,
IP18 6JA | 01502 725424
Cathedral-like St Edmund's, which dates from the 15th century, is one of Suffolk's finest Perpendicular churches. It is one of a chain of such churches that once stretched the entire length of Suffolk's coastline from Southwold to Felixstowe when the county was one of the richest in England.

Made of flint that gives it a subtle grey hue and standing in richly-planted gardens, St Edmund's would have been at the heart of medieval village life. Markets and village fairs would have taken place on the green next to the church, and festivals held inside under its high vaulted ceiling. Indeed, festivals are still held here. The church's 100-foot-high tower can be seen for miles.

When you approach the church, take a minute to study its exterior walls. It has superb examples of flushwork (flat planes of flint and ashlar), which are particularly fine at the west end of the tower. Here, panels of flint framed in stone rise above the window to a Latin inscription that translates as 'St Edmund Pray for Us'. Above that is chequerwork panelling of flint and stone. The two-storey south porch is just as good, with 'M' for St Mary picked out on the lower panels. Above the door, framed by two windows, is a modern statue of St Edmund, shown bound in the ropes that tied him to a tree when he was killed by Danish archers. St Edmund died in November 869 at the hands of Dutch invaders set on conquering swathes of East Anglian soil.The interior of the church is packed with interest. Some of its artifacts date back to the 15th century. The medieval rood screen, separating the nave and aisles from the chancel and chapels, is magnificent. It retains its original colour – a riot of reds and yellows – with paintings depicting the 12 apostles.

The painted and gilded pulpit and font cover are successful 20th-century restorations and re-creations of medieval decorative woodwork. The font itself is original, but has clearly seen better times. It is said that during the time of Henry VIII when he was breaking away from the Catholic Church the font was attacked by his followers and still bears axe marks.

Near the tower, look out for a figure dressed in armour with a sword in one hand and an axe in the other. Next to him is a bell. He is affectionately known as Southwold Jack. The figure is incredibly rare and is believed to date from when the church was built. He has worn well. Today, as in medieval times, he is made to raise his axe, which rings the bell to tell the congregation the service is about to start.

TAKE TO THE WATER

Coastal Voyager

coastalvoyager.co.uk
Stage S35, Blackshore, 8 Southwold Harbour, IP18 6TA | 07887 525 082
Open daily 8–4 (times vary)

If you fancy taking to the water around Southwold, then head for the harbour and the *Coastal Voyager*. A rigid inflatable boat with a deep V hull, *Coastal Voyager* can accommodate 12 in wraparound-style seats. Its 'Sea Blast' trip is not for the faint-hearted, though. The journey is high speed and fast; you should expect to get splashed. It follows a course around Sole Bay. For a calmer trip, you can try the *Coastal Voyager*'s 'River Blyth' cruise, which follows a steady course along the river past Walberswick to Blythburgh. It lasts three hours, including a pub lunch stop. If you are lucky, you may catch sight of seals that can often be seen playing in these quiet river creeks.

Waverley

waverleyexcursions.co.uk
0845 130 4647

Periodically, the *Waverley*, a lovely old sea-going paddle steamer, which is the last such vessel in the world, plies a route to Southwold. You can't miss its glorious pillar box red funnels that tower over its varnished wooden deck. The paddle steamer dates from 1947. At the end of its working life in 1975, it was famously bought by the Paddle Steamer Preservation Society for just one pound, and was fully restored. It is now a popular tourist attraction with trips around the British Isles during the summer months. Once on board, you can see its massive 2,100 horsepower steam engine and its famous paddle wheels, while meeting the captain, chief officer, the

▲ Adnams sign on brewery, Southwold

bosun and their crew. The *Waverley* has a dining saloon for breakfast, light lunches or evening dinner, a bar and the Caledonia tea room for light bites, plus a souvenir shop.

WATCH A FILM

Electric Picture Palace
www.exploresouthwold.co.uk
Blackmill Road, IP18 6AQ
07815 769565 | Open box office Tue 10.30–12 | tours Sun 2.30 film times vary

See a film or take a tour of this super 68-seat cinema that has been designed to resemble an early 1900s picture house. The Electric Picture Palace was opened in 2002 by the actor Michael Palin. New and old classic films are shown in seasons – spring through to winter. If you are Southwold for only a short time, you can take out a membership for just one season. Take a minute to look at the decor, the beautiful organ in front of the screen and the seating in the stalls and circle; all are designed to be authentic to the period.

EAT AND DRINK

The Blyth Hotel
blythhotel.com
Station Road, IP18 6AY
01502 722632

The Blyth ticks all of the contemporary style-led boxes needed to figure among Southwold's on-trend addresses. The beach is just a five-minute stroll away, and stripped pine floors, chunky wooden tables and a switched-on family- and dog-friendly attitude lend the place an appropriately seasidey vibe. Adnams ales are almost de rigueur in the brewery's home manor, so have a pint in the relaxed bar, then move into the classier environs of the contemporary restaurant, for appealing modern ideas built on local materials.

The Crown ◎◎
adnams.co.uk
90 High Street, IP18 6DP
01502 722275
Right in the centre of town, this Adnams' brewery-owned pub, restaurant and wine bar within a hotel has something for everyone. It's informal and lively throughout, whether you're in the pub-brasserie or the restaurant with its scrubbed pine tables. The Adnams wine list is as good as you'd expect with a great selection by the glass. The young and enthusiastic kitchen team turn out some appealing modern, rustic British dishes, with plenty of Mediterranean sunshine along the way, and good quality ingredients at the heart of everything.

▾ Southwold lighthouse

Sutherland House ◎◎
sutherlandhouse.co.uk
56 High Street, IP18 6DN
01502 724544
Dating back to the 14th century, this Grade II listed building on Southwold High Street is packed full of fascinating period details – most of the wooden beams come from battleships used in the Battle of Sole Bay (1672), plus there are ornate ceilings, coving and open fireplaces. In contrast the furniture cuts a contemporary dash. Relaxed, casual service helps the buzzy feel, and locally landed fish are a big part of the draw. The menu stalks a modern British path, ingredients are sourced with care and food miles are listed alongside each dish.

Swan Hotel ◎◎
adnams.co.uk
High Street, Market Place,
IP18 6EG | 01502 722186
The Adnams empire has things pretty tied up in Southwold, where it is the seaside town's brewer, main publican, wine merchant and hotelier. Just in front of the brewery, the Swan – its handsome bay-fronted Victorian facade occupying pole position among the boutiques – is the centre of operations. Inside, its 17th-century origins are revealed: there are wall

panels, genuine 18th-century oil paintings and gilt chandeliers, but time has not stood still, so it is all leavened with smart contemporary styling. Afternoon tea in the drawing room is something of a local institution, but try not to spoil your appetite for dinner in the smart dining room. As one would hope from a set-up with its roots deep in the local area, the provenance of the raw materials is emphatically regional, and the cooking is confident, full-flavoured stuff.

PLACES NEARBY

Picturesque Aldeburgh, famous as the home of composer Benjamin Britten and for its world-class music festival, lies along the coast (see page 52), while the ancient market town of Saxmundham is a 10-minute drive away (see page 238). You can learn all about Dunwich, the town lost to the sea and take walks on Dunwich Heath (see page 120) or play golf at nearby Halesworth Golf Club. Walberswick is a compact village and harbour lying just across the River Blyth from Southwold. It is a popular lunch spot, with a handful of eateries, including the Anchor and the Bell Inn. Your children will love the chance to see camels and other pets at the Oasis Camel Centre in Linstead, near Halesworth. For refreshment stops, head for the Randolph in Reydon or the Westleton Crown in Westleton.

Halesworth Golf Club
www.halesworthgc.co.uk
Bramfield Road, IP19 9XA
01986 875567 | Open daily including Bank Holidays
Situated in the heart of the Suffolk countryside with fine views over the Blyth Valley, the courses of the Halesworth Golf Club offer golfers of all levels a challenge. The nine-hole valley course is particularly suitable for the less experienced golfer.

The Anchor ❀❀
anchoratwalberswick.com
Main Street, Walberswick, IP18 6UA | 01502 722112
Mark and Sophie Dorber are responsible for ensuring that this striking Arts and Crafts pub on the Suffolk coast is more than just a village local. Mark, who oversees the drinks side, used to run a highly rated London pub, while Sophie, who once provided the catering on *Star Wars* film sets, and whose family has long-standing local connections, runs the kitchen. The menu suggests a beer or wine to accompany each dish. The adjoining wildflower meadow is perfect for a picnic, especially during the mid-August beer festival.

The Bell Inn
bellinnwalberswick.co.uk
Ferry Road, Walberswick, IP18 6TN | 01502 723109
Six centuries old and going stronger than ever, the Bell stands close to the Southwold ferry, the Suffolk Coastal Path

and the marshes. Character is certainly not in short supply, with oak-beamed ceilings, hidden alcoves, worn flagstone floors and open fires. Firm favourites on the menu are Brancaster mussels in cider; whole grilled Dover sole with lemon and herb butter; Parmesan and garlic-crusted chicken schnitzel; and steak, mushroom and Adnams ale pie. At the back is a family-friendly garden overlooking a creek and the beach; here too is the Barn Café, offering everything for a picnic.

Oasis Camel Park
oasiscamelcentre.co.uk
Orchard Farm, Linstead, IP19 ODT
07836 734748 | Open Apr–Nov daily 10.30–5
Along with the camels, which you can ride, there are donkeys, llamas and deer and small pets such as rabbits and guinea pigs which are cared for at this popular centre. Children can enjoy cuddle sessions with some of the animals, plus there are paddock walks, crazy golf, a mini-maze and a play area.

The Randolph
therandolph.co.uk
Wangford Road, Reydon, IP18 6PZ | 01502 723603
Built in 1899 by the Adnams brewery, this hotel was named after Lord Randolph Churchill, Sir Winston's father and a keen huntsman like the brewery's directors. The light and airy lounge bar, with contemporary high-backed chairs and comfortable sofas, overlooks a sunny, enclosed garden.

The Westleton Crown ◎◎
westletoncrown.co.uk
The Street, Westleton, IP17 3AD
01728 648777
This textbook red-brick Suffolk coaching inn may date from the 12th century, but there's nothing archaic about the gastronomic side of the operation. The Crown is still an endearingly cosy local with well-kept real ales, a log fire and ancient beams in the bar, while the modern conservatory restaurant is done out in a clean-cut style with mismatched scrubbed wood tables and a wall of sliding glass doors that opens up to the lovely terraced gardens. The food also keeps its feet planted in the present with some cleverly honed modern ideas wrought from first-rate local produce.

Stalham

If you want to know more about the history of the Norfolk Broads then Stalham is an ideal place to head for. Situated in the heart of the Broadlands, this lovely market town can trace its history back before the Domesday Book, and still has its original name, derived from 'stal', a pool of water, and 'ham', a settlement or village. Here, the Museum of the Broads tells how people lived and worked in the region, and how weather and fashions have left their legacy.

Evidence suggests that Stalham has been a prosperous place over the centuries. It lies on the old Roman road that connected the main north Norfolk towns and would have been a popular staging post for traders heading to Caister, Great Yarmouth and Lowestoft.

Much building has taken place over the years, with the Church of St Mary in the 15th century and the Jacobean manor house, Stalham Hall, in the 17th century. Progress was steady rather than rapid, and by the 1880s the town, largely self-sufficient, still had a population of only 852. Its economy was mainly based on agriculture and was a base from which to export grain and livestock by road and river, and eventually by rail. The town is connected to the River Ant by a dyke, with its own staithe, where wherries and other trading vessels could moor, while the town grew more prosperous when the railway came to Norfolk.

Today, with its narrow high street and weekly market, Stalham retains a worldly 'otherness'; it's a gentle and agreeable place where times gone by linger around every corner. It is home to one of the principal holiday boat hirers in Norfolk, and is perfectly placed for exploring the Broads, especially Hickling and Barton Broads (see page 203). Look out for Sutton Mill, near Stalham. It is the tallest tower mill in the country with nine floors and a fascinating collection of old farm machinery and tools.

VISIT THE MUSEUM

Museum of the Broads

museumofthebroads.org.uk

The Staithe, NR12 9DA

01692 581681 | Open Apr–Nov daily 10.30–5

Located right on the waterside in Stalham Staithe, one of the

▸ Sutton Mill, near Stalham

prettiest areas of the Broadlands. It's housed in four buildings, including a former wherry shed and a boat store. Moored up alongside is the museum's own boat, on which you can take a short trip. Inside the museum you'll see displays of memorabilia that tell of how thatching, eel-catching and boat-building have played a major role in local people's lives, from Roman times right through to the present day.

Stowmarket

A small but rapidly growing Suffolk market town, Stowmarket lies on the River Gipping just a few miles west of Ipswich. Its historic market square – it was granted a market charter by Edward III in 1347 – is surrounded by elegant Georgian and Victorian red-brick houses, most now used as shops and offices, while shiny new homes have been built around the town in recent years.

Stowmarket, or simply Stow as some locals refer to it, was one of England's major producers of malt which, when the river was developed as a canal, could be easily transported to Ipswich, and onwards to London. The railway brought further prosperity. It still has the air of a prosperous place today.

When you first arrive in Stowmarket you'll notice its green spaces and its many trees. The English poet John Milton (1608–74), who spent a great deal of time in the town, is said to have planted many of the trees. In front of the town council offices, housed in a former vicarage dating from the 1500s, is a huge tree, dubbed Milton's Tree.

Your visit to Stowmarket could include the Museum of East Anglian Life, one of the largest such attractions in Suffolk, and a visit to the fascinating John Peel Centre for Creative Arts. The townspeople have a liking for festivals; look out for its programme of events that includes the StowFest music festival.

VISIT THE MUSEUM

Museum of East Anglian Life

eastanglianlife.org.uk

IP14 1DL | 01449 612229 | Open Mar–Nov Mon–Sat 10–5, Sun 11–5; Nov–Mar Tue–Sat 10–5

The Abbot's Hall estate goes back to medieval times and part of the key to its years of efficiency was having its own farm, Home Farm. In the 1960s, the then owners of the estate, Misses Vera and Ena Longe, donated 70 acres of farmland, Home Farm, the hall itself, and gardens to be used as a museum after local collectors had amassed a huge array of historic local memorabilia. The result is the Museum of East Anglian Life, which features farming as well as day-to-day living. This all-weather museum, which opened its doors in 1967, is set in an attractive river valley site. It has seemingly endless woodland and riverside nature trails for you to follow. There are reconstructed buildings, including a working watermill, a smithy, a windpump, and the Boby Building that houses craft workshops.

The refurbished Abbot's Hall is open as part of the museum, and houses exhibitions across eight rooms. There are displays on Victorian domestic life, gypsies, farming and industry. These include working steam traction engines, the only surviving pair of Burrell ploughing engines of 1879, and a Suffolk Punch horse.

CATCH A PERFORMANCE

John Peel Centre for Creative Arts

johnpeelcentreforcreativearts.co.uk
Church Walk, IP14 1ET
01449 774678

You can see drama, comedy and concerts by local and national bands, acoustic artists and sometimes even circus acts at this arts centre based in the middle of town. It is named after John Peel, the radio presenter and DJ, who lived near here. His family helped to develop the arts centre as a memorial to John Peel, who died in 2004.

▾ Museum of East Anglian Life

PLAY GOLF

Stowmarket Golf Club

club-noticeboard.co.uk
Lower Road, Onehouse, IP14 3DA
01449 736473 | Open daily including Bank Holidays

The parkland course of the Stowmarket Golf Club is set in rolling countryside with river in play on three holes. There are many mature trees and fine views of the Suffolk countryside. A bar and catering facilities offering tea, coffee and sandwiches are available

EAT AND DRINK

The Buxhall Crown

thebuxhallcrown.co.uk
Mill Road, Buxhall, IP14 3DW
01449 736521

This 17th-century building has two bars, one very much in keeping with its origins, the other, the Mill Bar, dating from Georgian times. Bar snacks, light lunches and four-course meals are catered for; breads, biscuits, ice creams and sorbets are all freshly made on the premises.

Sudbury

Sudbury is an attractive town that has its roots in Saxon England. Then it was a small hamlet, but grew in status when its market was founded in around 1009. Further prosperity came when its weaving and silk industries expanded. If you wander around Sudbury today, you'll notice period cottages and merchants' houses that date back 600 years or more, built when the town was flourishing. It still has the feel of a thriving place.

The town is best known as the birthplace of two great men: Simon Sudbury (*c*.1316–81) and Thomas Gainsborough

▼ Gainsborough's House

(1727–88). Simon Sudbury was the Archbishop of Canterbury from 1375 until his death, and the Lord Chancellor of England in 1381. He invented the poll tax, which made him an unpopular man. During the Peasants' Revolt, Sudbury was in the Tower of London when a band of locals, enraged by the tax, gained entry, dragged him to Tower Hill and beheaded him. His skull is in the Church of St Gregory's and can be viewed, should you wish to do so.

Thomas Gainsborough was born in a beautiful Georgian-fronted brick house near Market Hill, in the centre of the town. Known as Gainsborough's House, it has been restored and houses a museum dedicated to the 18th-century landscape and portrait painter. You can see a statue of the painter outside the landmark Church of St Peter's on Market Hill

VISIT THE MUSEUM AND GALLERY

Gainsborough's House
gainsborough.org
46 Gainsborough Street, CO10 2EU
01787 372958 | Open Mon–Sat 10–5
Birthplace of painter Thomas Gainsborough, the house is open as a museum. Here you can see the most complete collection of his work on display anywhere in the world, including his first known portraits of a boy and a girl, a miniature of his wife, and some 20 portraits of rich clergymen, politicians and landowners. A small cabinet holds Gainsborough's personal items, such as his pocket watch, snuff box, pipe stopper and paint scraper. The walled garden, where exhibitions of sculpture are held in summer, contains a 400-year-old mulberry tree. A varied programme of temporary exhibitions on British art takes place throughout the year.

Sudbury Heritage Museum
sudburysuffolk.co.uk
Gaol Lane, CO10 1TL
01787 371880 | Open Mon–Fri 9.30–4.30
The Sudbury Heritage Museum contains a fascinating exhibition of photographs and memorabilia that tells the history of the town from prehistoric and Saxon times to the present day.

GO TO THE THEATRE

The Quay Theatre
quaytheatre.org.uk
Quay Lane, CO10 2AN
01787 374745
Housed in a converted granary, the Quay Theatre hosts a variety of drama, music shows, films and comedies.

PLACES NEARBY

The gorgeous village of Long Melford with its grand country mansions, Kentwell Hall and Melford Hall, is barely a five-minute drive away (see page 187).

Suffolk Heritage Coast

Suffolk Heritage Coast
An area dotted with impossibly pretty towns and villages, and with craggy coastlines, reed-fringed creeks bursting with wildlife, brilliant sunsets and sweeping skies, the Suffolk Heritage Coast is one of the finest stretches of land in England.

Here, some of the last wild lowland heaths in England sweep down to salt marshes. Harbours, once bursting with life in Suffolk's herring and fishing heyday, several of them the scene of battles, are now some of East Anglia's most select holiday resorts.

A total of 35 miles of the Suffolk Heritage Coast comes under the protection of being a designated Area of Outstanding Natural Beauty (AONB). Sand marsh and mudflats, along with acres of heathland, reedbeds and hay meadows, dykes, creeks and pools, grazing marshes and a variety of woodlands, provide the perfect habitat for many species of plants, birds and wildlife. Habitats such as these are severely threatened in lowland Britain.

▼ The Dunwich coast

The coast in Suffolk is deeply indented by the slow-flowing estuaries of the rivers Blyth, Alde, Deben and Orwell, and the River Stour on the Suffolk–Essex border. They may look picturesque, but they present issues such as silting. The coast is bounded by crumbling low sea cliffs and tidal shingle spits, which fight a constant losing battle against the ever-encroaching North Sea. The AONB's protection is vital along this stretch of coastline. It was bestowed on the area in 1969 and covers 156 sq miles from Lowestoft in the north to Felixstowe in the south; it includes three National Nature Reserves and the Minsmere RSPB Reserve, along with the Suffolk Heritage Coast coastline itself.

Dingle Marshes, near Leiston (see page 56), is one of the coastal reserves. Jointly owned and managed by the RSPB and the Suffolk Wildlife Trust, the reserve attracts breeding and wintering wildfowl and waders, including avocets, white-fronted geese, lapwings and redshanks. Nearby, the Orfordness–Havergate National Nature Reserve (page 231) has one of the country's largest vegetated shingle spits, formed when the River Alde was at one time diverted, which supports a number of rare invertebrates, particularly spiders and beetles.

▲ Dunwich Heath

Inland, ancient heathlands of heather and bracken, known as sandlings, were plentiful in medieval times when they provided grazing for huge flocks of sheep. Today, they are rare. At Dunwich Heath (see page 120), one of a just a few such heaths in the country, rare species of heather, gorse and broom can be seen. From July to September, the heath is a patchwork of colour with pink and purple heather vying for attention with the coconut-scented golden gorse.

Picturesque towns and villages, many with towering church spires, punctuate the rolling countryside of the Suffolk Heritage Coast. Southwold, one of the prettiest towns today and still a genteel holiday resort, has seen industry and battles, and has contributed much to the coastline's formidable heritage (see page 243). A port since Saxon times, it enjoyed prosperity thanks to the herring industry. However, it was the herring trade that was partly instrumental in starting three vicious naval battles here: the first in 1653 off Orford Ness, the second in 1664 near Lowestoft, and the Battle of Sole Bay in 1672, which was to be the first battle of the Third Anglo-Dutch War. Southwold, like other towns along the Suffolk coast, and that of its neighbouring county Norfolk, suffered from silting. Its herring industry collapsed as a result, and its fortunes waned, but all that changed in Victorian times when the town reinvented itself as a seaside resort at a time when it became fashionable to take coastal jaunts.

Today, when you visit Southwold, you'll see the pier dominates its seafront. It was originally built between 1899

▲ Woodbridge

and 1900 when the town was flourishing and, at over an eighth of a mile long, could easily accommodate the sea-going paddle steamers that plied along the coast in late Victorian times. During World War II it was split in two as a precaution against German invasion, and a mighty gale in 1955 destroyed chunks of its structure. It remained in a sorry state until 2001 when it was rebuilt and restored. In fact, Southwold's pier is down in recent history as the first to be built in England since the 1950s.

Aldeburgh, like Southwold, is a delightful town of pink- and blue-washed cottages and Georgian town houses that enjoyed a buoyant fishing and shipbuilding industry (see page 243). It, too, brought tremendous prosperity to the town, until its decline due to silting. Aldeburgh managed to turn its own fortunes around, not so much by becoming a seaside resort, but more because it was the home of 20th-century composer Benjamin Britten (1913–76) who, through his music, and the foundation of the highly respected Aldeburgh Festival, gave the town an international musical reputation. Snape Maltings concert hall, housed in a converted maltings building amid reeds and marshes on the outskirts of Aldeburgh, hosts a regular programme of concerts as well as the Aldeburgh Festival, which features some of the world's finest musicians (see page 52). Further south is the village of Orford (see page 231), which is famous for its beautifully preserved castle built by Henry II when it, too, was a thriving port, and Orford Ness, which is Europe's largest vegetated shingle spit and home to many birds and other wildlife (see page 231).

▲ Sutton Hoo burial mounds

Sutton Hoo

A short distance from the town of Woodbridge, at Sutton Hoo, is the Anglo-Saxon royal burial site of King Raedwald, where a vast treasure was discovered in a huge ship grave. Sutton Hoo is arguably one of the most vital archaeological sites in Britain, looked on by many as the first chapter of English history. Lying on a low spur of land above the River Deben, several large mounds were excavated in 1939 and one revealed a warrior's helmet and shield and a collection of gold ornaments in the remains of an 89 foot ship. The significance of this important discovery is incalculable.

When, in the early 5th century, the Romans withdrew from Britain, it left the way open for people from Denmark, Germany and the lower Rhine to settle here, displacing and even enslaving the remnant Celtic and Roman people. These early settlers were the Anglo-Saxons, and their language formed the basis of the modern English spoken today. Two hundred years later, new kingdoms were formed: Suffolk and Norfolk becoming the Kingdom of the East Angles, and thereby setting the foundations of England as a country.

Anglo-Saxon custom decreed that important people were buried beneath mounds, often along with precious goods as a sign of their wealth and importance. The burial of an entire ship is unique to East Anglia and Scandinavia, and the burial mound at Sutton Hoo was a prominent and fitting memorial to a powerful leader.

The National Trust exhibition hall at Sutton Hoo houses a full-sized reconstruction of the buried chamber and relates the history of how its treasures lay undisturbed for over 1,300 years. The burial mounds form part of a much larger estate, across which there are lovely walks with estuary views, across heathland and along woodland trails.

See **Land of Anglo-Saxon Kings,** page 36

Sutton Hoo

nationaltrust.org.uk/suttonhoo
IP12 3DJ | 01394 389700
Open see website for details

Discovered in 1939 and described as 'page one of English history', Sutton Hoo is the site of one of the most important archaeological finds in Britain's history. It is the complete seventh-century ship burial site of an Anglo-Saxon king, which had been missed by grave-robbers, and lay undisturbed for 1,300 years.

You can see displays that tell how Anglo-Saxon nobles lived, and how they went to war and founded a new kingdom in East Anglia. The centre-piece is a full-sized replica of an Anglo-Saxon warrior king's burial chamber. The discoveries at Sutton Hoo changed forever our perceptions of the 'Dark' Ages by revealing a culture rich in craftsmanship, trade and legend. The National Trust site has a small restaurant here.

Swaffham

Swaffham is an elegant sort of place, largely thanks to it having been a fashionable centre for well-connected people to attend balls, soirées and concerts in Regency and late Victorian times. One of the places they met was at the handsome Assembly Rooms, now a school, built between 1776 and 1778, which you can see as you stroll around the lively town centre. Lord Nelson himself is said to have favoured Swaffham as a weekend retreat.

People gathered in Swaffham for 'the season', and so many clergymen ranked among their numbers that the Bishop of Norwich was reported as being concerned that they were neglecting their parishioners. One of the most prestigious events in the days of the Regency was the annual hare coursing hosted by the Swaffham Club. This was established by Lord Orford, a nephew of the writer Horace Walpole, in 1786. By this time, though, Swaffham was already a prosperous town. It had buoyant wool and sheep industries, and a large market place where traders would come from all over Suffolk. The market place is still going albeit with no livestock. Today, you can see the large and ornate buttercross that marks its heart.

While you're out and about around Swaffham, take a minute to look at its village sign. It shows the legendary Pedlar of Swaffham. As the story goes, a local man called John Chapman went to London and met a stranger on London Bridge. The stranger told him about a dream in which he had discovered treasure in a garden, and the garden he described was the peddler's. The peddler set off home with great haste, discovered the treasure and donated his money to the town's church. Legend has it that the fabulous Tudor windows of the north aisle of the Church of St Peter and St Paul were paid for by Chapman.

◂ Swaffham village sign

Another famous local was Howard Carter (1874–1939), the eminent Egyptologist who discovered Tutankhamun's tomb in the Valley of the Kings and who is rumoured to have died prematurely as the result of the boy-king's curse. An exhibition of Carter's work in Egypt can be seen in the town museum.

VISIT THE MUSEUM

Swaffham Museum
swaffhammuseum.co.uk
London Street, PE37 7DQ
01760 721230 | Open daily
You can read all about the history of Swaffham, along with seeing an excellent exhibition dedicated to Howard Carter and his discoveries in Egypt. There are various exhibitions on display throughout the year.

PLAY GOLF

Swaffham Golf Club
club-noticeboard.co.uk
Cley Road, PE37 8AE
01760 721621 | Open Mon–Fri
This heathland course and designated wildlife site lies in the heart of Breckland country. It has excellent drainage and good all-year golfing.

PLACES NEARBY

Castle Acre is a picturesque, once fortified village just four miles or so away and is best known for its small castle and the rather dramatic remains of Castle Acre Priory. You could visit the gorgeous 15th-century moated Oxburgh Hall in nearby Oxborough (see page 232). Head for Newton-by-Castle Acre for a traditional country pub lunch at the George and Dragon. Watton, a short drive away, is the gorgeous parkland Richmond Park Golf Club.

Castle Acre Priory and Castle
english-heritage.org.uk
Stocks Green, PE32 2XD
01760 755394 | Open Apr–Jun and Sep daily 10–5; Jul–Aug 10–6, Oct–Nov Thu–Mon 10–4; Nov–Mar Sat–Sun 10–4
A castle mound was raised here by the Earls of Surrey in about AD 1080, and the first stone castle was added around the 11th century. Enormous earthworks were dug to protect it – great grassy ditches and ramparts swing around the castle, enclosing a sizeable portion of land. If you look carefully at the ground in the enclosure you might see the regular lines and grooves in the grass that are the foundations of former castle buildings.

The George and Dragon
newtongeorge.co.uk
Swaffham Road, Newton by Castle Acre, PE32 2BX | 01760 755046
If, like George Orwell, you could design your perfect pub (his was the fictitious *Moon Under Water*), then maybe this 1740-built, part-brick, part-flint, village inn near Swaffham will fit your bill. There's nothing imaginary about it. For a start, all the real ales are East Anglian, including the specially brewed Newton Bitter. Locally sourced food is fresh and

cooked to order. Phone the pub for jazz and Irish ceilidh nights dates. All this, and three acres of garden.

Richmond Park Golf Club
www.richmondpark.co.uk
Saham Road, Watton, IP25 6EA
01953 881803 | Open daily including Bank Holidays
The compact parkland course has mature and young trees set around the Little Wissey River and is spread over 100 acres o countryside. The river and oth hazards create an interesting but not daunting challenge. Facilities include a practice area and putting green and a club house with two restauran (the ground floor Pavilion Restaurant has a good view of the course). The Pro Shop is open seven days a week.

Thetford

The market town of Thetford has gone down in history as bein the place where Boudicca, the Queen of the Iceni tribe who lived in Norfolk around 2,000 years ago, spent most of her tim In later years, the town was the home of many East Anglian monarchs. It was also a bishopric and had a thriving wool industry. In short, Thetford was a prosperous place and one of the most important in south Norfolk. Today, the town is a pleasing place surrounded by the great expanse of the Thetfor Forest, the largest lowland pine forest in the country. If you ca into the High Lodge Visitor Centre, you'll find out all you need to know about the forest, plus there's a playground for the children, cycle hire, walking trails leaflets and the Go Ape high wire adventure course.

TAKE IN SOME HISTORY

Thetford Priory
english-heritage.org.uk
0870 333 1181 | Open daily 8–4
The Priory of Our Lady of Thetford belonged to the Order of Cluny, and was founded in 1103 by Roger Bigod, an old soldier and friend of William the Conqueror. Here the dukes and earls of Norfolk would have been buried. The remains are dramatic. You can see the walls of the church and cloister, and an almost complete gatehouse. This site gives you a glimpse of medieval religious life before the Dissolution of the Monasteries.

VISIT THE MUSEUM

Ancient House Museum
museums.norfolk.gov.uk
21–23 White Hart Street, IP24 1AA| 01842 752599
Open Apr–Sep Tue–Sat 10–5; Oct–Mar Tue–Sat 10–4
Life in and around Thetford ha been traced back to Neolithic times. The town's long history

▸ Thetford Forest

is told in this excellent museum housed in an early Tudor timber-framed house with beautifully carved beamed ceilings. Brass-rubbing facilities are available and there is a small period garden re-created in the rear courtyard.

WALK THE HIGH ROPES

Go Ape! Thetford

goape.co.uk/sites/thetford
High Lodge Forest Centre, Santon Downham, Brandon, IP27 0AF
0845 643 9215 | Open Apr–Oct daily; Nov Sat–Sun

You can burn some energy at Go Ape! Thetford. Set in the heart of the forest, this course has around 30 miles of bike and walking trails from which to explore 50,000 acres of woodland. The mother of all courses features a long crossing, over 85 foot long from platform to platform. And there's all the other vital Go Ape! ingredients, including high and long zip wires. But the adventure does not need to stop here. You can get off the beaten track and enjoy the latest forest adventure with Forest Segway.

PLAY GOLF

Thetford Golf Club

thetfordgolfclub.co.uk
Brandon Road, IP24 3NE
01842 752169 | Open Mon, Wed–Fri after 10, Tue, Sat–Sun and Bank Holidays after 2

Thetford Golf Club's course has a good pedigree. It was laid out by the fine golfer CH Mayo, later altered by James Braid and then altered again by another famous course designer, Mackenzie Ross. It is a testing heathland course with a particularly stiff finish.

EAT AND DRINK

Angel Inn

angel-larling.co.uk
Larling, NR16 2QU
01953 717963

Run for more than 80 years by three generations of the Stammers family, this 17th-century former coaching inn on the edge of Breckland and Thetford Forest Park has a good local feel and offers visitors a warm welcome. In the heavily beamed public bar, a jukebox, dartboard and fruit machine add to the entertainment, while the oak-panelled lounge bar has dining tables with cushioned wheel-back chairs, a wood burner and a huge collection of water jugs. Five guest ales, including a mild, are served, as well as more than a hundred whiskies. Menus make good use of local ingredients, and include lighter snacks. Each August the Angel hosts Norfolk's largest outdoor beer festival, with over 100 real ales and ciders.

Crown Hotel

the-crown-hotel.co.uk
Crown Road, Mundford, IP26 5HQ | 01842 878233

Originally a hunting lodge, this historic hillside inn on the edge of Thetford Forest dates back to 1652. Traditional, home-cooked food is served in the bars and two restaurants; perhaps pan-fried supreme of salmon with warm cherry tomato and basil salad or Jimmy Butler's slow-roasted pork belly with apple brandy sauce, baked apple and dauphinoise potatoes. In addition to the real ales and wines, there is a choice of over 50 malt whiskies. Being on a hill, the garden reached from the first floor.

PLACES NEARBY

Just a couple miles away is the village of Euston, where you could spend a good day at Euston Hall, or visit Grimes Graves, the site of Neolithic mines, in nearby Lynford. In the village of Weeting, a short drive from Thetford, is the remains of Weeting Castle. For local produce, and much more, try the Elveden Estate.

Euston Hall

www.eustonhall.co.uk
IP24 2QP | 01842 766366
Open Jul–Aug on selected days only 2.30–5 (Euston Hall will be closed in 2014)

You can see a magnificent collection of 17th-century courtly paintings on a visit to Euston Hall. One-time owner Henry FitzRoy's origins were indisputably Stuart, and Stuart portraits fill every corner. There is a portrait of Charles I painted by Van Dyck, and another of Charles II by Lely.

The house was originally built between 1666 and 1670 for the Duke of Arlington, Charles II's Secretary of State. He made a splendid match for his daughter Isabella when she was only five years old, betrothing her to Henry FitzRoy, the illegitimate son of the king and his mistress Barbara Villiers. Henry FitzRoy was made the Duke of Grafton, and Euston Hall, which he inherited from Arlington, has been the family home of the Graftons ever since.

Euston Hall was probably one of the first English country houses to have the luxury of a mechanically pumped water supply. The diarist John Evelyn visited Euston in 1671 and commented on the 'pretty engine' that pumped an abundant supply of water from a nearby canal for all the house's needs, with enough left over to run the fountains and a corn mill.

Henry FitzRoy enjoyed his inheritance for only five years before he died. His son, the second Duke, then commissioned Matthew Brettingham to remodel the house. Brettingham decided to face all three wings with red brick, as well as building the stable block between 1750 and 55, and these buildings remained untouched until they were destroyed by fire.

In 1902 a great fire raged at Euston Hall. The south and west wings were gutted, destroying, among other priceless treasures, the 18th-century ceilings painted by Verrio. Only the north wing remained. The burned wings were quickly rebuilt, but were demolished in 1952 so that the hall that can be seen today dates mainly from the 1740s.

Grimes Graves

english-heritage.org.uk
Lynford, IP26 5DE | 0870 333 1181
Open Mar–Sep daily 10–5
These unique and remarkable neolithic flint mines are the earliest remaining major industrial site in Europe. Using antlers as picks, prehistoric miners sank shafts and tunnels deep into the ground following seams of flint. It is possible to descend by a series of ladders to the bottom of one of the shafts to see how flint was extracted. A small exhibition area gives the site's history.

Weeting Castle

english-heritage.org.uk
Weeting, IP27 0RQ | 0870 333 11
Open at any reasonable time
Weeting Castle is an interestir yet ruined 11th-century fortifi manor house, standing in a moated enclosure. You can see the remains of a three-storey cross-wing and a brick ice house.

Elveden Cafe Restaurant

elveden.com
London Road, Elveden.
IP24 3TQ | 01842 898068
You can buy all manner of loca produce, such as wines, meat, vegetables, cheeses and chutneys, or simply stop to enjoy dishes from the temptin menu in its restaurant, at the 10,000-acre Elveden Estate no far from Thetford Forest. Its

▾ Grimes Graves near Weeting

cafe-restaurant is a stylish place with a beamed vaulted ceiling and expansive alfresco dining area. There's always a barbecue filling the air with tempting aromas in the summer. Open for breakfast, lunch and afternoon tea, the wide-ranging menu takes in unfussy, well-made classics. Bread is made in house – and goes well with dipping oils and olives; then there are dishes like homemade pork pie or caramelised onion tart to start, followed by mains at their most simple, using beef or venison from the estate. The Elveden Estate acts as a food hub for local producers in a complex of shops created within converted red-brick farm buildings.

Thorpeness

The village of Thorpeness, near Aldeburgh in Suffolk, is largely the creation of one man, the Scottish barrister, architect and playwright Glencairn Stuart Ogilvie. He inherited the Ogilvie estate of *c*.6,000 acres on the death of his mother in 1908. The land had been amassed by his father Alexander who made his fortune designing railways across the world.

Glencairn Stuart Ogilvie aimed to transform the tiny fishing hamlet of Thorpeness and the countryside that surrounded it into an upmarket holiday village for the middle classes to enjoy wholesome family holidays. Along with a colonial-style country club, complete with verandah, golf course, swimming pool and tennis courts, Ogilvie constructed a slice of England – mock Tudor and Jacobean cottages, almshouses, a working windmill and many architectural follies, including the House in the Clouds. This cleverly designed water tower was disguised as a weatherboarded and tile-hung house, and has become the dominant feature of the Thorpeness skyline. From a distance it appears to be lodged in the trees.

The town's focal point is the Meare, a shallow artificial lake with islands and play houses themed around the story of *Peter Pan*. Ogilvie clearly drew his inspiration from his friendship with the author J M Barrie. Until the 1970s most of Thorpeness remained owned by the Ogilvie family. Today many of the buildings have been sympathetically refurbished and in August the Meare is the location for a regatta and firework display.

EAT AND DRINK

The Dolphin Inn

thorpenessdolphin.com
Peace Place, IP16 4NA
01728 454994
Open lunch and dinner

A stone's throw from the shingle of Suffolk's Heritage Coast and in a conservation area, this community-focused free house replaced a 1910 predecessor, destroyed by fire in 1995. At the bar are real ales from Adnams and Brandon, nearly 20 wines by the glass, and bourbons and single malts in abundance. Look forward to River Deben blue mussels with smoked bacon; oven-baked chicken breast with sweet potato mash; or wild mushroom with white wine and Parmesan risotto. After a bracing walk on the beach, sit beside the fire and tuck into one of their homemade pies; in summer barbecues are held in the huge garden.

Thorpeness Hotel

thorpeness.co.uk

Lakeside Avenue, IP16 4NH

01728 452176

The Thorpeness Hotel has a superb golf course designed in 1923 by James Braid with a wide variety of holes lined with heather, gorse and silver birch. Understated modern styling makes the hotel interiors look trim, and there are of course grand views of the fairways from the main restaurant, the covered patio bar and terrace.

▼ The House in the Clouds

Walsingham

Walsingham is a village of two halves, divided by the River Stiffkey. Little Walsingham is the newer area of the two, and it tends to get all the attention because of shrines dedicated to Our Lady of Walsingham, while Great Walsingham, the original village, is the smaller. Both have a long history of pilgrimage, said to date back to the 11th century, or even before, and both have a wealth of fabulous period buildings.

The original shrine to Our Lady of Walsingham was, according to legend, built in 1061 after a devout local noblewomen, Richeldis de Faverches, had a vision in which the Virgin Mary led her to Nazareth. Richeldis was shown the house where the Virgin Mary learned that she would become the mother of Jesus, and was told to build a replica of the holy house in Walsingham. The house became a place of pilgrimage; indeed, it was one of the most famous shrines in medieval Christendom. Walsingham grew in significance. The Augustinian Canons built a priory here in 1153 in recognition of its importance. This was all but destroyed during the reign of Henry VIII, but you can still see the hugely dramatic remains standing in peaceful gardens. The original shrine was also destroyed during the Reformation, but some years later a 700-year-old chapel, known as the Slipper Chapel, was restored, and so pilgrims returned once again to the village. In 1934 it was named the Roman Catholic National Shrine of Our Lady.

In more recent times an Anglican church was built, and also dedicated to Our Lady of Walsingham. It has become a place of pilgrimage for Anglicans.

Walsingham is served by the Wells and Walsingham Light Railway in summer (see page 277).

TAKE IN SOME HISTORY

Walsingham Abbey Grounds and Shirehall Museum

walsinghamabbey.com
Common Place, NR22 6BP
01328 820510 | Open Apr–Oct daily 11–4

In the grounds of Walsingham Abbey are the spectacular ruins of the original Augustinian priory built here in the 1100s. At the entrance to the grounds is the Shirehall Museum housed in what was once a pilgrims' hostel and then for 200 years a Georgian courthouse. Here, you can see displays on the history of Walsingham and many local artifacts, such as old photos, tools and religious items. The priory ruins and museum stand in 20 acres of tranquil and picturesque gardens, which are famous for their dramatic display of snowdrops in February, with access to woodland and river walks across the ancient parkland.

Special events, such as performances of Shakespeare are often held.

SEE SOME LOCAL CHURCHES

National Shrine of Our Lady of Walsingham

walsingham.org.uk
Slipper Chapel, NR22 6AL
01328 820495

The delightful Slipper Chapel was built in the mid-14th century and had fallen into disrepair until its restoration in 1896. You can see a statue of Our Lady of Walsingham, to whom the chapel is dedicated, along with windows depicting the annunciation. See the Cloister Garden with its holy water fountain, the Chapel of the Holy Spirit and the Chapel of Reconciliation. The shrine remains a place of pilgrimage for Roman Catholics from around the world.

The Shrine of Our Lady of Walsingham

walsinghamanglican.org.uk
2 Common Place, NR22 6EE
01328 820255

In the centre of Little Walsingham is the Shrine to Our Lady of Walsingham for the Anglican Church. It is a modern building believed to stand on the site of the original 11th-century priory and represents the house in Nazareth which was the scene of the annunication. You can see a beautiful image of Our Lady of Walsingham carved in 1922 from a seal of the priory, and a Holy Well.

St Peter, Great Walsingham

Great Walsingham is much smaller than its neighbour Little Walsingham, and is dominated by the Church of St Peter. It is a fine 14th-century building with a 15th-century porch. It has no chancel, giving it a somewhat curtailed appearance, but this does not detract from the beauty of the windows, among the best of their kind.

The church's special treasure is its 40 benches dating from the 15th century. These still stand on their original wooden sills, a most unusual survival. The carving on many of the benches is exceptional, especially those with latticework backs. Some have linenfold panelled backs, a further refinement of medieval seating. There are carvings of saints on some of the benches, and others have animals and imaginary creatures on them.

Weeting

see **Thetford**, page 270

Wells-next-the-Sea

If you want to blend in with the locals, refer to this pretty town simply as Wells. This is a working harbour town with a quayside full to bursting with colourful fishing boats and dock equipment, even though it is no longer beside the sea. In fact, Wells is a mile or so inland on a muddy creek created by silting over the centuries.

The quay is dominated by the six-storey 1904 granary building, now converted into holiday accommodation. Its roofed overhead gantry spans the road. Behind the quay are narrow streets of flint houses, while inland a little are elegant Georgian and Victorian buildings.

On the seafront, is a memorial that commemorates the 11 lifeboat men who were lost at sea in 1880. Close by is Ware Hall House, a 15th-century timber-framed building that originally stood in Ware, Hertfordshire, but when the council wanted to demolish it, it was taken apart and moved to Wells by lorries and rebuilt, timber by timber and brick by brick, almost singlehandedly over 23 years, by its elderly owner Miss May Savidge. After her death in 1993, the house was completed by her niece.

A high embankment, known as 'The Bank', was constructed by Lord Leicester of nearby Holkham Hall (see page 154) in 1859, to reclaim an area of salt marsh and to help preserve the

▼ Wells-next-the-Sea

harbour. It now provides a pleasant walk to the beaches, woods and caravan and camping site north of the town, with the seasonal option of a ride on the narrow-gauge railway running alongside.

The vast sands stretch west to one of Britain's largest coastal nature reserves at Holkham Gap and are backed by dense coastal pinewoods, dunes and a fine array of lovingly preserved beach huts.

Locals collect samphire from the mudflats and salt marsh between the tides in summer. This coastal delicacy, a fleshy green plant, can be pickled or served freshly boiled with butt or malt vinegar.

▾ Wells-next-the-Sea beach

TAKE A TRAIN RIDE

Wells and Walsingham Light Railway

NR23 1QB | 01328 711630
Open Good Fri–Oct, daily

The railway covers the four miles between Wells and the neighbouring village of Walsingham (see page 273), and is the longest ten-and-a-quarter inch gauge track in the world. The line passes through some very attractive countryside, particularly noted for its wild flowers and butterflies. This is the home of the unique Garratt steam locomotive specially built for this line; two Garratt locos are now in service. A former Great Eastern Railways signal box is used as a tearoom at Wells.

EAT AND DRINK

The Crown Hotel

crownhotelnorfolk.co.uk
The Buttlands, NR23 1EX
01328 710209

This 17th-century former coaching inn overlooks the tree-lined green known as the Buttlands. The Crown's striking contemporary decor blends effortlessly with its old-world charm, and beneath the bar's ancient beams East Anglian ales and Aspall Cyder are on tap. Whether you eat in the bar, more formally in the restaurant, in the cheerful Orangery, or outside with great views, the menus offer traditional favourites, modern British cuisine, and internationally influenced dishes.

The Globe Inn

globeatwells.co.uk
The Buttlands, NR23 1EU
01328 710206

The Globe is a short stroll from the town's bustling quay and overlooks the leafy village green. It has a warm, welcoming bar and comfortable restaurant, with a sunny courtyard for alfresco drinking and dining. The menus take full advantage of the abundance of local produce from both land and sea – such as tender asparagus in early summer and game from the Holkham Estate in winter.

Three Horseshoes

Warham All Saints, NR23 1NL
01328 710547

This gem of a pub first opened its doors in 1725. Its rambling old rooms, including a gas-lit main bar, are stone floored with scrubbed wooden tables. A grandfather clock ticks away in one corner, and a curious green-and-red dial in the ceiling turns out to be a rare example of Norfolk Twister, an ancient pub game. Vintage posters, clay pipes, photographs and memorabilia adorn the walls, while down a step are old one-arm bandits. Woodforde's Sundew and Nelson's Revenge are served from the cask through a hole in the bar wall. Homemade soups, pies and puddings dominate the menu and a no-chips policy applies. Outside is a beer garden and courtyard

PLACES NEARBY

For a bite to eat nearby, try the Chequers Inn in Binham, or the Stiffkey Red Lion.

Chequers Inn
Front Street, Binham,
NR21 0AL | 01328 830297
Just a few miles from Wells on the north Norfolk coast, the Chequers is home to the Front Street Brewery, but even though they brew their own beer they still have guest ales, an extensive range of foreign bottled beers and a connoisseur's selection of rare and vintage beers. The pub has been owned by a village charity since the 1640s, and was originally a trade hall. Stones from nearby Binham Priory were used in its construction.

The Stiffkey Red Lion
stiffkey.com
44 Wells Road, NR23 1AJ
01328 830552
Dating from the 17th century, this comfortable inn has been a house and even a doctor's surgery in the course of its long life. Located on the north Norfolk coast, it is now a popular bolt-hole for walkers and birders stepping off the nearby salt marshes. Grab an old pew by one of the four log fires and warm up over a glass of Nelson's Revenge and locally sourced seasonal dishes such as salmon and crab fishcakes with homemade tartare sauce, or home honey-roasted ham with egg and chips, followed by classic spotted dick for dessert. Children's meals are available.

Welney

see **Ely**, page 128

West Stow

see **Bury St Edmunds**, page 80

▲ Windmill at Wicken Fen

Weybourne

see **Sheringham**, page 241

Wicken Fen National Nature Reserve

nationaltrust.org.uk/wickenfen

Lode Lane, Wicken, Ely, CB7 5XP | 01353 720274 | Open daily 10–5

You will be amazed by the sheer size of the fabulous Wicken Fen National Nature Reserve, Britain's oldest wetlands park and home to more than 8,500 species of plants and wildlife. A network of raised boardwalks and grass droves take you through reedbeds and flowering meadows ablaze with colour so you can easily see all areas of the reserve and witness nature at its most natural. Wicken is a top site nationally for molluscs, aquatic beetles, rove beetles and caddis flies.

Wicken Fen is one of only four 'wild' fens which still survive in the Great Fen Basin. Its importance is demonstrated by the fact that it is not just a National Nature Reserve, but also a Site of Special Scientific Interest, a Special Area of Conservation and a Ramsar site (an international wetland designation).

The nature of the wetland has played an important role in the social and economic life of the area, providing materials for bedding and animal feed, fish and fowl for food, and peat for fuel. Reeds were used for thatching roofs and the sedge went into the making of the ridge along the top of the roofs.

As well as a source of building materials, the marshes also provided people with water and food – waterfowl, fish and eels. Then, as the necessity to keep cattle grew, the fens were drained to provide grazing marshes, a series of open fields laced by a network of dykes, and dotted with windpumps that provided the power to push the water along the dykes. In time, this became a unique landscape, threatened for a while in the 1970s, as a move to develop arable land gained sway, but finally brought within the embrace of a National Park, which now holds the responsibility for the management and protection of this priceless landscape heritage.

▼ Wicken Fen

In the words of the Norfolk naturalist, the late Ted Ellis, the Fens, and in particular the Broads, are 'a breathing space for the cure of souls'. But they are more than that: these sometimes intimate nooks and crannies of reed-fringed pools, sometimes sky-laden expanses of open appeal, are a corner of heaven set aside for lovers of enchantment and the English countryside.

Today, Wicken Fen is a surviving fragment of the wilderness that once covered East Anglia, and can be explored along traditional wide droves and lush green paths, giving access to hides, two of which are equipped for wheelchairs. There's a boardwalk nature trail or you can hire a cycle or take a boat along fenland waterways. Wicken Fen has its own cafe for a light meal – and a welcome break from exploring – and a shop where you can buy bird food.

PLACES NEARBY

A short drive away is the enchanting Anglesey Abbey, Garden and Lode Mill (see page 99), the exhilarating university town Cambridge (see page 88) and Grantchester (see page 137).

Woodbridge

The riverside town of Woodbridge is full of character and is one of Suffolk's most engaging places. It rises from the banks of the hugely picturesque River Deben and is a mix of enchanting Tudor timber-framed cottages, elegant Georgian houses and grand Regency mansions. At the heart of the historic town, you'll see the parish church of St Mary. In fact, you can hardly miss the church since its noble 108-foot-high tower of flint and stone dominates the skyline. It stands in a churchyard of fantastically tall trees and table tombs.

Close by you'll find the 16th-century Shire Hall, resplendent in red brick with a curly Dutch gable. Its first floor is home to a museum that tells the story of the Suffolk Punch, a rare breed of working horse which was rescued from near extinction in the 1960s. In front is the Victorian Gothic parish pump, erected in 1876 and with separate troughs for horses and dogs.

Woodbridge is often full of yachting types who have taken on the challenge of the River Deben and its many sandbanks, and won. Its quayside bustles with sailing and fishing boats as it has for centuries. The scene is dominated by the elegant white weatherboarded facade of the Tide Mill. A mill has stood here since the 12th century; this one dates from 1793, worked until 1957 and is now a museum. It is operated by tidal water, artfully trapped in a pool behind the mill and used to drive the wheel when the tide has fallen. You can see it working naturally when the tide is right.

East of the town is the National Trust's Sutton Hoo, an evocative Edwardian house and estate with grassy burial mounds overlooking the estuary, where a celebrated Saxon ship burial and its treasures were discovered in 1939 (see page 262).

GET INDUSTRIAL

Woodbridge Tide Mill

woodbridgetidemill.org.uk
Tide Mill Way, IP12 1BY
01394 382815 | Open Easter–Oct daily 11–5

The machinery of this fabulous 18th-century mill has been completely restored in recent years and you can see how it works. It is operated using tidal power whenever the tide permits, but even at low water you can see it working by alternative power. If you time your visit right, you can catch one of its special milling days when the traditional process of making flour is demonstrated.

There are photographs and working models on display. Situated on a busy quayside, the unique building looks over towards the historic site of the Sutton Hoo Ship Burial.

PLAY GOLF

Woodbridge has some superb golf courses. Three of the best are listed here.

Seckford Golf Club

www.seckfordgolf.co.uk
Seckford Hall Road, Great Bealings, IP13 6NT | 01394 388000
Open daily including Bank Holidays

At the Seckford Golf Club the course is interspersed with maturing tree plantations, many bunkers, water hazards and undulating fairways, providing a challenge for all levels of golfer.

Ufford Park Hotel Golf and Spa

uffordpark.co.uk
Yarmouth Road, Melton, IP12 1QW
0844 477 6495 | Open daily including Bank Holidays

The Ufford Park Hotel course is set in 120 acres of ancient parkland with 12 water features and has been voted one of the best British winter courses. It enjoys excellent natural drainage and has a floodlit driving range and golf academy.

Woodbridge Golf Club

woodbridgegolfclub.co.uk
Bromeswell Heath, IP12 2PF
01394 382038 | Open Mon–Fri

The Woodbridge Golf Club's 18-hole heathland course requires strategic golfing skills to manoeuvre around.

EAT AND DRINK

The Crown at Woodbridge ◎◎

thecrownatwoodbridge.co.uk
2 Thoroughfare, IP12 1AD
01394 384242

A complete refurbishment saw the Crown triumphantly reopen for business a few years ago, and become one of the prime draws of this attractive riverside market town. It still feels very much an inn, with food served throughout a range of different eating areas, all pervaded by a relaxed, easygoing ambience and a good mix of keen local clientele. The main business is brasserie cooking of genuine flair, based on local materials and mixing culinary ideas to good effect.

Seckford Hall Hotel ❀❀
seckford.co.uk
IP13 6NU | 01394 385678
Approached by a sweeping drive, the imposing Tudor pile of Seckford – with its brick facade, soaring chimneys, carved-oak entrance door and well-preened grounds – is no less impressive than when Elizabeth I held court here.

10 famous people from Suffolk

- Benjamin Britten, composer
- John Constable, painter
- George Crabb, poet
- Thomas Gainsborough, painter
- Ralph Fiennes, actor
- Matthew Hopkins, witchfinder general
- Bob Hoskins, actor
- Alfred Munnings, painter
- Simon Sudbury, Bishop of London
- Thomas Wolsey, cardinal

A country-house hotel for the 21st century it may be, but its interior successfully blends its regal past with modern-day comforts. The main dining

▾ River Tide Mill in Woodbridge

room embodies that classical look, with oak panelling, rich tapestries, white linen and rich drapes, while the accomplished kitchen deals in country-house cooking with a modern spin.

Wilford Bridge
debeninns.co.uk/wilfordbridge
Wilford Bridge Road, IP12 2PA
01394 386141
On the other side of the River Deben from the pub – over Wilford Bridge, in fact – is Sutton Hoo, the famous ship burial site (see page 262). Mike and Anne Lomas have been running this free house for the last 20 years; Mike specialising in classic English dishes, especially seafood, such as haddock, salmon and prawn pie. In the bar, Adnams and John Smith's is joined by several guest ales.

Wroxham

Among the villages located on the Broads, Wroxham has long been regarded as the capital, although it's an accolade often challenged by adjacent Hoveton. The Norfolk village lies some eight miles northeast of Norwich. Attractively set on the River Bure, which runs right through the heart of the village, Wroxham is a centre for boat hire and holidays, and today, with Hoveton, has become a major tourist centre for the Broads.

Wroxham is where boating holidays really took off in the late 1800s. It has developed commercially over the years, with many hotels, tea rooms and gift shops springing up near the river.

One of the features of the village is Wroxham Bridge, built in 1619, a picturesque semi-circular road bridge that has very low

▼ The River Bure

headroom at high water. It's considered to be the second most difficult bridge to navigate after the one in the village of Potter Heigham. Many boats have hit the bridge and it's a key concern for anyone wanting to continue sailing upriver to the limit of navigation at Coltishall.
see **The Norfolk Broads**, page 203

TAKE A TRAIN RIDE

Bure Valley Railway
bvrw.co.uk
Aylesham Station, Norwich Road, Aylsham NR11 6BW
01263 733858
The 15-inch-gauge railway trains of the Bure Valley Railway run for nine miles between Wroxham and Aylsham. You can ride on any one of the five steam locomotives and one diesel that operate on the line.

PLACES NEARBY

A short drive from Wroxham is South Walsham, a quiet village in the heart of the Norfolk Broads. Here, you can spend some time enjoying boat trips and nature trails at the Fairhaven Woodland and Water Garden. Nearby, you will also find Hoveton (see page 160) and Ranworth (see page 234).

Fairhaven Woodland and Water Garden
fairhavengarden.co.uk
School Road, South Walsham NR13 6DZ | 01603 270449
Open Mar–Nov daily 10–5; Dec–Feb 10–4
Set in around 130 acres of ancient woodland, this gorgeous nature garden lies right next to the South Walsham Broad. If your family enjoys trips out on the water, birding from a boat or setting off to explore nature on foot, then this is the place to come.

In spring there are masses of primroses and bluebells, with huge colourful displays of rhododendrons and pink azaleas dotted around the gardens. You can see the sunny yellow of the candelabra primulas and some unusual plants growing near the waterways. Summer flowers include day lilies, ligularia, hostas, hydrangeas and flowering shrubs. In summer the wild flowers provide food for butterflies, bees and dragonflies.

The garden has its own restaurant and plant sales, plus a whole host of special events throughout the year.

Norfolk Mead Hotel
norfolkmead.co.uk
Church Loke, Coltishall, NR12 7DN | 01603 737531
The handsome old house in the heart of the beautiful Norfolk Broads has never looked so dapper. Refurbishment by new owners has given the Norfolk Mead a contemporary, country-chic look, never more so than in the restaurant, where period features are combined with white walls broken up with

abstract artwork, wooden floors and tables decorated with simple flower arrangements. Windows look out over the pretty gardens – a must for a pre- or post-prandial stroll down to the river – while the charming small bar offers a range of whiskies and real ales, with the bonus of a delightful sun-trap terrace. Chef Anna Duttson sources the finest, freshest local ingredients for her attractively presented modern British cooking with a local flavour.

Wymondham

It is difficult to believe that peaceful Wymondham was once the site of a bitter dispute between its parishioners and the abbey's Benedictine monks. The two parties could not agree. They did not like the times when each other rang their bells and they did not like sharing the church. Matters came to a head in the 14th century when the monks began to build a church tower, making it clear that this was going to be for their use only. In retaliation, in 1447, the townsfolk began to build their own tower – and then installed a peal of bells. The result is a church with two towers.The dispute dragged on for many years and was only laid to rest during the Dissolution, when the abbey buildings were destroyed and the monks expelled by Henry VIII.

TAKE IN SOME HISTORY

Wymondham Abbey

www.wymondhamabbey.org.uk
Wymondham NR18 0PH
01953 607062 | Open see website for details

Founded in 1107 by William d'Albini the abbey church of St Mary and St Thomas of Canterbury is well worth a visit. The first thing you notice is that the grand central tower is nothing more than a shell, with the great arch that once led to the abbey buildings open to the elements. This was the monks' tower, completed in 1409. It effectively divided the church in half, and left the parishioners staring at a blank wall, while the monks enjoyed the chancel. The east wall remained blank until the screen was erected in the early 20th century. Inside, the church is a delight. There are Norman arches in the nave and an angel roof, all drawing the eye forward to the gold extravaganza of the altar screen on the east wall.

VISIT THE MUSEUM

Wymondham Heritage Museum

wymondhamheritagemuseum.co.uk
10 The Bridewell, Norwich Road, NR18 0NS | 01953 600205
Open Mar–Nov 10–4

Featuring permanent exhibitions on the Wymondham Bridewell model prison (including a re-creation of a dungeon) and brushmaking, (once a major employer in the town), the Heritage Museum also hosts special displays and events throughout the year.

TAKE A TRAIN RIDE

Mid-Norfolk Railway
mnr.org.uk
Dereham Station, NR19 1DF
01362 690633 | Open Apr–Oct, Santa Specials in Dec and Jan
Operating on the old Wymondham to Wells-next-the-Sea branch line this heritage railway is a delight. It runs between Wymondham Abbey and Dereham (see page 116) and charter and excursion trains also use the line via the link with the national rail network at Wymondham station.

EAT AND DRINK

Number Twenty Four Restaurant ❀❀
number24.co.uk
24 Middleton Street, NR18 OAD | 01953 607750
A row of Grade II listed 18th-century cottages in the heart of Wymondham is the setting for this smart, family-run restaurant. The dining room is a period gem done out with linen-clothed, widely-spaced tables set against warm, soothing colours, and the vibe is good humoured and unstuffy. There is dedication to good old-fashioned hard work in the kitchen – everything is cooked from scratch and in tune with the seasons and local larder.

▾ Wymondham Abbey

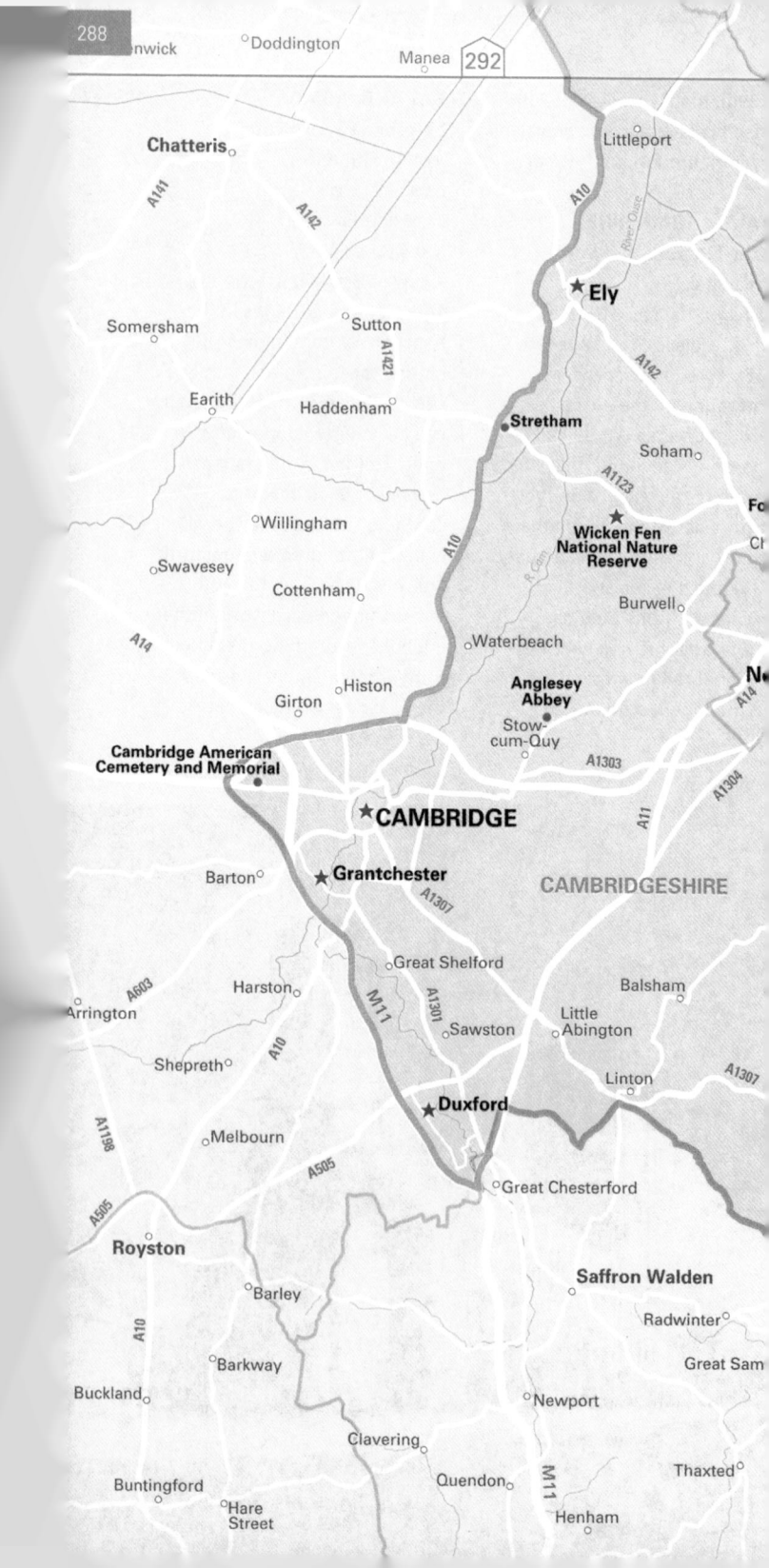
nwick
Doddington
Manea
292
Chatteris
Littleport
A141
A142
A10
River Ouse
Ely
Somersham
Sutton
A1421
A142
Earith
Haddenham
Stretham
Soham
A1123
Willingham
Wicken Fen National Nature Reserve
A10
Swavesey
R. Cam
Cottenham
Burwell
A14
Waterbeach
Histon
Anglesey Abbey
Girton
Stow-cum-Quy
A14
Cambridge American Cemetery and Memorial
A1303
A1304
CAMBRIDGE
A11
Barton
Grantchester
A1307
CAMBRIDGESHIRE
Great Shelford
A603
Harston
M11
A1301
Balsham
Arrington
Sawston
Little Abington
Shepreth
A10
Linton
A1307
Duxford
A1198
Melbourn
A505
Great Chesterford
A505
Royston
Saffron Walden
Barley
Radwinter
A10
Barkway
Great Sam
Buckland
Newport
Clavering
Thaxted
Buntingford
Quendon
M11
Hare Street
Henham

289
Hockham
Feltwell
Grime's Graves
293
Weeting Castle
Thetford Forest Park
Brandon
Go Ape! Thetford
A134
A4075
A11
Larling
East Harli
enheath
A1065
Thetford
A1066
Little Ouse River
Elveden
Euston Hall
Beck Row
A11
Mildenhall
A134
Honington
Stanton
rlington
River Lark
A1101
West Stow Anglo-Saxon Village
A1088
Tuddenham
Wyken Hall
Ingham
Ixworth
Flempton
A143
A1088
Kentford
A14
Thurston
Bury St Edmunds
Woolpit
ey
Ickworth House
A14
290
A134
Stow
A143
Lidgate
Whepstead
SUFFOLK
Rede
Hawkedon
Stradishall
Hartest
A134
Hitcham
Lavenham
Bilde
A143
Glemsford
Kentwell Hall
A1141
Cavendish
A1092
Melford Hall
verhill
Clare
Long Melford
Stoke by Clare
A1071
Sudbury
teeple umpstead
A134
Newton
Boxford
A1017
ESSEX
Great Yeldham
Stoke-b
Naylan
Castle Hedingham
A131
Denhan
Nayland
Bures
Finchingfield
Colne Engaine
Halstead
A134
at
dfield
Shalford
A1124
A120
Earls Colne

New Buckenham
294
Larling
Banham
East Harling
Kenninghall
NORFOLK
Pulham St Mary
Harleston
Burston
Garboldisham
Bressingham
Diss
Scole
Brockdish
Redgrave
Fressingfield
Hoxne
Botesdale
Brome
Stanton
Eye
Stradbroke
Wyken Hall
SUFFOLK
Finningham
Worlingworth
Brockford Street
Saxtead Green Post Mill
Debenham
Woolpit
Cretingham
289
Stowmarket
Helmingham
Needham Market
Coddenham
Hitcham
Great Blakenham
Witnesham
Claydon
Bildeston
Woodbridge
IPSWICH
Martlesham Heath
Hadleigh
Hintlesham
Copdock
Boxford
Nacton
Raydon
Capel St Mary
Stoke-by-Nayland
Holbrook
Shotley
Nayland
Denham Vale
East Bergholt
Dedham
River Stour
Manningtree
Harwi
ESSEX
Ardleigh
Wix
A11
A1066
A140
A143
A1088
A14
A1120
A12
A1214
A1071
A1156
A137
A134
A120
River Orwell

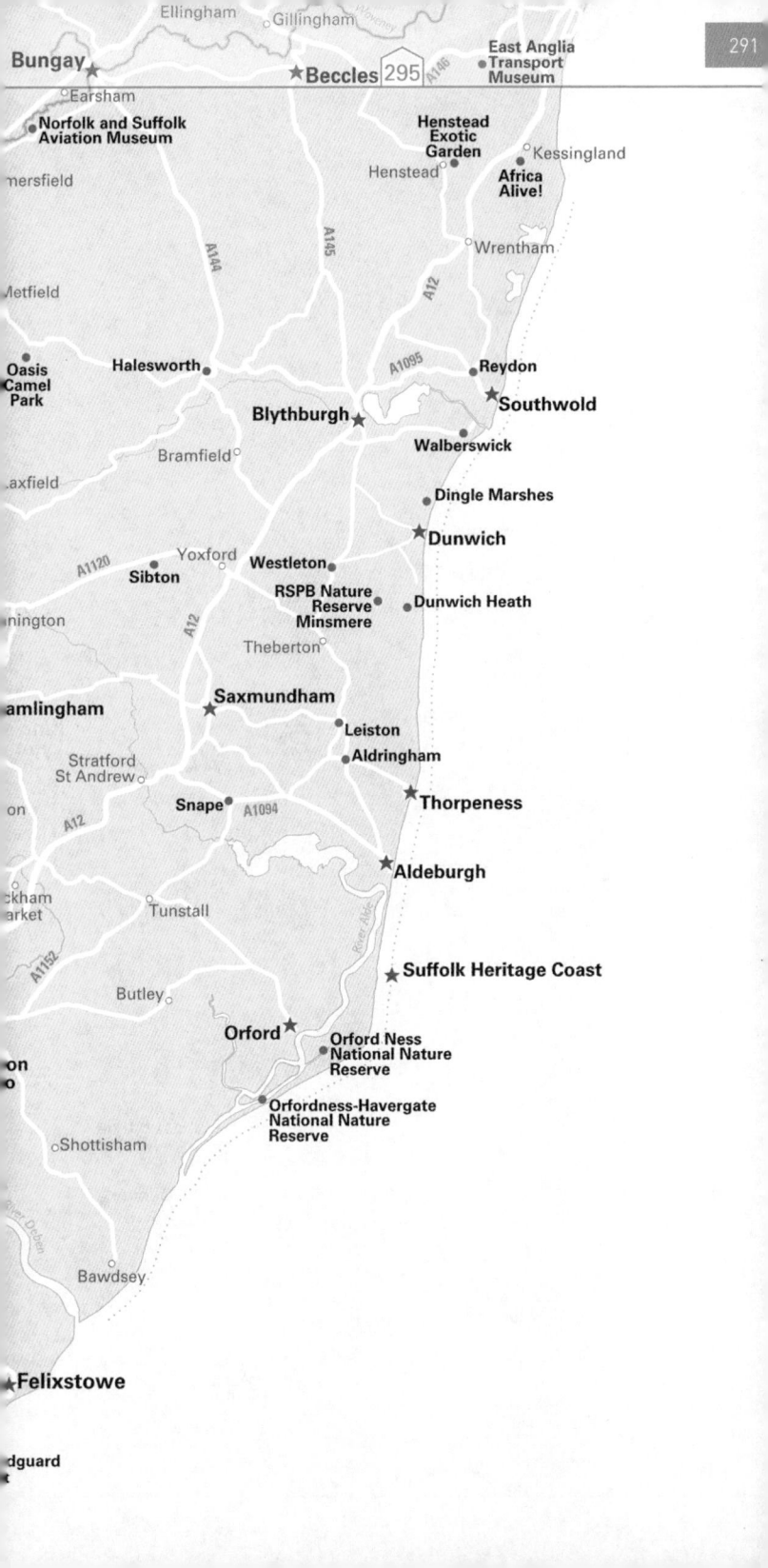
Ellingham
Gillingham
Bungay
Beccles
295
A146
East Anglia Transport Museum
Earsham
Norfolk and Suffolk Aviation Museum
Henstead Exotic Garden
Kessingland
Henstead
Africa Alive!
mersfield
A144
A145
Wrentham
A12
Metfield
Oasis Camel Park
Halesworth
A1095
Reydon
Southwold
Blythburgh
Walberswick
Bramfield
axfield
Dingle Marshes
Dunwich
A1120
Yoxford
Sibton
Westleton
RSPB Nature Reserve Minsmere
Dunwich Heath
nington
A12
Theberton
Saxmundham
amlingham
Leiston
Aldringham
Stratford St Andrew
Snape
A1094
Thorpeness
on
A12
Aldeburgh
ckham
arket
Tunstall
River Alde
A1152
Suffolk Heritage Coast
Butley
Orford
Orford Ness National Nature Reserve
on
o
Orfordness-Havergate National Nature Reserve
Shottisham
River Deben
Bawdsey
Felixstowe
dguard

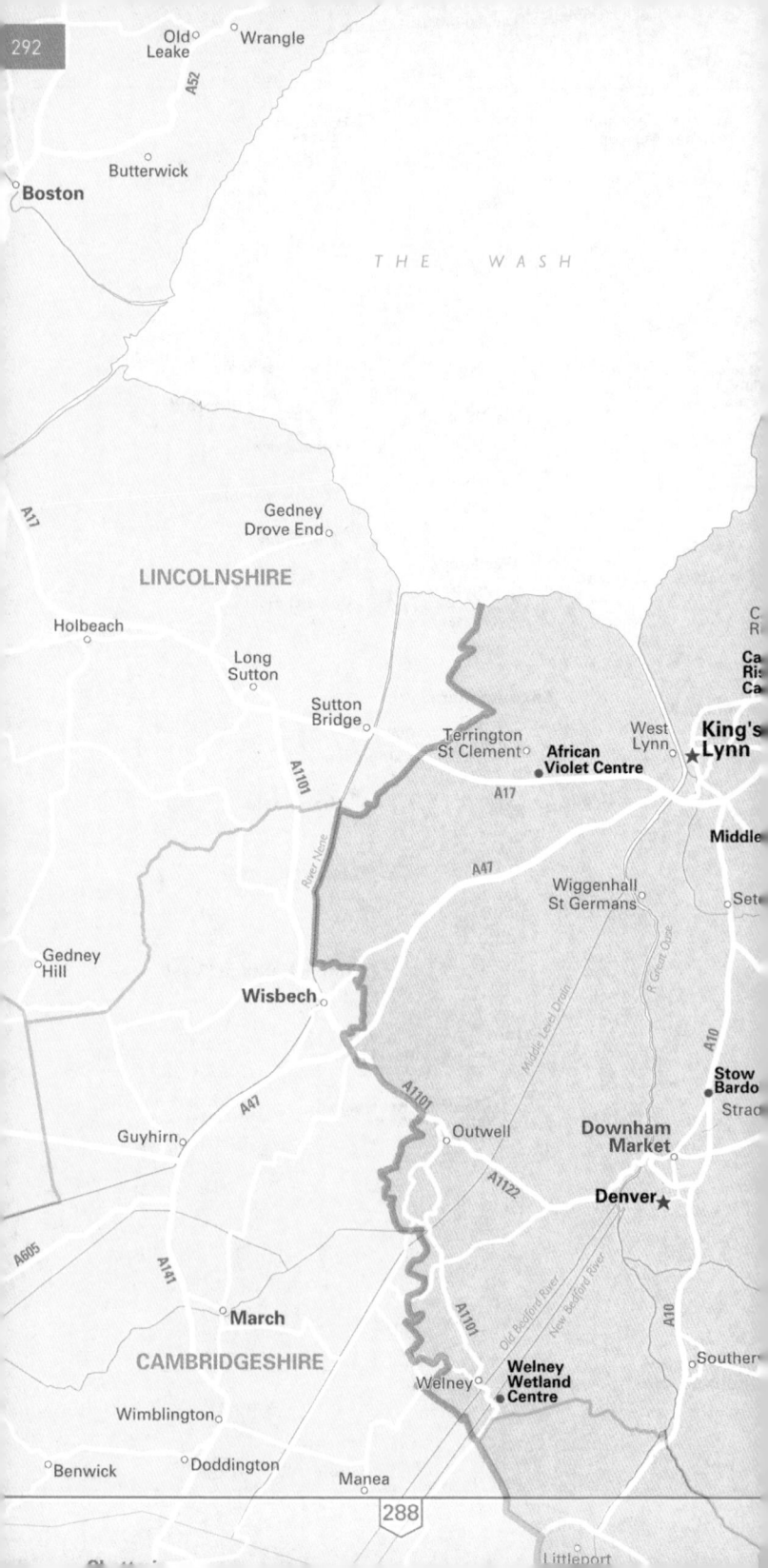
Old Leake
Wrangle
A52
Butterwick
Boston
THE WASH
A17
Gedney Drove End
LINCOLNSHIRE
Holbeach
Long Sutton
Sutton Bridge
A1101
River Nene
Terrington St Clement
African Violet Centre
West Lynn
King's Lynn
A17
A47
Wiggenhall St Germans
Gedney Hill
Wisbech
Middle Level Drain
R. Great Ouse
A10
Stow Bardo
A1101
A47
Guyhirn
Outwell
Downham Market
A1122
Denver
A605
A141
March
A1101
Old Bedford River
New Bedford River
A10
CAMBRIDGESHIRE
Welney
Welney Wetland Centre
Wimblington
Benwick
Doddington
Manea
288
Littleport

RSPB Nature Reserve Titchwell Marsh
Brancaster
Thornham
Titchwell
Brancaster Staithe
Burnham Overy Staithe
Burnham Deepdale
Burnham Market
Burnham Thorpe
Holkham
Holkham Hall
Wells-next-the-sea
Stiffkey
Wells & Walsingham Light Railway
Creake Abbey
North Creake
Walsingham
Norfolk Lavender
Docking
Sedgeford
Snettisham
Snettisham Park
Bircham Windmill
Great Bircham
Syderstone
Dersingham
Houghton Hall
Fakenham
Pensthorpe Nature Reserve
Fakenham Racecourse
Sandringham
West Newton
East Rudham
A148
South Raynham
Great Massingham
Grimston
Weasenham All Saints
A1065
Gayton
Litcham
Gressenhall Farm and Workhouse
Castle Acre Priory & Castle
Newton
Narborough
A47
NORFOLK
Swaffham
Necton
A1122
Fincham
Shipdham
A1075
Oxborough
A1065
Watton
Northwold
Methwold
Mundford
Great Hockham
Feltwell
Grime's Graves
Weeting Castle
Thetford
289
Brandon
A134
A4075
A11
Morston
Binham
Thursfo
A1607
North Elmham
294
Beetley
Dereham
Scoulto
Attle
Larling
East Harling

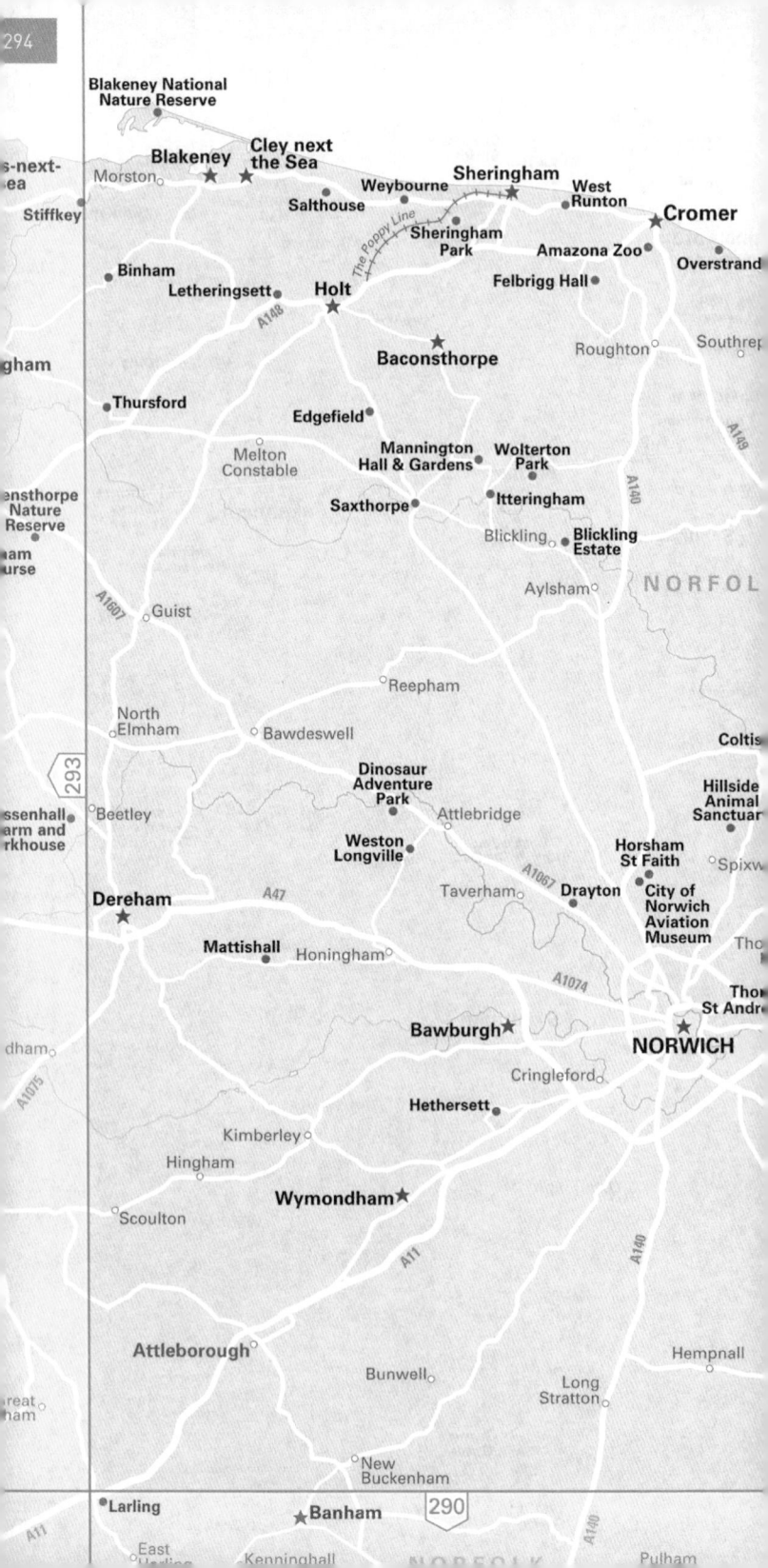
Blakeney National Nature Reserve
Blakeney
Cley next the Sea
Morston
Stiffkey
Weybourne
Salthouse
Sheringham
West Runton
Cromer
The Poppy Line
Sheringham Park
Amazona Zoo
Overstrand
Binham
Letheringsett
Holt
A148
Felbrigg Hall
Baconsthorpe
Roughton
Southrep
Thursford
Edgefield
Melton Constable
Mannington Hall & Gardens
Wolterton Park
A149
A140
Saxthorpe
Itteringham
Blickling
Blickling Estate
Aylsham
NORFOL
A1607
Guist
Reepham
North Elmham
Bawdeswell
Coltis
293
Dinosaur Adventure Park
Hillside Animal Sanctuar
Beetley
Attlebridge
Weston Longville
Horsham St Faith
Spixw
A1067
Taverham
Drayton
City of Norwich Aviation Museum
Dereham
A47
Mattishall
Honingham
Tho
A1074
Thor St Andr
Bawburgh
NORWICH
Cringleford
A1075
Hethersett
Kimberley
Hingham
Wymondham
Scoulton
A11
A140
Attleborough
Hempnall
Bunwell
Long Stratton
New Buckenham
Larling
Banham
290
East
Kenninghall
Pulham

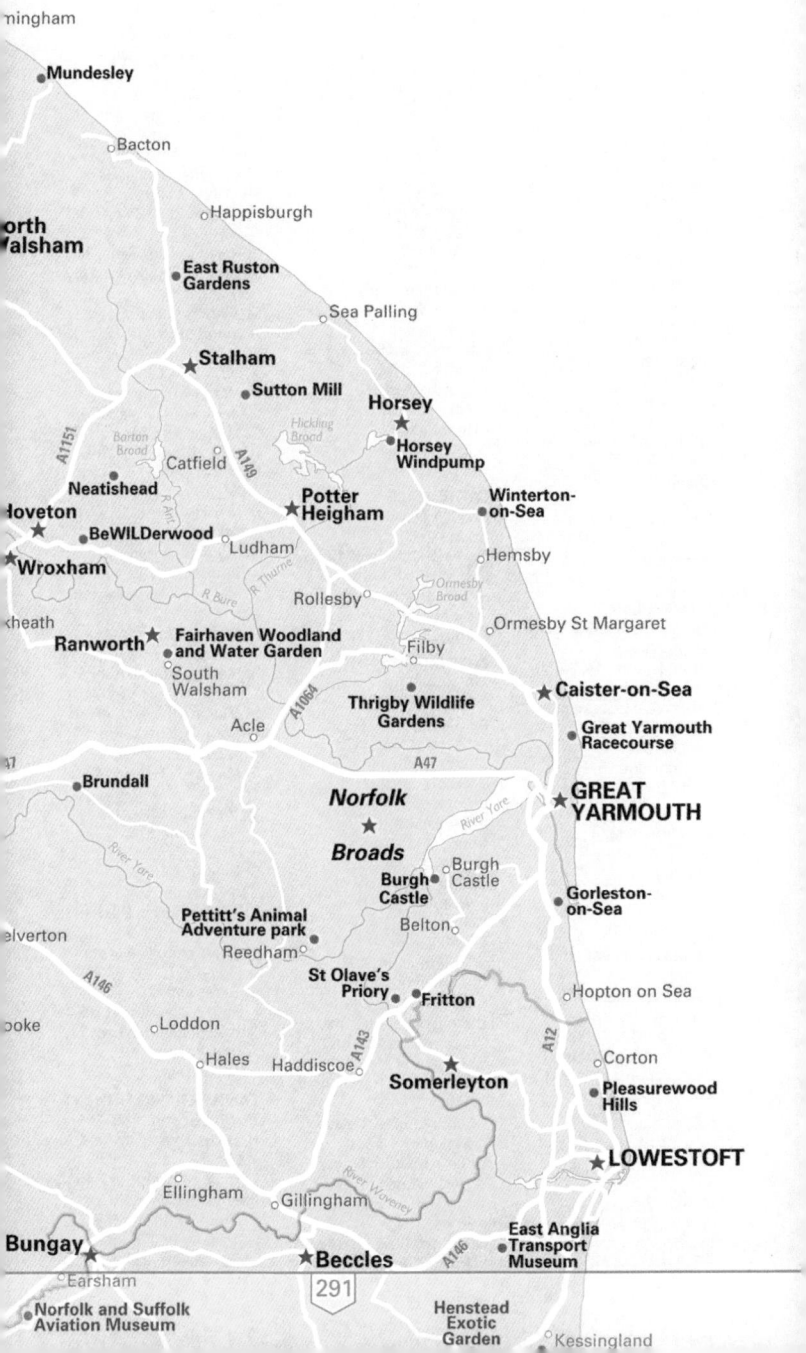
ningham
Mundesley
Bacton
Happisburgh
orth
Walsham
East Ruston
Gardens
Sea Palling
Stalham
Sutton Mill
Horsey
Horsey
Windpump
Hickling
Broad
A1151
Barton
Broad
Catfield
A149
Neatishead
Potter
Heigham
Winterton-
on-Sea
Hoveton
BeWILDerwood
Ludham
Hemsby
Wroxham
R Thurne
R Bure
Ormesby
Broad
Rollesby
Ormesby St Margaret
Ranworth
Fairhaven Woodland
and Water Garden
Filby
South
Walsham
A1064
Caister-on-Sea
Thrigby Wildlife
Gardens
Acle
Great Yarmouth
Racecourse
A47
Brundall
Norfolk
Broads
River Yare
GREAT
YARMOUTH
Burgh
Castle
Burgh
Castle
Gorleston-
on-Sea
Pettitt's Animal
Adventure park
Belton
Reedham
A146
St Olave's
Priory
Fritton
Hopton on Sea
Loddon
Hales
Haddiscoe
A143
A12
Corton
Somerleyton
Pleasurewood
Hills
LOWESTOFT
Ellingham
Gillingham
River Waveney
East Anglia
Transport
Museum
Bungay
Beccles
A146
Earsham
291
Norfolk and Suffolk
Aviation Museum
Henstead
Exotic
Garden
Kessingland

Index, themed

Page numbers in **bold** refer to main text entries

ABBEYS
Anglesey Abbey, Lode 99–100, 138, 200, 281
Creake Abbey, North Creake 72
Leiston Abbey 56–7
St Benet's Abbey, Norfolk Broads 205–6, 234
Walsingham Abbey Grounds and Shirehall Museum 273–4
Wymondham Abbey 286

ANIMAL ADVENTURES
Africa Alive!, Kessingland 14, 63, 193
Amazoma Zoo, Cromer 107
Amazonia World of Reptiles, Great Yarmouth 142
Banham Zoo 59
Hillside Animal Sanctuary, Frettenham 224–5
Hunstanton Sea Life Sanctuary 162
Oasis Camel Park, Linstead 251, 252
Pettitts Animal Adventure Park, Reedham 193
Pleasurewood Hills 14, 190–1
Sea Life Centre, Great Yarmouth 142, 144–5
Snettisham Park 166

ARCHAEOLOGY
Grimes Graves, Lynford 269, 270
Sutton Hoo 14, 16, 36–7, 43, 49, **262–3**, 282
University Museum of Archaeology and Anthropology, Cambridge 95
West Stow Anglo-Saxon Village 80

AVIATION & MILITARY
Atomic Weapons Research Establishment, Orford 230
City of Norwich Aviation Museum, Horsham St Faith 224
Cobra Mist, Orford 230
Imperial War Museum Duxford 13, 21, 123, 124
Muckleburgh Military Collection centre 241
Norfolk and Suffolk Aviation Museum, Flixton 74
RAF Air Defence Radar Museum, Hoveton 160

BOATING
Cambridge 90
Coastal Voyager, Southwold 248
Lydia Eva, Great Yarmouth 146
Maritime Museum, Lowestoft 190
Norwich Punting Co 219
RNLI Henry Blogg Museum, Cromer 104, 105
Time and Tide Museum, Great Yarmouth 140, 143
Waverley, Southwold 244, 248–9

CAMPSITES 48–9

CASTLES
Baconsthorpe Castle 58–9
Bungay Castle 73, 74
Burgh Castle 85, 147, 148
Caister Castle Car Collection 84–5
Castle Acre Priory and Castle 265
Castle Rising 181, 182
Framlingham Castle 133, 134–5
Norwich Castle 13, 18, 212–13, 215
Orford Castle 41, 228–9, 230, 231, 261
Weeting Castle 269, 270

CATHEDRALS
Ely Cathedral 10, 42, 47, 126–7
Norwich Cathedral 13, 47, 213–14, 216
St Edmundsbury Cathedral, Bury St Edmunds 76, 77

CHURCHES
All Saints' Church, Horsey 158
All Saints' Church, Sheringham 239
Church of St John, Oxborough 232
Church of St Mary, Baconsthorpe 58
Church of St Mary, Stalham 253
Church of St Mary, Woodbridge 281
Church of St Mary Magdalene, Sandringham 237
Church of St Mary and St Walstan, Bawburgh 60
Church of St Mary the Virgin, Diss 117
Church of St Mary the Virgin, East Bergholt 43, 110, 125
Church of St Nicholas, Blakeney 64, 65
Church of St Nicholas, North Walsham 210
Church of St Nicholas, Potter Heigham 233
Church of St Peter and St Paul, Cromer 104, 106
Church of St Peter and St Paul, Swaffham 264
Church of St Peter's, Sudbury 257
Church of St Withburga, Holkham 152
Holy Trinity Church, Blythburgh 67–8
King's College Chapel, Cambridge 10, 20, 89, 92
National Shrine of Our Lady of Walsingham, Slipper Chapel, Walsingham 273, 274
St Edmund, King and Martyr Church, Southwold 44, 244, 247–8
St Helen's, Ranworth 234
St James's Chapel Lindsey 174, 175
St John the Baptist Church, Duxford 123
St John church, Hoveton 160
St Margaret's Church, Cley next the Sea 102
St Margaret's Church, King's Lynn 177, 178–9
St Mary Church, Mildenhall 195
St Mary le Tower, Ipswich 170
St Mary the Virgin, Banham 59
St Mary the Virgin church, Dedham 112–13
St Mary's, Burnham Deepdale 69
St Mary's Church, Bury St Edmunds 76, 78
St Michael the Archangel, Framlingham 133, 135–6
St Michaels, Beccles 43, 61
St Nicholas' Chapel, King's Lynn 176, 177, 179
St Peter, Great Walsingham 274
St Peter Church, Duxford 123
St Peter church, Hoveton 160
St Peter and St Paul church, Lavenham 185
The Shrine of Our Lady of Walsingham, Walsingham 273, 274

FAMILY ENTERTAINMENT
BeWILDerwood 160, 161
Brancaster Activity Centre 69
Dinosaur Adventure Park, Lenwade 224, 225
Go Ape! Thetford 266, 268
Hillside Animal Sanctuary, Frettenham 224–5

Kid's Treasure Trail, Aldeburgh 54
Lowestoft 190–1
Oasis Camel Park, Linstead 251, 252
Pettitts Animal Adventure Park, Reedham 193
Pleasurewood Hills 14, 190–1

GARDENS
Abbey Gardens, Bury St Edmunds 77
Anglesey Abbey, Lode 99–100, 138, 200, 281
Blickling Estate 107, 108
Bressingham Steam and Museum Gardens 118
Cambridge University Botanic Garden 95–6
East Ruston Gardens 210–11
Fairhaven Woodland and Water Garden, South Walsham 285
Henstead Exotic Garden 61–2
Holkham Hall 41, 71–2, 152–3, 275
Ickworth House, Horringer 80
Mannington Hall and Gardens, Saxthorpe 156–7
Merrivale Model Village, Great Yarmouth 146
Pensthorpe Wildlife and Gardens, Fakenham 129–30
Sandringham House Gardens 237
Sheringham Park 240
Somerleyton Hall 241, 242–3
Thrigby Wildlife Gardens, Filby 85
Walsingham Abbey Grounds and Shirehall Museum 273–4
Wolerton Park, Erpingham 107
Wyken Hall, Stanton 80–1

GOLFING
Aldeburgh Golf Club 54
Alnesbourne Priory Golf Course, Ipswich 171
Bawburgh Golf Club 60
Beccles Golf Club 61
Brett Vale Golf Club, Raydon 150
Bungay and Waveney Valley Golf Club 74
Bury St Edmunds Golf Club, Bury St Edmunds 78
Caldecott Hall Golf and Leisure, Fritton 147, 148
Costessey Park Golf Course, Norwich 221
Cretingham Golf Club 136
De Vere Dunstan Hall, Norwich 221
Dereham Golf Club 116
Diss Golf Club 118
Eagles Golf Centre, King's Lynn 180
Eaton Golf Club, Norwich 221
Ely City Golf Club 128
Felixstowe Ferry Golf Club 132–3
Flempton Golf Club 80, 81
Fynn Valley Golf Club, Witnesham 174, 175
Gog Magog Golf Club, Cambridge 96
Gorleston Golf Club, Gorleston-on-Sea 147, 148
Great Yarmouth and Caister Golf Club 146
Halesworth Golf Club 251
Haverhill Golf Club 151
Heacham Manor Golf 151–2
Hintlesham Golf Club 173, 174
Hunstanton Golf Club 164
Ipswich Golf Club 171–2
King's Lynn Golf Club 180
Links Country Park Hotel and Golf Club, West Runton 107, 108
Links Golf Club, Newmarket 198–9
Mattishall Golf Course 117
Middleton Hall Golf Club, Middleton 181, 183
Mundesley Golf Club 107, 108
Newton Green Golf Club, Newton 202
Pirate's Cove Adventure Golf, Great Yarmouth 142
Rookery Park Golf Club, Lowestoft 192
Royal Cromer Golf Club, Cromer 106
Royal Norwich Golf Club 221
Royal West Norfolk Golf Club 69
Royal Worlington and Newmarket Golf Club, Worlington 200, 201
Rushmere Golf Club, Ipswich 172
Ryston Park Golf Club, Denver 116
Searles Resort Golf Course, Hunstanton 164
Seckford Golf Club, Woodbridge 282
Sheringham Golf Club 240
Sprowston Manor, Norwich 221, 222
Stowmarket Golf Club 256
Suffolk Golf and Spa Hotel, Bury St Edmunds 78
Swaffham Golf Club 265
Thetford Golf Club 268
Ufford Park Hotel Golf and Spa, Woodbridge 282
Wensum Valley Hotel, Golf and Country Club, Norwich 221, 222
West Suffolk Golf Centre, Mildenhall 195
Weston Park Golf Club, Weston Longville 225

HISTORIC HOUSES
Anglesey Abbey, Lode 99–100, 138, 200, 281
Blickling Estate 107, 108
Bridge Cottage, East Bergholt 112, 114, 125
Buckenham House, Southwold 244, 247
Christchurch Mansion, Ipswich 170
Euston Hall 269–70
Felbrigg Hall 107
Gainsborough's House, Sudbury 257
Holkham Hall 41, 71–2, 152–3, 275
Ickworth House, Horringer 80
Kentwell Hall, Long Melford 186, 187–8, 257
Madingley Hall 99
Mannington Hall and Gardens, Saxthorpe 156–7
Melford Hall, Long Melford 186, 188, 257
Old Merchant's House, Great Yarmouth 140, 143
Oliver Cromwell's House, Ely 126, 127
Oulton High House 28
Palace House, Newmarket 196–7
Sandringham House 236
Somerleyton Hall 241, 242–3
Ware Hall House, Wells-next-the-Sea 275
Wolerton Park, Erpingham 1–7
Wyken Hall, Stanton 80–1

MOTORING
Caister Castle Car Collection 84–5
East Anglia Transport Museum, Lowestoft 190

MUSEUMS AND GALLERIES
Aldeburgh Museum 54
Ancient House Museum, Thetford 266–8
Bressingham Steam and Museum Gardens 118
Bungay Museum 73, 74
Bygones Museum, Holkham 152
Caister Castle Car Collection 84–5
Cambridge University Botanic Museum 91
City of Norwich Aviation Museum, Horsham St Faith 224
Colman's Mustard Shop and Museum, Norwich 38, 219
Cromer Museum 105
Dunwich Museum 122
Easton Farm Park 136

Elizabeth House Museum, Great Yarmouth 143
Ely Museum 127
Fakenham Museum of Gas and Local History 129
Fitzwilliam Museum, Cambridge 12, 91, 93
Gainsborough's House, Sudbury 257
Great Yarmouth Potteries and Smoke House 144
Gressenhall Farm and Workhouse 117
Halesworth Airfield Museum 74
Hillside Animal Sanctuary, Frettenham 224–5
Imperial War Museum Duxford 13, 21, 123, 124
Ipswich Museum 170
Kettle's Yard, Cambridge 91, 94
Long Shop Museum, Leiston 57
Lynn Museum, King's Lynn 178, 180
Maritime Museum, Lowestoft 190
Mildenhall Museum 194, 195
Moot Hall, Aldeburgh 52–3
Moyse's Hall Museum, Bury St Edmunds 76, 77
Museum of the Broads, Stalham 253, 254
Museum of East Anglian Life, Stowmarket 254–5
National Horseracing Museum, Newmarket 197, 198
Norwich Castle 13, 18, 212–13, 215
Orford Castle 41, 228–9, 230, 231, 261
Oxborough Hall 232–3
RAF Air Defence Radar Museum, Hoveton 160
RNLI Henry Blogg Museum, Cromer 104, 105
Sainsbury Centre for Visual Arts, Norwich 218
Sandringham House Museum 236
Shire Hall, Woodbridge 281
Southwold Museum 244
Stained Glass Museum, Ely 128
Sudbury Heritage Museum, Sudbury 257
Swaffham Museum 265
The Forum, Norwich 217, 218
The Mo, Sheringham 240
The Museum of Cambridge 94
The Polar Museum, Scott Polar Research Institute, Cambridge 94–5
The Red House, Aldeburgh 54
The Rows and Greyfriars' Cloister, Great Yarmouth 140, 143
Thursford Collection 130–1
Time and Tide Museum, Great Yarmouth 140, 143
Tolhouse Museum, Great Yarmouth 143–4
Town House Museum, King's Lynn 178, 179
University Museum of Archaeology and Anthropology, Cambridge 95
Walsingham Abbey Grounds and Shirehall Museum 273–4
Woodbridge Tide Mill 281–2
Wymondham Heritage Museum 286–7
Yesterday's World, Great Yarmouth 144

MUSIC
Aldeburgh Music Festival 47, 52, 57, 67, 261
Ely Folk Festival 47
John Peel Centre for Creative Arts, Stowmarket 254, 255
Snape Maltings, Snape 47, 56, 57, 261
StowFest music festival 254
West Road Concert Hall, Cambridge 92

NATURE RESERVES
Blakeney National Nature Reserve 64, 65, 102
Dingle Marshes, nr Leiston 259
Heigham Holmes nature reserve 233
Holkham National Nature Reserve 152, 276
Minsmere RSPB Nature Reserve 25, 49, 56, 122, 238, 259
Orford Ness National Nature Reserve 229, 231–2, 259
RSPB Nature Reserve Titchwell Marsh 72–3
Wicken Fen National Nature Reserve 24, 99, 128, 138, 200, **279–81**

PIERS
Britannia Pier, Great Yarmouth 141–2, 145
Claremont Pier, Lowestoft 189, 190, 192
Cromer Pier 43
South Pier, Lowestoft 189, 190, 260–1
Southwold Pier 12, 244, 246
Wellington Pier, Great Yarmouth 141, 142, 145

PRIORIES
Alnesbourne Priory Golf Course 171
Castle Acre Priory an Castle 265
St Olave's Priory 147,
Thetford Priory 266

RAILWAYS 46
Bure Valley Railway 2
Mid-Norfolk Railway
North Norfolk Railwa Sheringham 240
Wells and Walsingha Light Railway 273, 2

SEA LIFE
Hunstanton Sea Life Sanctuary 162
Sea Life Centre, Grea Yarmouth 142, 144-

WETLANDS
Minsmere RSPB Natu Reserve 25, 49, 56, 238, 259
Welney Wetland Cent 128–9
Wicken Fen National Nature Reserve 24 128, 138, 200, **279–**

WILDLIFE ATTRACTI
Africa Alive!, Kessing 14, 63, 193
Alstrop Wood 202
BeWILDerwood, Hove 13, 160, 161
Blakeney National Na Reserve 64, 65, 102
Broadland Wildlife Ce 209, 235
Broads National Park Norfolk Broads 22- 203, 207, 208
Dingle Marshes, nr Leiston 259
Dunwich Heath 122
Fairhaven Woodland Water Garden, Sou Walsham 285
Heigham Holmes Na Reserve 233
Holkham National Na Reserve 152, 276
Minsmere RSPB Nat Reserve 25, 49, 56, 238, 259
Orford Ness National Nature Reserve 22 231–2, 259
Pensthorpe Wildlife Gardens, Fakenhar 129–30
RSPB Nature Reserv Titchwell Marsh 72
Sea Life Centre, Grea Yarmouth 142, 144
Thrigby Wildlife Gard Filby 85
Welney Wetland Cen 128–9
Wicken Fen National Nature Reserve 24 128, 138, 200, **279-**

Index, places

Page numbers in **bold** refer to main entries; page numbers in *italics* refer to town plans

A

Abbey Gardens, Bury St Edmunds 77
ADC Theatre, Cambridge 92, 96
Africa Alive!, Kessingland 14, 63, 193
African Violet Centre, King's Lynn 180
Aldeburgh 9, 10, 19, 46, **52–8**, 251, 261
Aldringham 56, 57
All Saints' Church, Horsey 158
All Saints' Church, Sheringham 239
Alnesbourne Priory Golf Course, Ipswich 171
Alstrop Wood 202
Amazona Zoo, Cromer 107
Amazonia World of Reptiles, Great Yarmouth 142
Ancient House Museum, Thetford 266–8
Anglesey Abbey, Lode 99–100, 138, 200, 281
Aspall Hall Farm 39
Assembly House, The, Norwich 217, 218
Assington 202

B

Backs, Cambridge 10
Baconsthorpe 58–9
Bacton 27
Banham 59
Barney 48
Barton Broad 203, 253
Bawburgh 60
Bawdsey Manor 229–30
Beccles 61–2, 193
Bedford 30
Belton 48
Berney Arms 208
BeWILDerwood, Hoveton 13, 160, 161
Binham 278
Bircham Newton 138
Bircham Tofts 138
Birmingham 32
Bisley 209
Blackfriars Friary, Ipswich 170
Blackfriars' Hall, Norwich 217
Blakeney 62–5
Blakeney Haven 62
Blakeney Point 62, 66
Blickling Estate 107, 108, 66
Blythburgh 67–8
Brancaster 69–73
Brancaster Manor salt marsh 69
Brancaster Staithe 69
Bressingham 73
Brett Vale Golf Club, Raydon 150
Breydon Water 204
Bridge Cottage, East Bergholt 112, 114, 125
Bridgewater Canal 31
Britannia Pier, Great Yarmouth 141–2, 145
Broadlands Wildlife Centre, Ranworth 209, 235
Broadman's Mill 208
Broads National Park, Norfolk Broads 22–4, 203, 207, 208
Brundell 225–6
Buckenham House, Southwold 244, 247
Bucklesham 49
Bungay 73–4
Bure Valley Railway, Wroxham 285
Bures 26–7
Burgh Castle 85, 147, 148
Burnham Deepdale 69
St Mary's 69
Burnham Market 71, 72
Burnham Thorpe 69, 71, 72
Burston 119
Bury St Edmunds 10, 28, 39, 46, *75*, **75–83**, 149
Buttermarket, Ipswich 168
Bygones Museum, Holkham 152

C

Caister-on-Sea 83–5, 147, 253
Caister Castle Car Collection 84–5
Caister Roman Fort 85
Great Yarmouth Racecourse 85
Caldecott Hall Golf and Leisure, Fritton 147, 148
Cam, River 88–90
Cambridge 8, 10, 19–20, 29–30, 33, 39, 41–3, *86–7*, **88–100**, 128, 138, 200, 281
Cambridge American Cemetery and Memorial, Madingley 99, 100
Castle Acre 101
Castle Acre Priory and Castle 265
Castle Rising 101, 181, 182
Cavendish 188
Christchurch Mansion, Ipswich 170
Church of St John, Oxborough 232
Church of St Mary, Baconsthorpe 58
Church of St Mary, Stalham 253
Church of St Mary, Woodbridge 281
Church of St Mary Magdalene, Sandringham 237
Church of St Mary and St Walstan, Bawburgh 60
Church of St Mary the Virgin, Diss 117
Church of St Mary the Virgin, East Bergholt 43, 110, 125
Church of St Nicholas, Blakeney 64, 65
Church of St Nicholas, North Walsham 210
Church of St Nicholas, Potter Heigham 233
Church of St Peter and St Paul, Cromer 104, 106
Church of St Peter and St Paul, Swaffham 264
Church of St Peter's, Sudbury 257
City of Norwich Aviation Museum, Horsham St Faith 224
Claremont Pier, Lowestoft 189, 190, 192
Clayrack 209
Cley next the Sea 18–19, 47, **101–3**
St Margaret's Church 102
Clippesby 48
Clopton Hall 26
Coastal Voyager (boat), Southwold 248
Cobra Mist, Orford 230
Colman's Mustard Shop and Museum, Norwich 38, 219
Coltishall 285, 285–6
Cornhill, Ipswich 168–70
Corpus Christi College, Cambridge 20, 29
Costessey Park Golf Course, Norwich 221
Creake Abbey, North Creake 72
Cretingham 136
Cromer 9, 46, 47, **103–9**
Custom House, King's Lynn 177

D

Dedham Vale 10, **110–15**, 125, 150
Dedham village 112–13, 115
Denver 116
Dereham 42, **116–17**
Dingle Marshes, nr Leiston 259
Dinosaur Adventure Park, Lenwade 224, 225
Diss 18, **117–19**
Dolphin House, Diss 117
Dragon Hall, Norwich 217–18
Drayton 226–7
Dunwich 16, 18–19, 41, **120–2**, 251
Duxford 99, **123–5**, 138

E

Earl Soham 133
East Anglia Transport Museum, Lowestoft 190
East Bergholt 110–12, 115, **125**
East Ruston Gardens 210–11
Easton 125, 136
Edgefield 156, 157
Edwardstone Woods 202
Elizabeth House Museum, Great Yarmouth 143
Elveden Estate 41–2, 269, 270–1
Ely 17, 19, 29, 33, 46, 99, **126–9**
Erpingham, Wolerton Park 107
Euston, Euston Hall 269–70

F

Fairhaven Woodland and Water Garden, South Walsham 285
Fakenham 10, **129–31**
Felbrigg 131
Felixstowe 9–10, 46, **131–3**, 243, 259
Fen Causeway 116
Filby, Thrigby Wildlife Gardens 85
Fitzwilliam Museum, Cambridge 12, 91, 93
Flatford Mill, East Bergholt 10, 112, 114, 125
Flixton, Norfolk and Suffolk Aviation Museum 74
Fordham 200, 201
Forum, The, Norwich 217, 218
Framlingham 133–7
Fressingfield 119
Frettenham 224–5
Fritton, Caldecott Hall Golf and Leisure 147, 148

G

Gainsborough's House, Sudbury 257
Go Ape! Thetford 266, 268
Gog Magog Golf Club, Cambridge 96
Gorleston Golf Club, Gorleston-on-Sea 147, 148
Grantchester 39, 99, **137–8**, 281
Great Bircham 138
Great Fen Basin 279
Great Hospital, Norwich 217
Great Ouse 30–1
Great Witchingham 38
Great Yarmouth 9, 10, 19, 40, 42, 44, 46, 83, 85, **139–48**, 193, 205, 208, 243, 253
Gressenhall 149
Greyfriars Tower, King's Lynn 177
Grimes Graves, Lynford 269, 270
Grimston 181, 183
Guildhall, Norwich 217
Guildhall of Corpus Christi, The, Lavenham 184, 185

H

Hadleigh 10, **149–50**, 173
Halesworth Airfield Museum, Haleswor 74
Halvergate 23
Happisburgh 27
Harwich, Essex 132
Havergate Island 229
Haverhill 150–1
Heacham 151–2
Heigham Holmes Nature Reserve 233
Hemingford Grey 99
Henstead Exotic Garden 61–2
Herringfleet 208
Hethersett 226
Hickling Broad 233, 253
Hillside Animal Sanctuary, Frettenham 224–5
Hintlesham 173
Hippodrome, Great Yarmouth 145
Holkham 152–4
Hollesley 49
Holme 205–6
Holt 47, 59, **155–7**, 240
Holy Trinity Church, Blythburgh 67–8
Horringer, Ickworth House 80
Horsey 158–60
Horsey Mere 233
Horsham St Faith 224
Houghton Hall, King's Lynn 182–3
Houghton Mill, King's Lynn 31, 99
House in the Clouds, Thorpeness 271
Hoveton 160, 209, 235, 284, 285
How Hill, Norfolk Broads 209
Hunstanton 42, 151, **162–7**

I

Ickworth House, Horringer 80
Imperial War Museum Duxford 13, 21, 123, 124
Ingham 80, 82
Ipswich 8, 46, 47, 149, 150, **168–75**
Isle of Ely 17
Itteringham 107, 109
Ixworth 80, 81–2

J

John Peel Centre for Creative Arts, Stowmarket 254, 255

K

Kentwell Hall, Long Melford 41, 186, 187–8, 257
Kersey 9, 186
Kessingland 49, 63
Kettleburgh 133
Kettle's Yard, Cambridge 91, 94
King's College, Cambridge 10, 15, 20, 4 89, 92
King's Lynn 28, 46, **176–83**

L

Lake Lothing 189
Landguard Fort, Felixstowe 132
Lavenham 9, 18, 41, 150, **184–6**
Leiston 49, 56–7
Lenwade 224, 225
Letheringsett 156, 157
Lincoln 30
Lindsey, St James's Chapel 174, 175
Linstead, Oasis Camel Park 251, 252
Long Melford 186–8, 257
Kentwell Hall 186, 187–8, 257
Melford Hall 186, 188, 257
Long Shop Museum, Leiston 56, 57

Lowestoft 9, 19, 46, 147, **189–93**, 208, 242, 253, 259
Ludham 47, 209
Lydia Eva (steam drifter), Great Yarmouth 146
Lynford, Grimes Graves 269, 270
Lynn Museum, King's Lynn 178, 180

M

Madingley 194
Malthouse Broad 234
Mannington Hall and Gardens, Saxthorpe 156–7
Manningtree 112
Maritime Museum, Lowestoft 190
Martello Tower, Aldeburgh 53, 54
Mattishall Golf Course 117
Meare, Thorpeness 271
Melford Hall, Long Melford 186, 188, 257
Merrivale Model Village, Great Yarmouth 146
Mid-Norfolk Railway, Wymondham 287
Middleton Hall Golf Club, Middleton 181, 183
Mildenhall 194–5
Mildenhall Treasure 194
Minsmere RSPB Nature Reserve, Sandringham 25, 56, 122, 238, 259
Mo, The, Sheringham 240
Monks Eleigh 174, 175
Moot Hall, Aldeburgh 52–3
Moyse's Hall Museum, Bury St Edmunds 76, 77
Muckleburgh Military Collection centre, Weybourne 241
Mundesley 27
Museum of Cambridge, The 94
Museum of East Anglian Life, Stowmarket 254–5

N

National Horseracing Museum, Newmarket 197, 198
National Shrine of Our Lady of Walsingham, Walsingham 273, 274
Newmarket 10, 46, **196–201**
Newton 99, **202**
Newton Green Golf Club 202
Newton-by-Castle Acre 265–6
Norfolk Broads 22–4, 44, 48, 160, 189, **203–9**, 217, 233, 253, 281
Norfolk Lavender, Heacham 151
Norfolk and Norwich Food and Drink Festival 47
Norfolk and Suffolk Aviation Museum, Flixton 74
North Creake, Creake Abbey 72
North Norfolk Railway (Poppy Line), Sheringham 240
North Walsham 48–9, **210–11**
Church of St Nicholas 210
Paston College 210
Norwich 8, 9, 18, 40, 43, 46, 208, *212–13*, **212–27**

O

Oasis Camel Park, Linstead 251, 252
Old Merchant's House, Great Yarmouth 140, 143
Oliver Cromwell's House, Ely 126, 127
Orford 21, 39, 56, **228–32**, 261
Orford Ness 21, 229–31, 259, 261
Oulton Broad 189
Oulton High House 28
Overstrand 107, 109
Oxborough 232–3, 265
Oxborough Dirk 232

P

Palace House, Newmarket 196–7
Paston College, North Walsham 210
Pavilion Theatre, Cromer 104, 105–6
Peterhouse, Cambridge 20, 92
Pettitts Animal Adventure Park, Reedham 193
Pirate's Cove Adventure Golf, Great Yarmouth 142
Pleasurewood Hills, Lowestoft 14, 190–1
Polar Museum, The, Scott Polar Research Institute, Cambridge 94–5
Poppy Line (North Norfolk Railway), Sheringham 240
Potter Heigham 233, 285

Q

Quay Theatre, The, Sudbury 257
Queens' College, Cambridge 20, 43–4, 90–1
Queens' College Mathematical Bridge, Cambridge 90–1
Queensberry House, Newmarket 197

R

RAF Air Defence Radar Museum, Hoveton 160
RAF Lakenheath, Mildenhall 194
RAF Mildenhall, Mildenhall 194
Ranworth 209, **234–5**, 285
Ranworth Broad 234
Raydon, Brett Vale Golf Club 150
Red House, The, Aldeburgh 54
Rede 80, 83
Reedham 209, 235
Reydon 251, 252
Ringstead 167
RNLI Henry Blogg Museum, Cromer 104
Roman history, Caister Roman Fort 85
Rookery Park Golf Club, Lowestoft 192
Ross Hall, Beccles 28
Rows, The and Greyfriars' Cloister, Great Yarmouth 140, 143
Royal Cromer Golf Club, Cromer 106
Royal Norwich Golf Club 221
Royal West Norfolk Golf Club, Brancaster 69
Royal Worlington and Newmarket Golf Club, Worlington 200, 201
RSPB Nature Reserve Titchwell Marsh 72–3
Rushmere Golf Club, Ipswich 172

S

Sainsbury Centre for Visual Arts, Norwich 218
St Benet's Abbey, Norfolk Broads 205–6, 234
St Edmund, King and Martyr Church, Southwold 44, 244, 247–8
St Edmundsbury Cathedral, Bury St Edmunds 76, 77
St George's Guildhall, King's Lynn 177
St Helen's, Ranworth 234
St James's Chapel, Lindsey 174, 175
St John the Baptist Church, Duxford 123
St John church, Hoveton 160
St Margaret's Church, Cley next the Sea 102
St Margaret's Church, King's Lynn 177, 178–9

St Mary Church, Mildenhall 195
St Mary le Tower, Ipswich 170
St Mary the Virgin, Banham 59
St Mary the Virgin church, Dedham 112–13
St Mary's, Burnham Deepdale 69
St Mary's Church, Bury St Edmunds 76, 78
St Michael the Archangel, Framlingham 133, 135–6
St Michaels, Beccles 43, 61
St Nicholas' Chapel, King's Lynn 176, 177, 179
St Peter, Great Walsingham 274
St Peter Church, Duxford 123
St Peter church, Hoveton 160
St Peter and St Paul church, Lavenham 185
Salthouse 103
Sandringham 15, **236–7**
Saxmundham 238, 251
Saxtead 133, 136
Saxtead Green 239
Saxthorpe 239
Scallop, The, Aldeburgh 53
Sea Life Centre, Great Yarmouth 142, 144–5
Seahenge, Lynn Museum, King's Lynn 178
Seckford Golf Club, Woodbridge 282
Sedgeford 166
Sheringham 26, 46, 47, 59, **239–41**
Shire Hall, Woodbridge 281
Shotley 174–5
Shrine of Our Lady of Walsingham, The, Walsingham 273, 274
Slipper Chapel, Walsingham 273, 274
Snape 52, 56, 57–8, 261
Snape Maltings, Snape 47, 56, 57, 261
Snettisham 166
Somerleyton 9, **241–3**
South Pier, Lowestoft 189, 190
South Walsham 243
Southwold 9, 19, 25, 40, 46, 47, **243–52**, 260–1
Sprowston Manor, Norwich 221, 222
Stained Glass Museum, Ely 128
Stalham 253–4
Stanton 80, 82
Stow Bardolph 181, 183
StowFest music festival 254
Stowmarket 28–9, 47, **254–6**
Stretham 128, 129
Sudbury 202, **256–7**
Suffolk Golf and Spa Hotel, Bury St Edmunds 78
Suffolk Heritage Coast 22, 25, **258–61**
Summer in the City festival, Cambridge 47
Sutton Hoo 14, 16, 36–7, 43, 49, **262–3**, 282
Sutton Mill, Stalham 253
Swaffham 42, **264–6**
Sweffling 133
Swilland 174, 175

T

Theatre Royal, Bury St Edmunds 78
Thetford 42, **266–71**
Thornham 166, 167
Thorpe St Andrew 227
Thorpeness 56, **271–2**
Thrigby Wildlife Gardens, Filby 85
Thurne Dyke 208
Thursford 130–1
Time and Tide Museum, Great Yarmouth 140, 143
Titchwell Marsh 72–3
Tolhouse Museum, Great Yarmouth 143
Town House Museum, King's Lynn 178, 179
Trinity College, Cambridge 20, 21, 39, 4
Trinity Guildhall, King's Lynn 177
Tuddenham Mill, Tuddenham St Mary 200–1
Turf Fen 208, 209

U

Ufford Park Hotel Golf and Spa, Woodbridge 282
University of Cambridge 19–21, 29, 42–4 88, 91, 92, 93, 95–6
University of East Anglia 40, 217

W

Walberswick 251–2
Walsingham 273–4
Wandlebury 99
Wandlebury Ring 99
Ware Hall House, Wells-next-the-Sea 2
Warren Hill, Newmarket 197
Waverley (paddle steamer), Southwold 244, 248–9
Weavers' Way 233
Weeting 275
Wellington Pier, Great Yarmouth 141, 14 145
Wells and Walsingham Light Railway 27 277
Wells-next-the-Sea 42, 47, 71, **275–8**
Welney 278
Wensum Valley Hotel, Golf and Country Club, Norwich 221, 222
West Lynn 178
West Road Concert Hall, Cambridge 92
West Runton, Links Country Park Hotel and Golf Club 107, 108
West Stow 278
West Suffolk Golf Centre, Mildenhall 19
Westleton 251, 252
Weston Longville 226
Weston Park Golf Club 225
Weybourne 240, 279
Whepstead 80, 82
Wicken Fen National Nature Reserve 2 99, 128, 138, 200, 279–81
Willis Faber and Dumas, Ipswich 170
Willy Lott's Cottage, East Bergholt 112, 114, 125
Winterton-on-Sea 148
Witnesham, Fynn Valley Golf Club 174, 175
Wolerton 107, 108–9
Wolerton Park, Erpingham 107
Wolsey Theatre, Ipswich 170, 171
Woodbridge 49, 262, **281–4**
Worlington, Royal Worlington and Newmarket Golf Club 200, 201
Worstead 47
Wroxham 209, 235, **282–6**
Wyken Hall, Stanton 80–1
Wymondham 286–7

Y

Yesterday's World, Great Yarmouth 144

The Automobile Association wishes to thank the following photographers and organisations for their assistance in the preparation of this book.

Abbreviations for the picture credits are as follows – (t) top; (m) middle; (b) bottom; (l) left; (r) right; (c) centre; (AA) AA World Travel Library.

Trade Cover: nagelestock.com/Alamy
SS Cover: AA/T Mackie

4b AA/T Mackie; 4tl AA/T Mackie; 4tr AA/T Mackie; 5r AA/C Coe; 5bl AA/T Mackie; 8–9 AA/T Mackie; 11 AA/L Noble; 12t Richard Bowden/Alamy; 12b AA/L Noble; 13t AA/T Mackie; 13m AA/M Birkitt; 13b Courtesy of BeWILDerwood; 14t Courtesy of Pleasurewood Hills; 14m PhotoDisc; 14b David Lyons/Alamy; 15t AA/L Noble; 15m Skyscan Photolibrary/Alamy; 15b AA/T Mackie; 16–7 Jon Gibbs/Alamy; 18 AA/A Baker; 19 Clearview/Alamy; 20–1 AA/L Noble; 22 AA/A J Hopkins; 23tr PhotoDisc; 24 AA/S&O Mathews; 25 AA/T Mackie; 26 T.M.O.Landscapes/Alamy; 27 Heritage Image Partnership Ltd/Alamy; 30 International Photobank/Alamy; 32 AA/T Mackie; 33 Rod Edwards/Alamy; 34–5 AA/M Birkitt; 36 QEDimages/Alamy; 38 AA/T Mackie; 39 AA/T Mackie; 40 AA/J Tims; 42 AA/A Baker; 43 The National Trust Photolibrary/Alamy; 44 AA/C Coe; 45r AA/M Birkitt; 47 67photo/Alamy; 48 AA/A Burton; 50–1 AA/T Mackie; 53 AA/T Mackie; 55 AA/T Mackie; 62–3 PhotoDisc; 64 AA/T Mackie; 67 AA/T Mackie; 70–1 AA/S&O Mathews; 76 AA/A Baker; 77 AA/A Baker; 81 AA/M Birkitt; 83 Courtesy of Caister Castle Car Collection; 84 AA/A Baker; 88l AA/L Noble; 88–9 AA/L Noble; 89r AA/L Noble; 90 AA/M Moody; 92 AA/C Coe; 93 travelbild.com/Alamy; 95 Geoffrey Robinson/Alamy; 100 AA/M Birkitt; 101 AA/T Souter; 104–5 AA/T Mackie; 110 AA/S&O Mathews; 111 AA/T Mackie; 112–3 AA/T Mackie; 115 AA/S&O Mathews; 118–9 AA/T Mackie; 120 AA/T Mackie; 124b Steve Vidler/Alamy; 124t AA/M Birkitt; 126 AA/T Mackie; 127 David Lyons/Alamy; 132 AA/A Baker; 134 AA/D Forss; 140–1 Kathy Wright/Alamy; 142 AA/T Mackie; 146–7 AA/A Baker; 153 AA/T Mackie; 154 Skyscan Photolibrary/Alamy; 156 Stuart Sneddon/Alamy; 158–9 AA/M Birkitt; 161 Courtesy of BeWILDerwood; 163 AA/T Mackie; 165 AA/L Whitman; 168–9 Peter Smith/Alamy; 171 AA/A Baker; 176 Howard Taylor/Alamy; 179 AA/A Baker; 181 AA/R J Edwards; 184 AA/T Mackie; 186 AA/T Mackie; 187 AA/M Trelawny; 191 Courtesy of Pleasurewood Hills; 192–3 Mark Dyball/Alamy; 196–7 AA/M Birkitt; 198bl Courtesy of National Horse Racing Museum; 198–9 Courtesy of National Horse Racing Museum; 199r Courtesy of National Horse Racing Museum; 203 AA/T Souter; 204–5 AA/T Mackie; 205r Jon Gibbs/Alamy; 206 AA/C Coe; 207 AA/T Mackie; 208 AA/T Mackie; 209 AA/C Coe; 211 AA/S&O Mathews; 212 AA/L Whitman; 213 AA/A Baker; 214 AA/R Ireland; 215 AA/A Baker; 216 AA/T Mackie; 217 AA/L Whitman; 219 AA/T Mackie; 221 AA/T Mackie; 228 AA/T Mackie; 230 AA/S&O Mathews; 234 AA/T Mackie; 237 AA/T Mackie; 240 AA/S&O Mathews; 245 AA/T Mackie; 246 eye35/Alamy; 249 AA/T Mackie; 250 AA/T Mackie; 253 AA/A Baker; 255 AA/M Birkitt; 256 AA/S&O Mathews; 258–9 AA/T Mackie; 260–1 AA/T Mackie; 261r AA/T Mackie; 262 The National Trust Photolibrary/Alamy; 263 David Lyons/Alamy; 264 Simon Pocklington / Alamy; 267 AA/A Baker; 270 AA/M Birkitt; 272 AA/S&O Mathews; 275 AA/T Mackie; 276 nobleIMAGES/Alamy; 278–9 AA/T Mackie; 280 The National Trust Photolibrary/Alamy; 283 AA/S&O Mathews; 284 AA/A Perkins; 287 Robert Estall photo agency/Alamy

Every effort has been made to trace the copyright holders, and we apologise in advance for any unintentional omissions or errors. We would be pleased to apply any corrections in any following edition of this publication.

Series editor: Rebecca Needes
Author: Carole French
Copy editor: Janet Law
Designer: Liz Baldin
Proofreader: Sandy Draper
Indexer: Lisa Footitt
Digital imaging & repro: Ian Little
Art director: James Tims

Additional writing by other AA contributors. Lore of the Land feature by Ruth Binney. Some content may appear in other AA books and publications.

Has something changed? Email us at travelguides@theaa.com.

'WE KNOW BRITAIN'

The AA was founded in 1905 as a body initially intended to help motorists avoid police speed traps. As motoring became more popular, so did we, and our activities have continued to expand into a great variety of areas.

The first edition of the AA Members' Handbook appeared in 1908. Due to the difficulty many motorists were having finding reasonable meals and accommodation while on the road, the AA introduced a new scheme to include listings for 'about one thousand of the leading hotels' in the second edition in 1909. As a result the AA has been recommending and assessing establishments for over a century, and each year our professional inspectors anonymously visit and rate thousands of hotels, restaurants, guest accommodations and campsites. We are relied upon for our trustworthy and objective star, Rosette and Pennant ratings systems, which you will see used in this guide to denote AA-inspected restaurants and campsites.

In 1912 we published our first handwritten routes and our atlas of town plans, and in 1925 our classic touring guide, *The AA Road Book of England and Wales* appeared. Together, our accurate mapping and in-depth knowledge of places to visit were to set the benchmark for British travel publishing.

Since the 1990s we have dramatically expanded our publishing activities, producing high quality atlases, maps, walking and travel guides for the UK and the rest of the world. In this new series of regional travel guides we are drawing on over a hundred years of experience to bring you the very best of Britain.